Birding

IN ATLANTIC CANADA

Birding

IN ATLANTIC CANADA

ACADIA/L'ACADIE

Roger Burrows

JESPERSON PRESS LTD.

Jesperson Press Ltd.
39 James Lane
St. John's, Newfoundland
A1E 3H3

Cover and text design: Jesperson Press Ltd., St. John's, NF
Cover illustration: Robert Villani, Kew Gardens, N.Y.
Typesetting, Printing and Binding: Jesperson Press Limited, St. John's, NF

Appreciation is expressed to *The Canada Council* for its assistance in publishing this book.

The publisher acknowledges the financial contribution of the *Cultural Affairs Division* of the *Department of Culture, Recreation and Youth, Government of Newfoundland and Labrador* which has helped make this publication possible.

Canadian Cataloguing in Publication Data

Burrows, Roger, 1942-

   Birding in Atlantic Canada

   Includes bibliographical references and index.
   Partial contents: v. 3. Acadia/L'Acadie.
   ISBN 0-920502-87-3 (set) -- ISBN 0-921692-09-9
(v. 3)

1. Bird watching -- Atlantic Provinces -- Guide-
books.   2. Birds -- Atlantic Provinces --
Geographical distribution.   I. Title

QL685.5.A9B867 1988   598 .07234715   C88-098644-1

Acknowledgements

by Roger Burrows

Apart from brief visits in 1974 and 1976, all my birding in Prince Edward Island was telescoped into a seven-month stint in 1975 during which I logged a creditable 208 species. My birding in New Brunswick has been restricted to two very short periods of residence in the Kouchibouguac area in 1976 and 1978 and several fleeting visits, mainly to Fundy National Park, St. Andrews and the Sackville area, although I added a few more sites in the summer of 1989. A 228 species total is, however, still way behind the province's resident birders. My visits to Quebec are even more limited, but I finally visited the Gasp! in June 1989 and increased my provincial total to 148.

This hardly qualifies me as an expert on the region. And yet, the amount of material published by the various bird and naturalist societies has enabled me to produce a guide comparable to the two previous guides in this series. The checklists provided by the two Quebec regional societies, together with seasonal summaries contained in Le Kakawi and in the pages of the New Brunswick Naturalist were a big help, as were answers to my original questionnaire mailed out in 1980. More recently, those who went through the site manuscripts and corrected errors and omissions have made an immeasurable contribution, especially considering my limited first-hand experience of the region. Anyone mentioned in the text as a contact has provided information, and I would like to thank each and every one for sharing birding knowledge and offering encouragement.

Dedication

This book is dedicated to my good friends Hank and Joanne Deichmann, who have suffered many a sleepless night wondering, among other things, what possesses me to set out in a blizzard to make a Christmas Bird Count. They still don't know, and neither do I.

Table of Contents

Preface

by Henrik Deichmann

With the release of this third book in the *Birding in Atlantic Canada* series, Roger Burrows has fulfilled a goal to produce current guides for all of Atlantic Canada, quite a feat considering the previous lack of regional guides.

New Brunswick, with its remote forested valleys, rolling landforms and rugged coastlines, offers terrific birding. Tentative results from the recently-completed Maritime Breeding Bird Atlas project indicate that the province will lead Nova Scotia in confirmed breeding species. But New Brunswick is equally renowned for its migration watching, too. The first International Hemispheric Shorebird Reserve was created at Mary's Point in the upper Bay of Fundy, and Grand Manan draws vagrant birds like a magnet to the lower Bay of Fundy.

Prince Edward Island's pastoral landscape, wild dunes and remote shores offer the dedicated birder quite a challenge while affording the possibility of a wide variety of species during a short visit. The province also boasts a successful conservation effort in its protection of endanged Piping Plovers close to a busy national park holiday beach. Close by, the Iles de la Madeleine have a flavour all their own and deserve to be seriously explored by birders.

The forgotten part of Atlantic Canada for many visiting birders is the Gaspé, the maritime heart of Quebec. Located north of New Brunswick, this blend of Scottish and Acadian culture provides a refreshing change from the commercialism to the south, and its birdlife is as varied as its heritage. This book offers some personal recommendations on how to combine the two aspects.

I have copies of Roger's two previous books and this book will join them in my bookcase. But I'll need many more, as I know my New Brunswick-born friends and relatives will be clamoring for them. Thanks, Roger, for helping make us "birding literate" in Atlantic Canada.

Introduction

Canada's smallest province, Prince Edward Island, is also one of its flattest. There are no mountains on the island, but there is a backbone of rolling hills to provide habitats for many species rarely seen along the coastlines. PEI also has its red soil, a product of the old red sandstone still found in its crumbling cliffs. This soft rock, mixed with alluvial clays, has created a rich soil used to grow the island's best-known crop, potatoes. Some of the country roads are also built with the local material and are best avoided in spring when they would mire even the world's best rally drivers. Fortunately, most of the main roads have a less malleable surface and are open year-round, except at times in winter when blowing snow can be a major hazard. The roads are most crowded in summer when PEI's tourist industry is at its peak.

Tourist Information Centres are located at many points, including Charlottetown's Royalty Mall, and the province also maintains centres at Aulac, NB, and Caribou, NS. The best source of information is, however, Geoff Hogan who has written a book on the island's more common birds and has a store in Charlottetown that caters to the needs of resident and visiting birdwatchers. Shellfish, especially lobsters and locally clams and oysters, are the main catch of the fishing industry, but Irish moss, a red algae, is also harvested on the north shore. PEI was part of Acadie and known as Ile Saint Jean until 1769.

New Brunswick is, after Quebec, the most francophone province in Canada, but it owes much of its early development to Empire Loyalists who, in the mid-1700s, left the United States to settle in its southwest corner. Acadians were already living in the southeast and many more arrived and settled in the northern half of the province. This created an interesting mix of cultural traditions reflected in placenames. Tourism is well established in the southwest and growing in other parts of the province, and signage is better than in most of Atlantic Canada. The province operates Tourist Information Centres throughout the province, and has produced a useful birdwatching brochure.

Dairy farming is locally important, as are potatoes. The herring weirs of the Fundy coast and the crab and lobster fisheries of the northeast coast reflect the different characteristics of the Bay of Fundy and Gulf of St. Lawrence fisheries. Dulse is a popular seaweed among New Brunswickers who also harvest "fiddleheads", the uncoiled shoots of ferns. And, contrary to their nickname, I have yet to see a resident choke a herring!

The St. Lawrence River has always been an important water link from the interior of Canada to the markets of Europe, and remains a lifeline for the province of Quebec and a major influence on the lives of the people who live along its banks and along the coastlines of the Gulf of St. Lawrence. Communities on the South Shore are much larger and more diversified in terms of industry. Most of Maritime Quebec has retained its French culture, traditions and language, but the communities along the north shore of Chaleur Bay are more English and Scottish in nature. The Gaspé is a unique area with the highest mountains in Atlantic Canada and the largest **Northern Gannet** colony in North America at Bonaventure Island. The fishery provides most of the jobs on the Gaspé, although tourism is rapidly overtaking it as the region becomes better known.

The province has a number of Tourist Information Centres at access points and major towns. There are also several privately-operated information centres at places like Rimouski, Percé, Port-Daniel and Carleton. Birding is not yet a major pastime, but birding is good even in winter, and the Gaspésie society in particular is very visible in the summer months.

Most of the region is accessible by road with border crossings from Maine in both New Brunswick and the northwest corner of Maritime Quebec. Quebec and Labrador now have road connections from Baie Comeau to Labrador City, and rail connections from Sept Iles to Labrador City. The North Shore Highway will eventually link Tadoussac, Les Escoumins, Sept-Iles, Baie-Comeau and Godbout with the South Shore and coastal Labrador. This would greatly enhance birding opportunities and make round trips throughout Atlantic Canada a real possibility.

Prince Edward Islanders are embroiled in debating the merits of a tunnel or bridge, but the province is at the moment accessible only by car ferry from Cape Tormentine in New Brunswick or Caribou in Nova Scotia—the latter service is much less popular and may well be discontinued. The Bay of Fundy car ferry connects Digby, Nova Scotia, and Saint John, New Brunswick, and provides an excellent pelagic trip at times. A ferry from Souris, Prince Edward Island, to the Iles de la Madeleine is also recommended, and there are local ferry services in Quebec connecting the North and South Shores of the St. Lawrence River and the communities further east along the North Shore. Rail service is being downgraded throughout the region, but there are still connections with most major towns. SMT and Voyageur provide excellent local bus services in New Brunswick and Quebec, and Acadian Lines has connections to Nova Scotia and Prince Edward Island.

International flights make scheduled stops at Moncton International Airport in New Brunswick, and there are daily flights to and from other parts of Atlantic Canada and Montreal, Quebec City, Toronto and Ottawa. Other major airports are located at Charlottetown, PEI, Saint John and Fredericton, NB, and Rimouski, Quebec. Air Canada, Canadian Airlines International and Quebecair are the long distance carriers, but a number of local airlines provide internal flights, especially in Quebec.

It should be noted that not all observers send in their sightings to *American Birds*, and that less than a third of New Brunswick's Christmas Bird Counts are published in the magazine. This gives a misleading picture of the wealth of birdlife in the region. Much of the basic data in this book comes from personal experience and from information contained in the publications mentioned above and listed in the Bibliography. I have, however, lived a total of just 14 months in the three provinces, so my knowledge of parts of Quebec and New Brunswick is rather limited. The many birders who live in the region have provided me with a wealth of information, some of it going back ten years when I first conceived the idea of a regional guide. Some of those people have since died, and I hope this book is a fitting testimonial to the help they provided. To those who remain, I hope you find your favourite area has received proper recognition in terms of its birdlife.

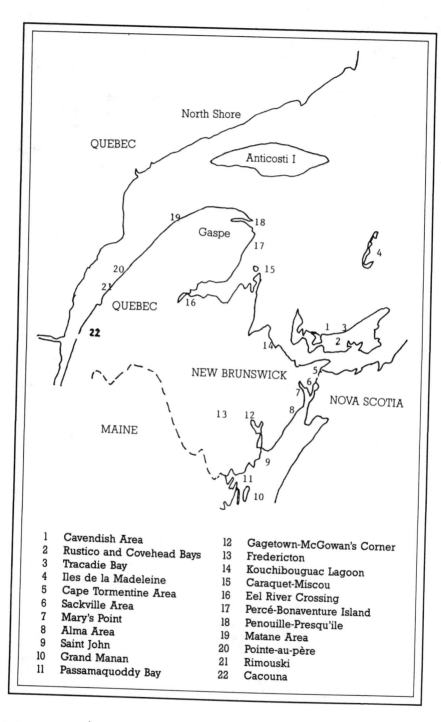

1	Cavendish Area	12	Gagetown-McGowan's Corner
2	Rustico and Covehead Bays	13	Fredericton
3	Tracadie Bay	14	Kouchibouguac Lagoon
4	Iles de la Madeleine	15	Caraquet-Miscou
5	Cape Tormentine Area	16	Eel River Crossing
6	Sackville Area	17	Percé-Bonaventure Island
7	Mary's Point	18	Penouille-Presqu'ile
8	Alma Area	19	Matane Area
9	Saint John	20	Pointe-au-père
10	Grand Manan	21	Rimouski
11	Passamaquoddy Bay	22	Cacouna

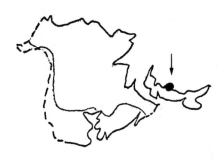

CAVENDISH AREA

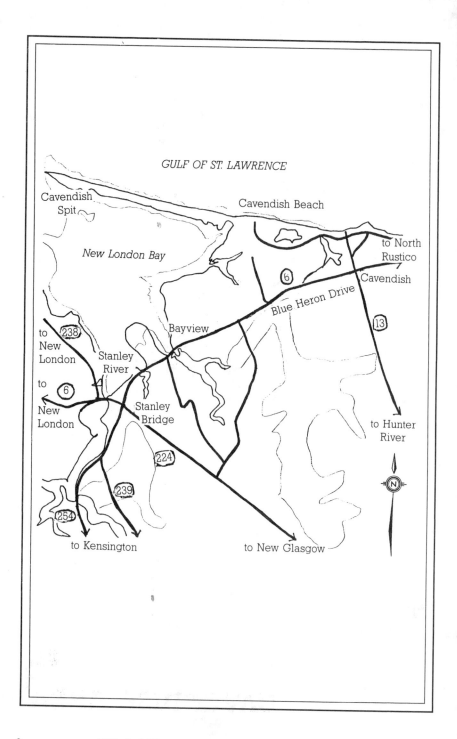

The western section of Prince Edward Island National Park takes in the coastline between North Rustico and Cavendish spit. There are two distinct habitats along the shoreline — the sand beaches and backing dunes of Cavendish and the sandstone cliffs and woods east of Orby Head. Both are located off Blue Heron Drive (Highway 6) but can be reached by taking Highway 15 north from Hunter River. Most of the best sites are easily accessible from Cavendish campground or from one of the many trailer sites and campgrounds outside the national park. Several are within walking distance and provide very enjoyable excursions.

The long walk along the Cavendish sandspit is rarely very productive in summer unless you want to check out reports of a summering **Snowy Owl** or see a **Piping Plover** — the nesting area is marked off when the plovers are on territory and should be avoided to allow the **15+ pairs** to raise their young in peace. It is worth the effort, however, in spring and early fall.

The saltmarshes by New London Bay are an attraction for spring migrants, especially **Canada Goose, Black Duck, Mallard and Great Blue Heron**. The scrubby growth is good for songbirds, particularly sparrows, and there are sometimes **Snow Bunting and Lapland Longspur** around before the main influx. **Northern Gannet, Great Cormorant and Black Guillemot** appear in the bay in late April, and there are a few **Greater Scaup, Common Goldeneye, Oldsquaw, White-winged and Surf Scoters** until mid May.

In fall the area is taken over by shorebirds on their way south. There are usually a few **Short-billed Dowitcher, Least and Semipalmated Sandpipers** probing in the wet mud, but the largest counts are at the end of the sandspit which is a good example of a primary dune on the move. There have been three-figure fall counts of **Semipalmated and Black-bellied Plovers, Ruddy Turnstone, Red Knot, Least and Semipalmated Sandpiper, and Sanderling**, plus smaller numbers of **Piping Plover, Hudsonian Godwit, Willet, Spotted Sandpiper, Greater and Lesser Yellowlegs, Short-billed Dowitcher, White-rumped Sandpiper, and Dunlin**. There have been sightings of **Whimbrel and Curlew Sandpiper** on the Cavendish sandspit in fall.

While the saltmarsh is most productive in late July and August, the sandspit is the better location later in the migration period. Good numbers of gulls and terns also gather along the sandspit in late summer and fall, especially **Bonaparte's and Ring-billed Gulls**. Any groups of terns flying by should be scrutinized for **Caspian and Black Terns**.

Birding the long sandy beach by Cavendish campground is virtually impossible during the hottest part of the day, but the beaches are empty in the early morning when many birds are on the move. This is a good place to take a dawn stroll as there are often rafts of diving ducks in the surf. **Surf and White-winged Scoters** pass by in early May, well after the first returning **Great and Double-crested Cormorants** and with the last of the northbound **Oldsquaw**, and there may be large rafts of **Black Scoter** on calmer days. A late July **Marbled Godwit** is the rarest shorebird reported off Cavendish Beach. The backing dunes and mixed forests shelter a wide range of passerines in spring and summer, which explains the presence of **Northern Harrier, Short-eared Owl and American Kestrel** and the abundance of red foxes. A few shorebirds arrive in mid May, but ducks continue to provide the main interest. Parties of **Greater Scaup** float nonchalantly offshore, while **Common Eider** fly by with the main contingent of scoters. Once the flocks of **Bank Swallow** arrive to decimate the insect population in early June, it's time to switch your attention elsewhere until the fall migration.

The first groups of returning shorebirds patrol the beach in mid July, and by the end of the month the parties can be quite large. **Sanderling** form the bulk of the birds along the beach, with a few parties of **Ruddy Turnstone, Red Knot and Semipalmated Sandpiper** for company. **Least Sandpiper** rarely stray from the marsh margins, but **Spotted Sandpiper** can often be seen around tentsites in the early morning, especially after rainstorms. **White-rumped Sandpiper** pitch into any open area in October when few other shorebirds are around. A few birds of prey pass through in August and September after the nesting pairs have left, and there have been fall records of **Red-tailed Hawk and Peregrine**. Once most of the shorebirds have left, the area is taken over by restless flocks of **Snow Bunting and Lapland Longspur**, which usually appear in October and stay until early December. There is also a return movement of loons, cormorants and scoters with all species represented.

The golf course located alongside the Lake of Shining Waters is perfect for leisurely strolls through the woods and alongside the pond. The grassy expanses are popular with the swirling flocks of **Snow Bunting** in mid April, and any grass visible through the melting snow is seized upon by the first **American Robin** and blackbird returnees.

A little later, it's possible to find **Bobolink**, and on very rare occasions an **Eastern Meadowlark** may show up on the golf course, but the greatest variety of birds in early May are on and around the pond. **Great Blue Heron** reappear in mid April, and are quickly followed by **Canada Goose** and dabbling ducks. The geese have raised a brood on the pond several years in a row. **Pied-billed Grebe** sometimes join them in early May, when **American Bittern, Blue-winged Teal and Ring-necked Duck** join already-established **Black Duck**. **Common Snipe and Killdeer** also nest in the area and flush to cover as **Northern Harrier and Short-eared Owl** quarter the golf course and fields from mid May.

The lush vegetation around the lake guarantees a good hatch of insects most years, making it the best place to look for **Ruby-throated Hummingbird, Alder Flycatcher and Northern Parula**. There have been a few sightings of **Eastern Phoebe**, and careful checks could turn up **Brown Thrasher and Gray Catbird** in the secondgrowth and thickets. **Purple Finch** families are raised among the conifers on the west side of the pond.

The first broods of ducks are often in the water before the main tourist influx, but many nesting songbirds have a hard time coping with errant golf balls, family pets and children. A stroll along the Balsam Hollow trail is recommended for anyone wanting to cache a few warblers. The shaded woods of balsam fir, red maple, white and yellow birch are aglow with colourful flowers in the late spring and early summer and provide good photographic opportunities year round even if the warblers are uncooperative. **Great Crested Flycatcher, Eastern Wood-pewee and Red-eyed Vireo** have been reported in summer along the trail.

The open waters of Clarks Pond are often windswept, which makes canoeing rather hazardous. Along its shores, red foxes find a good selection of small mammals and birds to feed their kits. Some **Black Duck and Green-winged Teal** probably breed, but most of the ducks using the pond are migrants. There are several access points to the pond, which is at its best in spring and fall, and you don't have to walk far to get a good view. In spring, small parties of **Greater Scaup and Common Goldeneye** may be joined by **Barrow's Goldeneye and Northern Shoveler**, both of which are now regular. **Caspian Tern** may also appear in early May, but the pond is generally avoided by gulls and terns until much later in the year, although there has been at least one spring visit by an **Ivory Gull**.

The best time to visit is undoubtedly in the fall, when the pond can be covered with a wide variety of waterfowl. From early October to mid November, Clarks Pond is the staging area for over **1000 Greater Scaup** and up to **200 Common Merganser**. The first birds arrive in the third week of September, when there are a few **Blue-winged Teal** around, but the main influx is in October. **Black Duck and Green-winged Teal** are found in the hundreds, and are joined by smaller numbers of **Mallard, Northern Pintail, Ring-necked Duck and Hooded Merganser** as the month progresses.

By the end of October, the peak has been reached, but the flocks may include a few **Bufflehead** among the **Common Goldeneye and Red-breasted Merganser** parties. At the same time, there is a build-up of **Bonaparte's Gull** roosting on the pond with a few **Caspian Tern**, and a check off the Cavendish shore for **Iceland Gulls** is in order. The pond freezes over in winter, but many of the ducks linger if the weather remains mild.

Cavendish itself is best avoided during the peak summer months, but it does provide good birding during migration periods before tourists arrive and after they depart. Large flocks of **Common Grackle, Red-winged and Rusty Blackbirds, and Brown-headed Cowbird** arrive in mid April and "harmonize" during the night—believe me, they beat heavy metal bands for noise and lack of melodic content! **Killdeer and American Robin** arrive at the same time, and are often put to flight by **Northern Harrier and Short-eared Owl** checking out the farm fields behind the community. During the summer there are a few breeding swallows, but the most active insectivores are **Common Nighthawks**.

The sandstone cliffs east of Cavendish offer a sharp contrast to the sand dunes and beaches to the west. This is an excellent area to study intertidal life in the pools left among the rocks at low tide. The precipitous nature of the cliffs and their crumbly texture make this a dangerous place to be when the tide is coming in, but the scene changes completely at low tide. Orby Head is one of the few places where you can expect to see **Black Guillemot** in summer, and there is a good chance of adding **Common Eider and Purple Sandpiper** in May. **Peregrines** are also possible here in spring. Another regular spring and fall visitor is the **Caspian Tern**. While the coastline offers its best birding in spring and fall, the Cape Turner picnic area and the short Brook Valley trail are best visited in summer.

Most songbird species can be expected in spring, including such rarities as **Brown Thrasher, Solitary Vireo and Rose-breasted Grosbeak**, and several stay to breed. A few pairs of **Bobolink** are to be seen on the inside of the Brook Valley trail. Warblers are a feature of fall migration from late August to mid September, and many of the northern breeders, including **Cape May, Bay-breasted and Blackpoll Warblers**, can be found at this time.

The small pond just north of North Rustico — Rollings Pond — is part of the PEI Wildlife Park, so any birds on its waters should be checked for signs of being pinioned. Most wild waterfowl occur in spring, when **Black Duck, Blue-winged Teal and Ring-necked Duck** are regular, but I have also seen **Common Goldeneye** on the pond in mid September. By mid May good numbers of earlier warblers, especially **Yellow, Yellow-rumped and Palm Warblers**, can be seen flycatching around the pond. June and September are the best months for gulls and shorebirds.

The last section of the park shoreline leads to North Rustico harbour which can provide a temporary sanctuary to windblown vagrants in spring and fall. The spring break up is more likely to bring flocks of **Common Eider, Oldsquaw** and scoters. The small sandy beach is an ideal place to look for gulls in spring — the harbour flock has included a **Glaucous Gull** up to mid June. Shorebirds are less regular in spring, but the tidal pools and waveswept seaweed sometimes attracts southbound migrants from mid July to early September. I have seen both **Tundra Swan and Bald Eagle** flying over the ice by North Rustico in late April, as well as a fairly sedentary **Snowy Owl** in early May.

Other places to visit from this area
The best place to see migrants is probably North Cape at the extreme tip of the western peninsula. Pelagics are regularly seen from May to late October, with **Northern Gannet, Great Cormorant, Red-throated Loon, Horned and Red-necked Grebes** in spring and fall. A few **Northern Fulmar, Greater and Sooty Shearwaters** are occasionally driven close to shore, and the gull flocks almost certainly attract the **Parasitic and Pomarine Jaegers** seen more often from the Magdalenes. **200+ Caspian Tern** at one time in fall give an indication of what could be seen if more visits were made here. Offcourse songbirds are also likely, especially in fall. An unsubstantiated record of **250+ Purple Martin** in mid September and **5 Scarlet Tanager** in mid August are examples of the numbers of birds that occasionally appear.

Other areas are very lightly reported so I have had to rely on *American Birds* summaries which highlight rarities. The Tignish area was visited by Stu Tingley in fall and proved productive with a **Fulvous Whistling Duck** in mid August, and both **Gadwall**

and Western Sandpiper in early-mid September. On my late summer visit to Tignish I found a few shorebirds around the estuary of the Miminegash River. The Alberton area turned up a **Caspian Tern and Merlin** as well as small numbers of ducks and shorebirds. **Northern Harrier, Short-eared Owl and American Kestrel** share the open areas, and there are often good numbers of **Horned Lark**, swallows, blackbirds and sparrows on migration. The woods around Alberton are quite varied, and there have been August sightings of **Blue-gray Gnatcatcher and Scarlet Tanager**.

The Northumberland Strait shore from Bonshaw via Crapaud to the Borden ferry has rather more ponds and marshes for **Pied-billed Grebe, American Bittern, Mallard, Green- and Blue-winged Teal, Northern Pintail, American Wigeon, Ring-necked Duck, Northern Harrier, Common Snipe, Swamp and Sharp-tailed Sparrows**. There are several access points, but birding visits are so few I hesitate to recommend a choice. Some beaches have shorebirds — but nothing to rival the North Shore. **American Kestrel, Killdeer, American Woodcock, Common Nighthawk, Barn Swallow, Bobolink and Song Sparrow** are fairly widespread in summer.

The farmlands around Kensington have a fluctuating population of **Ring-necked Pheasant and Gray Partridge**, although finding them is sometimes a problem. The best route is Highway 2 which passes through the northern section of the Bonshaw Hills. A visit in summer could turn up a brood of **Killdeer** or an **Upland Sandpiper**. On my few visits, birds of prey were quite often seen perched on telegraph poles or farm fences. **Red-tailed Hawk, Short-eared Owl and American Kestrel** appeared to be widespread, and **Sharp-shinned Hawk and Northern Harrier** more local.

The most productive waterfowl site west of the national park is Indian River in the eastern section of Malpèque Bay. This has been the point of expansion for many western ducks in the last decade. Apart from regular nesting by **Black Duck, Green- and Blue-winged Teal**, the marshes have attracted **Mallard, Northern Pintail, Gadwall, American Wigeon and Northern Shoveler. Redhead and Ruddy Duck** have prospected the area enough to suggest breeding is imminent if it hasn't already taken place. The saltwater coves and bays nearby probably have a higher number of migrant and nonbreeding diving ducks, but the most surprising breeding record is of **Greater Scaup. Ospreys** are regular nesters at Indian River, and there have been sightings of **Little Blue Heron** in spring.

The coastline between Royalty Point and Cape Tryon is composed of steep cliffs and several ponds which attract waterfowl, gulls and shorebirds, and could easily turn up a few vagrants. **Wilson's Phalarope** is now becoming quite regular along the Gulf shore, but **Red-necked Phalarope** is just a distinct possibility from late July to mid October. This is also the best time for large numbers of gulls and terns which roost on the ponds close to Highway 20. **Killdeer and Bobolink** are both conspicuous and noisy in their individual ways by the roadside. The cliffs offer an excellent view of the rafts of **Common Eider, Black, White-winged, and Surf Scoters, Oldsquaw and Greater Scaup** found inshore in late spring and fall. **King Eider** is a distinct possibility by Cape Tryon, especially in the late fall and early spring. There are also good numbers of **Common and Red-throated Loons, Horned and Red-necked Grebes** in April and October.

The most conspicuous birds, however, are the **Great and Double-crested Cormorants** of a thriving mixed colony near Cape Tryon. There are usually close to **200 pairs of Great Cormorant** and perhaps **600 pairs of Double-crested Cormorant** nesting on ledges and slopes on the cliffs. Several roads lead off Highway 20 beyond French River, and the adults can be seen flying to and from the cliffs all summer. There is also a large nesting colony of **Bank Swallow** along the cliffs, and **Common Ravens** and **Rock Doves** also nest at Cape Tryon.

Double-crested Cormorant

The estuary section of the Hunter River which empties into Rustico Harbour is very popular with **Great Blue Heron**, and it's not unusual to find the first birds back at Rusticoville by late April when the first parties of **Canada Goose** are also evident. About a month later, the last of the diving ducks are ready to leave, but there may be a few **Surf Scoter** present until mid June. North Rustico and South Rustico on either side of the Hunter River both have extensive saltmarshes which warrant a closer look if you have time to spend in the area.

A detour along Highway 224 from Stanley Bridge to New Glasgow is worth taking to avoid crowds and to study the Bonshaw Hills. There is always a chance of finding **Northern Goshawk and Merlin** along the road, and the neighbouring marshes of Hunter

River close to New Glasgow are excellent for dabbling ducks in spring and fall, and gulls and shorebirds from May to early October. **Northern Pintail and American Wigeon** are both quite common, and I have seen a few **Caspian Tern** as late as early October. **Ring-billed Gull** are plentiful into November. Further upstream, there is a good lookout point for fair numbers of both **Canada Goose and Brant**—the latter only in spring.

The Bonshaw Hills form the sandstone and shale backbone of Prince Edward Island. Only 500 feet in height, they, nevertheless, provide an extensive watershed for many streams flowing to both coasts. Erosion is a problem, both in the hills themselves and in farmfields and roads where gullies may be a major hindrance in spring and early summer. Roadside seeding programs have been designed to reduce runoff, and some farms have been abandoned. This has led to white spruce parklands and a variety of breeding habitats.

The woodland birdlife is probably more varied than anywhere else on the island, but few people have taken the time to explore the hills and farms. **Red-tailed Hawk** share the woodlots and fields with a few **Northern Goshawk and Merlin**, and there are sometimes **Broad-winged and Cooper's Hawks** among the summering **Sharp-shinned Hawk and American Kestrel**. I have seen **Great Horned, Barred and Short-eared Owls** here, and I suspect all other species found on the island occur regularly. The mixture of woods, hedges and fields is perfect for **Ring-necked Pheasant, Ruffed Grouse and Gray Partridge**, and **Mourning Doves** are quite common in open areas, feeding in loose flocks on grain left in fields in early winter.

All the island's nesting passerines can be looked for. Woodpeckers are widespread, as are flycatchers, thrushes, warblers and sparrows. **Gray Catbird** are heard more often than they are seen in the hedgerows and overgrown thickets, where an occasional **Brown Thrasher** may join them. Some of the farms are still operating, so permission should be sought before exploring woodlots or crossing fields. **Bobolink and Rose-breasted Grosbeak** are regular nesting species.

RUSTICO AND COVEHEAD BAYS

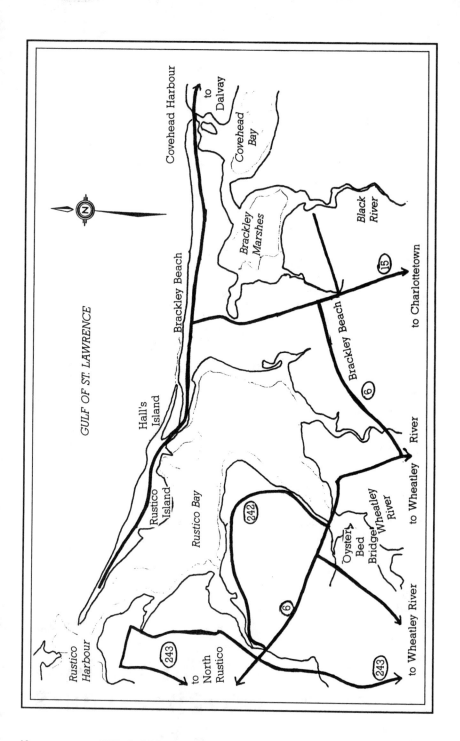

The central section of Prince Edward Island National Park is a rich mixture of sand beaches, dunes, tuckamoor, saltmarshes, mudflats and shallow waters unmatched anywhere else on the island. This is one of the most productive birding sites in Atlantic Canada from May to September, and it warrants more than a day's visit to do it justice. I spent seven months in the park in 1975 and conducted daily counts late April to early November—this was by far the best area in terms of variety of species and numbers. You could camp at Stanhope Beach then, but I suspect the only campground is now at Rustico Island—more distant from the main shorebird and larid action but closer to the ducks and marshbirds.

The most westerly location is Rustico Island—a long and rapidly-eroding spit of land cutting off Rustico Bay. This was indeed an island until the causeway was built, but its existence is now threatened by the action of wind and waves. The paved section of the road is disappearing at a surprising rate and there are justifiable fears that the encroaching dunes will threaten the **Great Blue Heron** colony occupying a group of trees on the edge of the campground. This colony has already moved several times as trees have been blown down by fall and winter storms. The nesting terns have fared even worse, and there are now only a few satellite pairs of **Common and Arctic Terns** along the inner shoreline. A few pairs of **Piping Plover** cope very well with the conditions, as do the many breeding **Spotted Sandpiper**.

Most spring waterfowl are concentrated along the Rustico Bay shore. The earliest birds are **Canada Goose, Black Duck and Common Goldeneye**, but between the end of April and mid-May there may be as many as **370 Brant**, and **100+ Common Goldeneye and Red-breasted Merganser**. All three scoters are possible, and there is no shortage of **Common Loon, Northern Gannet, Great and Double-crested Cormorants** in the choppy waters off the tip. Birds of prey are regular visitors to Rustico Island—with **Northern Harrier, Snowy and Short-eared Owls** from late April. Shorebirds are less often seen, but a few do appear along the muddy bay shore where **Great Blue Heron** find the best feeding. Most appear in late May, when parties of **Black-bellied Plover** and a few **Whimbrel, Lesser Yellowlegs and White-rumped Sandpiper** join the groups of **Semipalmated Plover, Greater Yellowlegs, Least and Semipalmated Sandpipers**.

The mixed woods around the campsites are favoured by most songbirds, and this is one area deserving extra scrutiny in spring. The first birds to appear are swallows, **Horned Lark** and finches, but by the second week of May, the warblers, thrushes and sparrows are beginning to pour in to fill the woods and clearings with song. Most of the rarer park visitors have been seen here. I found **Northern Mockingbird, Brown Thrasher, Gray Catbird, Winter Wren, Alder Flycatcher, Black-throated Blue and Mourning Warblers, Rose-breasted Grosbeak and White-crowned Sparrow** without too much difficulty between early May and mid June. Many birds stay around to nest, but increased use of the campground and beach has limited breeding success.

By the second week of July the first shorebirds are returning, and it's not too long before 15 or more species can be counted along the shoreline on an early morning visit at mid to low tide. I tried a few shorebird walks for those park visitors willing to start out before 7 a.m., and they were very successful. Some species are relatively common, although far below their Covehead Bay totals. Typical fall shorebird high counts are **45 Black-bellied Plover, 25 Greater Yellowlegs, 20 Least Sandpiper, 30 Semipalmated Sandpiper and 80 Sanderling**, together with a dozen or so **Semipalmated Plover and Ruddy Turnstone**. **Piping Plover, Lesser Golden-plover, Whimbrel, Lesser Yellowlegs, Red Knot, Dunlin, White-rumped Sandpiper and Hudsonian Godwit** appear in smaller numbers, and there may be a few **Black-bellied Plover, Greater Yellowlegs, White-rumped and Semipalmated Sandpipers, and Sanderling** to late October.

Waterfowl are another fall feature of Rustico Island with numbers rivalling those of Covehead Bay. The first **Common Loon** appear in early August, and are quickly followed by **Greater Scaup, Surf Scoter and Common Eider**. By mid September, **Northern Gannet** can be seen inshore, and they have reached totals of over **200** in mid October. **Great and Double-crested Cormorants** stream by in untidy skeins of **15-50** birds at the same time as the dabbling ducks reach their peak in September. **540 Black Duck** are joined by a few **Mallard, Northern Pintail and Green-winged Teal**. **300+ Canada Geese** may be present in October.

Diving ducks arrive a little later, but they reach impressive numbers in Rustico Bay and along the Gulf shore. As many as **500 Greater Scaup and 400 Red-breasted Merganser** stage here with **60 Common Eider and 25 Oldsquaw** between late September and mid October, and there are regular visits by all three scoters and **Common Merganser**. At the same time, **Common Loon** reach a peak and attract a few **Red-throated Loon and Red-necked Grebe**. Gulls and terns are also conspicuous on the sandflats where I have seen several hundred **Herring and Bonaparte's Gulls** as well as **20+ Caspian Tern** and a few **Iceland and Ring-billed Gulls**. **Arctic Tern** hang around until October.

The peak migration of warblers lasts from late August to the end of September, and flocks are easy to locate. **Yellow, Magnolia, Yellow-rumped, Black-throated Green and Blackpoll Warblers** are particularly common in September. **White-crowned Sparrow** are found along the roadside in late September and early October, when **White-throated, Swamp and Song Sparrows** are also common. **Rose-breasted Grosbeak** is also regular in September, and almost every passerine recorded on Prince Edward Island has appeared here at one time or another in fall. Notable rarities like **Yellow-breasted Chat and Orange-crowned Warbler** have occured on Rustico Island in early September. A few **Horned Lark, Snow Bunting and Lapland Longspur** persist into

December, but the peninsula is usually bleak and birdless until the return of the first ducks in mid April.

The small headland known as Hall's Island rates a special mention as the best place to study the gull and tern flocks on the sandflats and the rafts of diving ducks offshore. This is probably the best location in the park to observe **Oldsquaw, Common Eider** and scoters in May, when I have counted **30 Common Eider, 20 Surf Scoter, 15 Oldsquaw** and a few **Black and White-winged Scoters, Mallard and Greater Scaup** inshore. Many birds feed very close to the bluff which is covered with crowberry and juniper. **Black-bellied Plover and Sanderling** feed along the shore in late May when they are put to flight by passing **Northern Harrier and American Kestrel.**

In the fall there are fewer ducks inshore, but the same species fly by in tight flocks past the **Common and Red-throated Loons** on the water. There are, however, far more shorebirds, gulls and terns on the sandflats. Most of the **Bonaparte's Gull and Caspian Tern** spend their time crouched on the sandflats, although a hatch of insects or a "wreck" of moon snails will send them into a frenzy of excitement—the tiny **Bonaparte's Gulls** are fascinating to watch as they hawk for flies while the less buoyant **Herring and Ring-billed Gulls** do a number on moon snails. A few songbirds nest in the sparse growth on the headland, but most prefer the better cover of the campground woods where they are less likely to end up in the diet of a red fox or **Short-eared Owl.** Songbirds are just as common in fall as in spring at Rustico Island. A telescope is handy for searching among the flock on Rustico Beach for **Common Black-headed Gull.**

The area around the Highway 15 entrance to Brackley Beach can sometimes be a rewarding location in spring and fall. The small marsh and the roadside extension of Covehead Bay are both productive in spring. The first arrivals in late April are **Pied-billed Grebe, American Bittern and Greater Yellowlegs,** followed by **Brant, Northern Pintail, Ring-necked Duck, Willet, Lesser Yellowlegs and Least Sandpiper** in May.Most birds of prey arrive around the same time with **Northern Harrier, Peregrine, Merlin and American Kestrel** all in evidence. Many of the waterfowl linger into June when songbirds are on territory.

By late August the families are breaking up and the open woods are filled with flycatchers and warblers. It's worth strolling through the woods between the tennis courts and the beach and around the group campground area to find rarer birds like **Olive-sided, Alder and Yellow-bellied Flycatchers, and Chestnut-sided Warbler.** I have noted **Warbling Vireo and Northern Oriole** in the secondgrowth at Brackley Beach, and species like **Yellow-breasted Chat and Indigo Bunting** are certainly likely.

The extensive saltflats and marshes lining Covehead Bay are one of the top birding spots in Atlantic Canada. Except for a brief period in the winter, when there are only a few flocks of **Common Goldeneye, Common and Red-breasted Mergansers** in the bay and parties of **Snow Bunting and American Tree Sparrow** in the dunes and fields, Brackley Marshes are always alive with large numbers of birds. Even in summer when the migrants leave and the beaches are crammed with holidaymakers, there are breeding **Willet and Sharp-tailed Sparrow** to discover and a chance to flush up a **Northern Harrier or Short-eared Owl** from the dune grasses.

A visit in early April reveals the earlier waterfowl, and by the end of the month the first **Canada Goose and Brant** have appeared. Almost every species of dabbling duck has been seen from April to late June when up to **110 Black Duck, 100 Green-winged Teal and 60 Northern Pintail** share the waters with small numbers of **Mallard, American Wigeon, Blue-winged Teal and Northern Shoveler**. Geese numbers are even more impressive with up to **520 Brant and 180 Canada Geese** recorded. Most of the **Canada Geese** leave by late April, but the **Brant** flocks linger until late May. Diving ducks are in good numbers, too, with **Greater Scaup, Ring-necked Duck and Red-breasted Merganser** the commonest species to early May and **Oldsquaw** likely on the Gulf side.

Birds of prey move through the area from early April, with most birds leaving by mid May, although there have been a few reports of **Snowy Owl** well into early June. Shorebirds appear in small numbers from late April, with **Black-bellied Plover, Lesser Golden-plover and Greater Yellowlegs** the most likely to be seen until the short but impressive passage of **Least Sandpiper** in the second third of May. At this time there may be as many as **500 Least Sandpiper** strung out across the spartina flats with a few **White-rumped and Semipalmated Sandpipers**. Songbirds are much less frequently seen as there is little cover on the saltmarshes, but swallows, **Horned Lark** and sparrows sometimes arrive in good numbers in early May.

The marshes really come into their own in the late summer—anyone planning a visit should try to time it for late July to mid September to get the greatest variety of species. Numbers of shorebirds can be extremely high, and it's not difficult to get within a few feet of feeding flocks close to the road at mid tide. **Greater and Lesser Yellowlegs, Short-billed Dowitcher, Least and Semipalmated Sandpipers** are among the first birds to return in July, and later on the flocks of **Semipalmated Plover, Pectoral and White-rumped Sandpipers** are more evident. The spartina-glasswort flats of Brackley Marshes and Covehead will sometimes turn up a **Buff-breasted or Baird's Sandpiper**, and **Western Sandpiper, Ruff and Wilson's Phalarope** are all possible on Brackley Marshes in fall.

At one time or another from mid July to early November it's possible to count **1000 Semipalmated Sandpiper, 300+ Semipalmated and Black-bellied Plovers, Greater and Lesser Yellowlegs, Pectoral, Least and White-rumped Sandpipers, and 100+ Short-billed Dowitcher and Dunlin** at low tide. Smaller numbers of **Lesser Golden-plover, Whimbrel, Hudsonian Godwit, Willet and Red Knot** are also present on the flats. The marshes are used for roosting and feeding by up to **50 Great Blue Heron**.

Waterfowl are also plentiful in fall, but the first flocks wait until mid September to put in an appearance. **Green-winged Teal and Red-breasted Merganser** are the first to stage, but a visit between late September and mid November can produce up to **1250 Canada Geese, 1550 Black Duck** and much small numbers of **Northern Pintail, Green- and Blue-winged Teal, and Red-breasted Merganser**. **Gadwall and Mallard** are recorded each fall, but **American Wigeon** are not as regular as in spring. You may find a **Lesser Scaup or Ruddy Duck** on Covehead Bay in mid October. A few gulls use the marshes, but most prefer Rustico Island and Covehead Harbour.

After the last **Northern Harrier** has left and the late broods of **Sharp-tailed Sparrow** have dispersed, there are a few parties of **Snow Bunting and Lapland Longspur** searching for grass seeds in the dunes as **Horned Lark and Water Pipit** flocks inspect the marshes. Few stay for the Christmas Count which has rarely produced much in the typical cold weather of an island winter. Birds of prey and woodpeckers are found in small numbers, along with the odd **Great Blue Heron, Canada Goose, Mallard, Greater Scaup, Harlequin, Red-breasted Merganser, Ring-necked Pheasant, Glaucous Gull, Mourning Dove, Boreal Chickadee, Red-breasted Nuthatch, Brown Creeper, Bohemian Waxwing, Northern Shrike, Dark-eyed Junco, Common Grackle, Purple Finch and White-winged Crossbill.**

The 1988 count had 45 species, but only **Black Duck, Common Goldeneye, Great Black-backed and Herring Gulls, American Crow, Common Starling, Snow Bunting and House Sparrow** reached three figures. Next in numbers were **Rock Dove, Blue Jay, Black-capped Chickadee and Evening Grosbeak**, with small counts of **Oldsquaw, Barrow's Goldeneye, Common Merganser, Gray Partridge, Ruffed Grouse, Iceland Gull, Horned Lark, Common Raven, Golden-crowned Kinglet and American Robin.**

The entrance to Covehead Bay is at the bridge by Covehead Harbour where giant bluefin tuna were landed in large numbers. In spring the harbour area is excellent for diving ducks, especially **Common Goldeneye and Red-breasted Merganser**, and sometimes a few **Greater Scaup, Oldsquaw and Surf Scoter** offshore. Dabbling ducks are less common, with **American Wigeon and Northern Shoveler** until early June—the latter nesting by Covehead Pond where **Willet** nest.

The commonest spring shorebirds are **Greater Yellowlegs and Least Sandpiper**, but **Piping Plover** are regular on the sandbar from late April, and there have been **Ruff and Short-billed Dowitcher** in the marshy area by the Covehead road. **Caspian Tern** join the harbour gulls in May and June, and there are always a few pairs of **Arctic Tern** in the small colony of **Common Tern** by the roadbridge.

Willet

Covehead shows its colours in fall when huge numbers of gulls and shorebirds pass through. The birdlife is very similar to that of the Brackley Marshes, but the sandy nature of the flats make them more attractive to **Black-bellied Plover, Red Knot, Sanderling, Caspian Tern and Bonaparte's Gull** in fall. The first birds arrive in early July soon after the last northbound birds have left, and the flocks are in a constant flux.

Black-bellied Plover are extremely common with a normal maximum count of **300**, and there may be almost as many **Semipalmated Plover and Lesser Golden-plover**. The highest counts are reserved for **1200 Semipalmated Sandpiper, 1150 Sanderling and 800 Lesser Yellowlegs**, but maximum counts of **300 Least Sandpiper, 170 Greater Yellowlegs, 135 Dunlin, 115 Short-billed Dowitcher and 100 White-rumped Sandpiper** are impressive, too. Counts of **Killdeer, Ruddy Turnstone, Whimbrel, Hudsonian Godwit, Red Knot and Pectoral Sandpiper** are also into double figures. Many of these birds move to Brackley Marshes at mid tide when the sandbar gets covered, so the best time to scope the flocks is at low tide.

Gulls and terns also like the sandbar at low tide, and this is one of the best places on Prince Edward Island to see **Bonaparte's Gull and Caspian Tern** in the fall. The first birds appear in mid-late July, when **Ring-billed Gull** is regular, and the larger flocks are a feature of early August-mid October. As many as **190 Great Black-backed, 450 Herring and 520 Bonaparte's Gulls, 130 Common and 45 Caspian Terns** have been counted, and the flocks are always worth checking for rarer species after storms. **Great Blue Heron** often feed in the area, and a walk through the marsh grasses may surprise a **Ring-necked Pheasant or Mourning Dove** at any time in the fall and winter.

Dabbling ducks are quite common in late August and September, but the largest waterfowl numbers are reserved for geese and diving ducks. **Red-breasted Merganser** reach a peak of **550** in mid October, about the same time as **200 + Canada Geese and Black Duck** can be counted. Several **Greater Scaup, Surf Scoter and Common Goldeneye** stage at the same time. By the time the last ducks and shorebirds have left and the odd **Northern Harrier, Peregrine and Merlin** have passed by, there are only a few late flocks of **Horned Lark, Snow Bunting and Lapland Longspur** to face the long winter.

Other places to visit from this site

The southward extension of Rustico Bay towards Wheatley River is one of the richest shellfish grounds in the area. The mudflats by Oyster Bed Bridge are popular with marshbirds and shorebirds, but it is the wintering flock of **Barrow's Goldeneye** that draws most comments—I have counted **57** in early April and there are always birds present from late winter to early spring. Most other diving ducks peak in late April, when **Greater Scaup and Surf Scoter** fish among the flocks of **Common Goldeneye, Common and Red-breasted Mergansers**. **Canada Goose and Brant** may also appear in good numbers in late April and May—especially if disturbed from their favourite Brackley Marshes. **Great Blue Heron** are numerous when the ducks pass through and there may be a few shorebirds in late May. Most ducks reappear in October after the small numbers of terns and shorebirds have left, and a stop by the Highway 6 bridge is in order to check them out.

The Brackley Beach farmlands are well worth inspecting, but you should talk to the local farmers first. Most open-country birds nest in the fields and woodlots, including **Red-tailed Hawk, Killdeer, Cliff Swallow, Bobolink and Vesper Sparrow**. I found most of the usual nesting songbirds in summer and migrants in May and September. Thrushes and warblers are plentiful on migration, and the wide range of cover makes finding a few rarities quite likely. There are also a few freshwater ponds alongside the road — these are noticeably attractive to **Solitary Sandpiper** in late August-early September. The section between Harrington and Brackley Beach may also be quite productive, but I had few opportunities to check out the upper reaches of the Black River. The woods are composed largely of secondgrowth and young conifers, and boreal finches may be quite widespread here.

The first pond on the shore side of the park road east of Covehead Harbour is known as John Archies Pond. This is a seasonal pond and its birdlife varies with the amount of water or mud present. Spring **Gadwall and Northern Shoveler** are not unknown. During a wet summer it's used by ducks, including broods of **Black Duck, Blue-winged Teal and American Wigeon**, but is most productive after a dry spell when the oozy mud is favoured by large numbers of shorebirds. A few ducks and shorebirds may be present in May and June, when the nesting **Yellow Warbler, Common Yellowthroat and Swamp Sparrow** are in full song, but the main influx comes in mid-late July and lasts until early October in a good year. Other interesting summer visitors have included **Northern Fulmar, Osprey and Ruby-throated Hummingbird**, and the occasional **Common Black-headed Gull** may turn up along the beach.

Semipalmated Plover and Semipalmated Sandpiper are the commonest shorebird species, but **Killdeer, Greater Yellowlegs, Short-billed Dowitcher, Least and White-rumped Sandpipers** are also regular. A few **Lesser Yellowlegs and Dunlin** appear if the pond is muddy, and **Mallard and Northern Pintail** use John Archies Pond in fall if the water level is high enough. It is one of the few places that has reported a **Wilson's Phalarope** in late summer. Rarer species are less likely near Covehead, but the small marsh on the Stanhope side of the harbour has produced **Ruff, Curlew and Stilt Sandpipers, and Wilson's Phalarope**. There has also been a fall report of a **Red-necked Phalarope** — long overdue as the park interpretation symbol was for a long time this species although there had been no park record!

Stanhope Beach has a second, somewhat larger, pond which can be counted on for breeding ducks, including **American Wigeon**, and quite often **Pied-billed Grebe**. Duck numbers are usually small, but most freshwater species occur in spring and fall. The surrounding secondgrowth and scrub has the usual selection of thrushes, warblers and sparrows, and a glimpse may be caught of the few **Eastern Kingbird and Gray Catbird** on the other side of the Gulf Shore road. This is also a good place to look for **Northern Shrike, Evening Grosbeak, Red Crossbill and Bobolink** in early spring. Stanhope Beach can also be a good spot for a seawatch. In late April flocks of **Common Eider, Surf Scoter and Ring-necked Duck** can be looked for, and during September there are a few **Common Loon, Northern Gannet and Greater Scaup** close to shore. **Red-throated Loon and Horned Grebe** are less regular. One of the **Ring-necked Pheasant** from the Stanhope farmlands has also showed up here. The sandy beach, especially at the Long Pond outlet, attracts good numbers of shorebirds and gulls in the early fall. August-early September see groups of **Bonaparte's and Ring-billed Gulls**. **Black-bellied Plover and Sanderling** may also attract a **Lesser Golden-plover** to the grassy margins.

The woods around Stanhope are less productive than those on the Long Pond Loop, but those along the Bubbling Springs trail are usually good for boreal species such as **Black-backed Woodpecker, Gray Jay, Boreal Chickadee, Red-breasted Nuthatch, Gray-cheeked Thrush, Cape May and Bay-breasted Warblers** early in the summer and into fall. The cottage developments have drawn a few pairs of **Gray Catbird** and are popular feeding spots for swallows and thrushes in summer. Birds of prey are irregular, although there have been **Sharp-shinned Hawk and American Kestrel** in summer and **Rough-legged Hawk and Short-eared Owl** on migration.

Long Pond is the only freshwater lake in the eastern end of the park with suitable nesting habitat for good numbers of waterfowl, so the presence of a few pairs of **Black Duck, Green- and Blue-winged Teal** is not surprising. The lake is also a good place to look for **Ring-necked Duck and Bufflehead** in early May, although the best waterfowl season is certainly fall. **Pied-billed Grebe and Ring-necked Duck** move from their nesting areas in September and are joined by small numbers of **Northern Pintail, American Wigeon and Gadwall** at the end of the month. At the same time, diving ducks start to appear and the hundreds of **Common Goldeneye** may be joined by a few **Lesser Scaup, Barrow's Goldeneye, Bufflehead, Ruddy Duck and Hooded Merganser**.

By the end of October it's possible to add **Mallard and Greater Scaup** to the tally. **American Bittern** can be seen until October. The trail itself loops round Long Pond and is probably the best place to study nesting songbirds. Nearly every passerine found in the national park occurs here, including a few hard to find anywhere else like **Least Flycatcher, Gray Catbird, Solitary Vireo, Northern Parula, Northern Oriole and Rose-breasted Grosbeak**. I have also recorded **Philadelphia Vireo and Nashville Warbler** along the Long Pond trail and found **Sora and Sedge Wren** in the wetter margins. The trail is also a good chance to see mammals.

The best location on Hillsborough Bay is a 7-mile peninsula ending at Point Prim. The furthermost point is reached by taking Highway 209, and I would recommend parking about two miles from there and walking from a small spit on the Hillsborough Bay shore around the point and back on the Pinette Harbour shore. The round trip of less than 5 miles is sure to yield good numbers of most common shorebirds in August and September, including **Ruddy Turnstone and Willet**. Ducks can be seen offshore with **Great Cormorant**, but the best dabbling duck habitats are the marshes and pools opposite Pinette Point. This is private land, so the usual comments on seeking permission apply. The small estuaries to the east at Pinette Harbour and Gascoigne Cove have extensive saltmarshes for dabbling ducks and shorebirds. **Blue-winged Teal** are especially common in late August — when flocks of **100** are not unusual. **Mallard** are also increasing among the **Black Duck** flocks. The offshore mussel beds attract large parties of **White-winged, Black and Surf Scoters** during the early summer, and other diving ducks are common in April and October. There could be a few **Gadwall and Northern Shoveler** in the Pinette Harbour dabbling duck flocks.

TRACADIE BAY

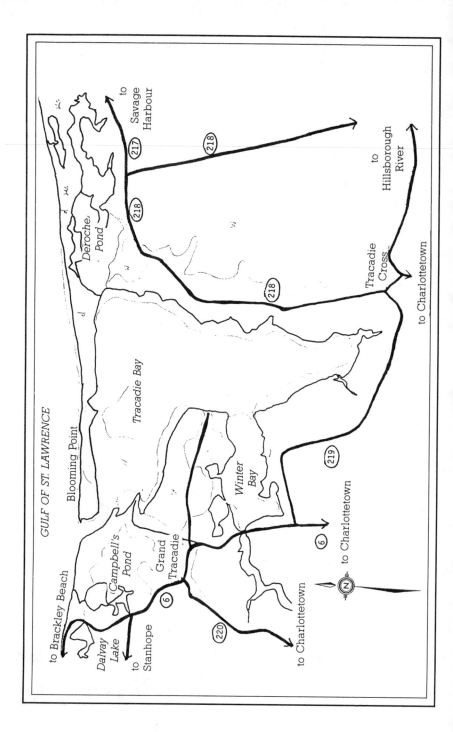

GULF OF ST. LAWRENCE

Blooming Point

Deroche Pond

Tracadie Bay

Winter Bay

Campbell's Pond

Grand Tracadie

Dalvay Lake

to Brackley Beach

to Stanhope

to Charlottetown

to Charlottetown

to Charlottetown

to Charlottetown

to Savage Harbour

to Hillsborough River

Tracadie Cross

217

218

218

218

219

6

6

220

N

Although the waters and marshes of Tracadie Bay are not included within the boundaries of Prince Edward Island National Park, they play an important part in providing additional habitats for birds. Tracadie Harbour is reached by driving north off Highway 6 along the minor road in Grand Tracadie. Most of the local fishermen fish for lobster, scallop and oyster, and the narrow channel is negotiable only at mid and high tides.

The national park spans Tracadie Bay from the tuckamoor and dunes northeast of Dalvay to the similar habitats of Blooming Point. If time is restricted, a walk to the harbour entrance by way of Campbell's Pond is in order. This is a little known gem of a habitat providing a summer haven for nesting ducks. **American Wigeon** nest here with **Black Duck, Green- and Blue-winged Teal, and Ring-necked Duck. Pied-billed Grebe, Mallard and Northern Pintail** are all found in late summer and may nest. **Osprey** are a regular feature in summer, when **Northern Harrier, Short-eared Owl and American Kestrel** patrol the dunes.

The western and southern margins of the pond by the park road have a good number of nesting songbirds. **Alder Flycatcher, Gray Catbird, Solitary Vireo and Rose-breasted Grosbeak** are all present, and rarer warblers like **Bay-breasted, Canada and Wilson's Warblers** may join them in the thicket growth along the stream and pond edges. **Eastern Kingbird and Red-winged Blackbird** like the marshy edges, and swallows hawk over the waters from May to late September. The stand of pine near the pond also provides a year-round home for **Pine Grosbeak, Red and White-winged Crossbills, and Pine Siskin**, but they are not always visible.

The birdlife of Tracadie Bay is very similar to that of the larger tidal flats and marshes of Rustico and Covehead Bays, but numbers are generally much lower. Ducks overwinter in the area, including a small flock of **Barrow's Goldeneye**. By late April the early migrants have begun to stream through, with **Northern Pintail, White-winged Scoter and Piping Plover** among the more interesting species. Ducks dominate into mid May, and there are usually a few **American Wigeon** feeding in the grassy marshes. Later on the shorebirds take over. For some reason the marsh is attractive to species not normally associated with spring migration such as **Hudsonian Godwit**, and there are always a few **Piping Plover and Willet** on hand until late in the month. **Piping Plover** were not breeding in the area in the 1970s, but likely are now. June may also produce late-migrating **Bonaparte's Gull and Caspian Tern**, and the feeding gull flocks may contain a few **Ring-billed Gull**. **Red-winged Blackbird, Bobolink and Sharp-tailed Sparrow** are the best nesting songbirds.

Things start to pick up again in mid July, when up to **30 Great Blue Heron** can be counted at low tide, and it is about this time that the first gull parties should be checked for **Common Black-headed Gull and Caspian Tern**. By the end of the month the flats and marshes are filled with restless parties of shorebirds, which share the area first with gulls and terns and then with waterfowl.

Almost all the eastern shorebird species are represented. **Lesser Yellowlegs, Short-billed Dowitcher, Semipalmated Plover, Least and Semipalmated Sandpipers** dominate early in August, and **Black-bellied Plover, Greater Yellowlegs, and Red Knot** replace them until early September. **Black-bellied and Semipalmated Plovers, Red Knot, Dunlin, White-rumped Sandpiper and Sanderling** swell the ranks of **Greater Yellowlegs and Semipalmated Sandpiper** until the end of migration in late October. Other species such as **Piping Plover, Killdeer, Hudsonian Godwit, Ruddy Turnstone and Pectoral Sandpiper** can be expected at any time. I didn't spend enough time here in 1975 to see any rarities, and reports are lacking.

The mixed gull and tern flocks are best counted at low tide when they roost on the sandbar north of the spit road. They are a noticeable feature from mid July to October, when parties of **Bonaparte's Gull and Common Tern** are still present. Maximum counts for the various species are indicative of the numbers involved during this period — **70 Great Black-backed Gull** in early August, **370 Herring Gull** in early September, **380 Bonaparte's Gull** from mid to late September, and **85 Common Tern** in late August. There are also a dozen **Caspian Tern** in early September and a few **Ring-billed Gull** throughout the fall.

Waterfowl start to reappear in late August, when dabbling ducks are more conspicuous, but only really begin to build up in mid September, when **350 Black Duck** are joined by a few **Mallard, Northern Pintail, American Wigeon, Green- and Blue-winged Teal**. Late in the month the first **Canada Geese** appear, and the **Black Duck** count reaches **500** on the eastern shores where food is more readily accessible and hunters are less of a problem. By mid October there may be **650 Canada Geese and 1000 Black Duck** in Tracadie Bay, and there can be as many as **215 Greater Scaup and 60 Red-breasted Merganser** on hand until the wintering flock is established in early November, when the first **Oldsquaw, Common and Barrow's Goldeneyes** arrive.

The relative isolation of Blooming Point which guards the entrance to Tracadie Bay makes it difficult to assess its birdlife on the same terms as similar dune habitats on Cavendish and Dalvay beaches which I was able to study on a regular basis. However, a few visits in early summer have shown this is a good place to look for northbound passerines, particularly the rarer flycatchers and warblers. The national park has given special protective status to Blooming Point. This is partly as a result of the existence of a few pairs of **Piping Plover** on sandy beaches undisturbed by tourist hordes, and partly because of the plantlife found in the relict forests along the spit. The mixed colony of **Common and Arctic Terns** need all the protection they can get as summer storms and high tides often inundate nests on the exposed tip facing Dalvay Beach. Blooming Point has provided a rare midsummer record of a **Wood Duck**.

The coastal tuckamoor and relict forests provide nesting habitats for songbirds in summer, while fall offers a good opportunity to study loons, waterfowl and shorebirds on both sides of the point. Access to Blooming Point is best made by canoe, but inexperienced canoeists should be aware that there is a very strong tide in the channel — crossing should not be attempted if the wind gets up. The water is very shallow at low tide which means getting out and dragging a loaded canoe over the sandbars. I can vouch for the effort as I helped line a canoe across the sand flats at low tide. An alternative access is by way of the minor road along the eastern shore of Tracadie Bay and a long hike along the spit. This is a good alternative if it is planned as an adjunct to a visit to Deroche Pond.

Deroche Pond is one of the best places on the Gulf shore to see waterfowl at close range, and a visit between April and October is almost certain to add a few species to an island list. The pond received a limited amount of protection, but there was still hunting in the area until the Island Nature Trust purchased its 142 acres. Several ducks nest in the fringing vegetation, and this appears to be a good candidate for breeding by **Northern Shoveler, Redhead and Ruddy Duck** — all of which are regular on spring migration.

Waterfowl

Pied-billed Grebe has bred, and there is a good chance of adding **Gadwall, Lesser Scaup, Bufflehead and Hooded Merganser** on a fall visit. **Horned Grebe** are fairly common offshore and the Point Deroche coast also receives regular visits from more pelagic species. Rails almost certainly breed, and there is a good chance of adding a stray heron or egret to your list in late summer. Songbirds are also conspicuous on migration, and the secondgrowth and scrubby forest lining Highway 219 turns up some interesting species.

Other places to visit from this site
The dirt road branching off the national park housing area road past Dalvay Pond leads through mixed and coniferous woods to two ponds serving as the park's sewage lagoon. Depending on the level of the water in the ponds, they can be very popular with

waterfowl and shorebirds. The left lagoon is usually mud or shallow water and is rarely used, but the right one is a small pond that has attracted surprising numbers of **Blue- and Green-winged Teal, Common Goldeneye and Ring-necked Duck**. The margins of this pond are used by shorebirds in September, when I have seen small numbers of **Solitary and Least Sandpipers**. More surprising visitors to the Dalvay sewage lagoon in September were **Pectoral and Stilt Sandpipers, and Wilson's Phalarope**.

The abundance of birds didn't go entirely unnoticed by the resident birds as I saw an immature **Northern Goshawk** making a few unsuccessful sallies at the teal on two visits. The scrubby growth and forest have a few nesting songbirds, especially **Yellow- bellied and Alder Flycatchers** and warblers, but they are most productive in spring and fall. I saw a **Northern Shrike** checking out the area in late April, and sparrow numbers were very high in May and late September. The imposing lakeshore manor of Dalvay-by-the-Sea was built in 1896 by the Scottish president of the Standard Oil Company, Alexander MacDonald. It now serves as the local hotel.

Dalvay Lake itself is very low in plant and animal food, although a few **Black and Ring- necked Ducks** find it worthy of passing interest in the fall. The much smaller Dalvay Pond on the other side of the road is much more attractive and offers **Blue-winged Teal and Ring-necked Duck** in early and later summer. **American Bittern** hide out in the wet margins, and it's worth following the boardwalk of the Reeds and Rushes trail to look for songbirds and occasional **Solitary and Least Sandpipers**.

Dalvay Beach is more for shorebirds, which are less harried than those gathered on the popular Stanhope and Brackley beaches. **Piping Plover** are sometimes present, but the usual migrants are **Black-bellied Plover and Sanderling**. Most birds have left by mid September, but this is about the time to look for **Red-throated Loon and Old- squaw** as they start to move south. The following month can be quite stormy which explains the number of **Leach's and Wilson's Storm-petrels** rescued on the lawns and roadsides. There have also been some October visits to Dalvay Beach by rarities like **Northern Fulmar and Arctic Loon**. Early November is a good time to look for **Common Redpoll and Red Crossbill** and the first **Northern Shrike** before the snowflakes and **Snow Bunting** flocks take over the beach.

Charlottetown is the cultural and commercial centre of Prince Edward Island, while the only other city, Summerside, is its industrial and military centre. Many of the buildings in the Old Town date from the 1860s when the idea of Canada was first discussed in what is now Province House. Prince Edward Islanders, with typical foresight and caution, waited a few years before embracing confederation — thereby gaining some important concessions on transportation and communication. The city of Charlottetown is attractively placed at the junction of several river estuaries and below the rugged Bonshaw Hills which cut across the island.

Most of the island's birders live in Charlottetown, including Geoff Hogan, who has written a bird guide and runs the "Bird's Eye" store in town. His feeders and seed helped sustain two overwintering **Pine Warbler** recently. Dan McAskill compiles both Prince Edward Island Christmas Bird Counts. The Hillsborough count is notable mainly for its **5500+ Common Starling** and good totals for **Canada Goose, Black Duck, Common Goldeneye, Common Merganser** and gulls.

Just north of the Hillsborough River bridge on the east side of town, the suburb of East Royalty has the best local birding with small numbers of shorebirds from mid July to mid October. **Black-bellied Plover, Killdeer, Greater and Lesser Yellowlegs** pass through in parties of two dozen or more, and there are smaller numbers of **Semipalmated Plover, Spotted Sandpiper, Short-billed Dowitcher, White-rumped and Semipalmated Sandpipers**. The East Royalty area has also turned up a **Willet**. There are also **Common Tern** nests on piles in the river.

To the east of Charlottetown, the tidal Hillsborough River flows into Hillsborough Bay although its source is very close to the Gulf of St. Lawrence shore near Savage Harbour. Almost every section of the river yields some birds year round, and access points are found all along Highway 2 on the north bank and Highway 21 on the the south bank. Several pairs of **Osprey** nest in the Mount Stewart area, and are widespread in summer. Other birds of prey are often noted, including **Rough-legged Hawk** in winter.

Herons are also extremely common along the river — **Great Blue Heron** numbers are quite high. Rails may well be widespread, although nesting populations of both **Sora and Virginia Rail** are unknown. The southern banks of the Hillsborough River have also attracted a few stray **Common Moorhen**, which are rumoured to have bred. There have been occasional **Little Blue Heron, Black-crowned Night Heron, and Snowy Egret** along the Hillsborough River in summer and the odd **Great Blue Heron** lingers into winter.

Dabbling ducks are certainly plentiful and nest along the river. I have seen broods of **Black Duck, Green- and Blue-winged Teal, Northern Pintail and Mallard**, and I suspect **American Wigeon, Gadwall and Ring-necked Duck** families are also raised most summers. **Lesser Scaup** may be disturbed from the more placid sections of the river on migration. **Northern Shoveler and Hooded Merganser** have also been found in late December, along with a few very late songbirds.

Access to the shore is possible at several points between East Royalty and Mount Stewart, but permission should be sought before entering private pasturelands. Winter counts have indicated the potential of the area by turning up **310 Common Merganser** and a few **Gray Partridge**, but the count of **1260 American Crow** is likely to excite no-one but a fervent corvid fan.

ISLES DE LA MADELEINE

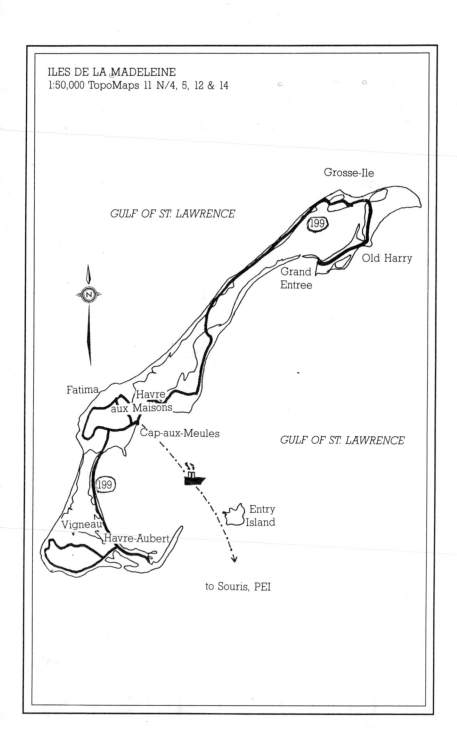

ILES DE LA MADELEINE
1:50,000 TopoMaps 11 N/4, 5, 12 & 14

Grosse-Ile

GULF OF ST. LAWRENCE

199

Old Harry

Grand
Entree

N

Fatima

Havre
aux Maisons

Cap-aux-Meules

GULF OF ST. LAWRENCE

199

Entry
Island

Vigneau

Havre-Aubert

to Souris, PEI

Souris is the terminal for the 85-mile car ferry trip to the Iles de la Madeleine. Excellent roads giving access to sites in the archipelago make it worthwhile to take the car ferry from PEI rather than flying. This ferry is a good opportunity to look for pelagics, and is often quite productive in terms of numbers of **Leach's Storm-petrel and Greater Shearwater**. **Wilson's Storm-petrel, Sooty Shearwater and Red Phalarope** are also fairly common in these waters. **Manx Shearwater** are becoming much more frequent in late summer and early fall—with **15** being counted off Grosse Ile in early September. The location of the archipelago also makes the ferry route a place to look for migrating **Sabine's Gull**, which prefer a more oceanic route than other arctic gulls. **Red-throated Loon, Red-necked Grebe, Pomarine and Parasitic Jaegers, and Red-necked Phalarope** also pass by on their way between the Labrador and Quebec coasts heading south. **Dovekie** sometimes appear in September, but the most likely time is November when more than **1200** were killed in an oil spill. Ducks are conspicuous in spring and fall, and shorebirds are also plentiful enough to look for rarities.

Located in the Gulf of St. Lawrence 70 miles from Prince Edward Island and 60 miles from Cape Breton, the archipelago of the Iles de la Madeleine is made up of twelve islands and islets, all but five of which are uninhabited. Air and sea connections have reduced the isolation of the islands somewhat, but this is still a very out-of-the-way place to visit. Champlain first reached the islands in 1534 and named Ile Brion after the French Grand Admiral of the time, but the archipelago's name comes from Madeleine Fontaine, wife of the first French noble to settle. Most of the islands and islets have both French and English names—a reminder of the conflicts between England and France.

Several locations have turned up birds in the winter months. The most productive has been Havre-aux-Maisons with all three scoters, none of which regularly winter in the archipelago. A **Bald Eagle** at Vigneau and **Common Black-headed Gull** at Havre-aux-Basques are more in line with what might be expected. Grand Entrée has sheltered **20 Mourning Dove** in early December, but the fact that the islands have a handful of winter sightings of **Dark-eyed Junco** most years indicates a lack of cover. The **Horned Lark** that wintered one year at Havre Aubert Island did not have that problem. Grosse Ile has provided **Bufflehead and Boreal Owl** in winter. The Magdalene archipelago's first **Hoary Redpoll** was found at Grand Entrée in late February, and a **Long-eared Owl** at La Vernière in early January proves that this species does occasionally wander to the Gulf of St. Lawrence.

Spring tends to be a quiet time of year on the archipelago, although there are parties of **Black Scoter** winging by and usually a few **Roseate Tern** with the returning **Common and Arctic Terns** in late May. **Greater Shearwater** sometimes appear in good numbers off Old Harry. Shorebirds are rare but **Ruddy Turnstone** has been seen at Havre-aux-Basques in late May. What were likely three **Black-tailed Godwit** were reported at Havre-aux-Maisons in the first half of May. Other European visitors included a drake **Eurasian Wigeon** in mid June. Havre-aux-Basques has had **Black Tern** in late May, while Havre-Aubert provided the first archipelago **Yellow-headed Blackbird** in the third week of May. Even better were a **Bobolink** at Havre-aux-Maisons in early April and a **Harris' Sparrow** at Cap-aux-Meules at the end of May.

By June, the **40+ pairs of Piping Plover** on the island beaches have young, and both **Common Black-headed Gull and Roseate Tern** have nested. There are also **Caspian Tern** in the colony at Havre-aux-Basques most years, and this site is a regular stop for a pair of **Gadwall** which successfully raised young in 1987. **Wood Duck** are also appearing regularly in summer, but a family of **Virginia Rail** at Grosse Ile and of **Long-eared Owl** at Grand Entrée in late July and early August have to be considered unusual.

A **Scarlet Tanager** at Grand Entrée on two occasions in summer, and the odd **Rose-breasted Grosbeak** indicate that southern species do appear, as does the island's second **Indigo Bunting** at Brion Island in mid June. An unmated pair of **Rufous-sided Towhee** at Havre-aux-Maisons provided the archipelago's second and third records. Old Harry is another productive site in summer with a **Green-backed Heron** appearing two summers in a row and a **Ruff** in early August. Fatima has also attracted an **Eastern Bluebird** in June, a **Ruff** in mid July and a **Ruddy Duck** in late July. **Snowy Egret** has also appeared at Pointe de l'Est in early summer. Other landbirds include **Black-billed Cuckoo** at Havre-Aubert in early July and **Chimney Swift** at Point-aux-loups in early June.

Much more likely to be seen are the first returning parties of shorebirds in early July. **Shortbilled Dowitcher** is usually the first species to arrive and numbers build to as many as **650** by mid July. **Whimbrel and Hudsonian Godwit** may also appear as early as late June, **Willet** are seen from early June to September, and **Ruff** are irregular in mid July-early August, along with **Wilson's Phalarope**. The number of **Whimbrel** passing through can be guaged by the **1000** counted at Havre-aux-Basques in early August. At the same time there were **400 Hudsonian Godwit**. Among the better American shorebirds, an **American Oystercatcher** at Havre-Aubert in late June, a **Long-billed Curlew** at Etang-des-Caps in early August, and a **Black-necked Stilt** at Havre-aux-Basques in early July are outstanding.

There have been occasional **Great Egret and Little Blue Heron** late in the summer, and a few sightings of **Snow Goose, Wood Duck, Bufflehead, King Eider and Ruddy Duck**. Other interesting summer reports have been from Fatima where **American Coot** have had young in August, **Virginia Rail** have been seen in early July and a **Ruff** has been seen in mid July. **Roseate Tern** are clinging on to their only nesting sites in the Gulf of St. Lawrence, with Point aux Loups the usual location. The common nesting passerines are **Horned Lark and Savannah Sparrow** on the dunes and a few **Veery** in the woods.

Perhaps the most famous site in the archipelago actually lies outside it — 15 miles to the northeast, in fact. Rochers des Oiseaux (Bird Rock) lies right in the middle of one of the busiest shipping lanes in the west Atlantic. The first lighthouse was built in 1870 and proved to be the hardest to construct of the ten built around the Gulf of St. Lawrence. One reason was the difficulty of landing anywhere around the island's 100-ft cliffs. This has not seemed to bother the 40,000 birds of a dozen species — mainly **Northern Gannet** — that have nested here since long before the first fishermen arrived in the 1500s and harvested boatloads for food.

Landings can be made on windless days, but these are rare and helicopters are the only feasible method of transportation for the lightkeepers and visitors. Apart from **Northern Gannet**, there are large numbers of **Black-legged Kittiwake** and somewhat smaller numbers of **Razorbill, Atlantic Puffin, Common and Thick-billed Murres**. Brion Island has nesting **Great Cormorant and Atlantic Puffin**, and there is a small colony of **Leach's Storm-petrel**. Brion Island has also attracted nesting pairs of **Common Eider and Black-backed Woodpecker**. This site has also attracted a party of **Great Blue Heron**, summering **Snowy Owl** on several occasions, and the odd **American Coot and Boreal Owl** in summer.

Shag Rock, appropriately enough, has a small number of **Great Cormorant**. The islets are accessible from Grosse Ile at the northern end of the archipelago, and fishermen might charter their boats. Grosse Ile is itself a good site with several June and July records of **Willet**, a rare family group of **Virginia Rail** and parties of shorebirds later in the summer. This location has provided **Bufflehead and Boreal Owl** in winter and parties of prospecting **Manx Shearwater** in September.

The islands are best known for their impressive showing during the fall shorebird migration. Several species, such as **Whimbrel, Lesser Golden-plover, Hudsonian Godwit, Red Knot and Lesser Yellowlegs**, are commoner here than anywhere else in Atlantic Canada, and a few pairs of **Piping Plover** breed on each sand beach.

Lesser Yellowlegs

Many flocks of shorebirds number in the **hundreds** and some total many **thousands** — sometimes mixed and sometimes single species. **Stilt Sandpiper** are regular in fall. **Marbled Godwit** can be looked for in late August-early September on the Madeleines, and a few more visits may turn up some of the Eurasian shorebirds which doubtless occur here.

The relative isolation precludes the arrival of many birds of prey, but those **Snowy Owl** that do make it in winter often stay through the summer. A few **Horned Grebe** nest in the vicinity of East Point, and several other waterfowl species, especially **Northern Pintail and Greater Scaup**, also nest. Many small islets in the larger lagoons support breeding colonies of **Great Blue Heron and Double-crested Cormorant**, and both **Snow Geese and Common Eider** are regular in fall.

Fall is the best time of year for rarities, which have included a critically-observed adult **Arctic Loon** at Grand Entrée in early October. The archipelago's first **American Woodcock** was at Havre-aux-Maisons in early October, the same time a **Buff-breasted Sandpiper** visited Fatima. Raptors generally avoid the islands, but the first **Red-tailed Hawk** was seen at Leslie in mid fall, and the first **Northern Hawk Owl** was at Havre-aux-Maisons mid-October. **Black and Roseate Terns** have been seen in early September, and there are sometimes **Northern Fulmar**, too. Unusual landbirds include a **Yellow-billed Cuckoo** at Grosse Ile in late September, **Ruby-throated Hummingbird** at Cap-aux-Meules in early August, **Townsend's Solitaire** at Old Harry in late August, **Eastern Wood-pewee** at Fatima in mid August, the first **Orange-crowned Warbler** at Havre-Aubert in late August, and a **Field Sparrow** at Old Harry in late October.

Other places to visit from this site

Gulls are common in the Souris area, which has more fishing activity than many other parts of the island. **Bonaparte's Gull** are common in fall when **Common Black-headed Gull and Black-legged Kittiwake** are likely, and **Iceland Gull** may sometimes outnumber other gulls in winter flocks. More observations are needed to put the Souris area on the map for birders. The saltmarshes of Colville and Rollo Bays and the tidal portion of the Souris River are all accessible from the Kings Byway — Highway 2. A late July **Curlew Sandpiper** and mid September **Gadwall** at Souris indicate more visits would pay off. There is a wide variety of habitats here, especially for waterbirds.

The inlets at Savage Harbour, St. Peter's Lake and St. Peter's Bay are good places to look for waterfowl and gulls. **Brant and Canada Goose** both appear in the spring, and diving ducks are regular on migration. The spit of land beyond Crow Bush Cove Provincial Park on the eastern shore of Savage Harbour looks attractive for shorebirds and may well have a few **Piping Plover** in the summer. **Caspian Tern** are a common sight in early May, when a few ducks are always present. The spits protecting the mouth of St. Peter's Bay may rate a visit for shorebirds, but I regret I never had the time to check them out.

The North Lake-East Point area looked very interesting on my only visit. Pelagics certainly pass by close to shore if the winds are right, and I'm sure an enterprising birder could add a few species to the provincial list by spending time between late June and early October. Shorebirds use North Lake, Diligent Pond, South Lake and Basin Head as staging and feeding areas, as do waterfowl. Nesting birds include **Northern Harrier, Short-eared Owl and Common Tern**, but I suspect the coast from East Point to Basin Head would yield far more. Winter is very bleak, but **Snowy Owls** are regular winter residents and flocks of **Snow Bunting and Lapland Longspur** not uncommon. The Basin Head area is ideally placed to attract strays year round, but the only rarities I know of are some late October **Harlequin**, a late October **Little Gull** and a mid November **Tundra Swan**. **Roseate Tern, Laughing and Sabine's Gulls** are definite possibilities, although they are rarely recorded on the island.

The most-visited site in eastern Prince Edward Island is probably Brudenell River Provincial Park, which lies next to a popular country club near Georgetown. The river marshes and golf course are well used by shorebirds, and this is a prime candidate for **Buff-breasted Sandpiper** visits—I have seen both **Piping Plover and Lesser Golden-plover**. The mudflats and rocks are occupied by most of the commoner shorebirds, especially **Greater and Lesser Yellowlegs**. Ducks are also common, with some birds staying very late into the early winter.

The north shore appears to have a wider range of habitats. The two-mile long spit off Poverty Beach that almost blocks access to Murray Harbour has good numbers of gulls and terns, and almost certainly roosting shorebirds at high tide. The Murray Harbour estuary has also produced an early summer **Great Egret**. Gary Schneider is a good contact in Montague.

The ferry terminal at Wood Islands was becoming a more popular departure and arrival point when facilities were improved, but there are plans (not entirely dependent on the proposed fixed link with New Brunswick) to discontinue the service. The trip can sometimes produce pelagics, but most birds pass north of the island. It is, however, one of the best places to see **Red-throated Loon** in May and October, but **Red-necked and Horned Grebes** are less frequent on the run. **Common Eider, White-winged and Surf Scoters** are extremely common in mid channel, and **Oldsquaw and Black Scoter** are regularly seen on migration. There is a chance of **Harlequin and King Eider** in May. **Red and Red-necked Phalaropes** pass through the Northumberland Strait, but sightings are rare and far from guaranteed, even during peak migration in May and late August-early September. The terminal itself has a few shorebirds at low tide well into October, and the coastal thickets of alder, bayberry and wild rose can be productive during migration.

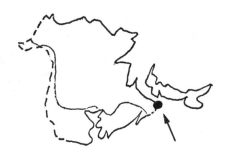

CAPE TORMENTINE AREA

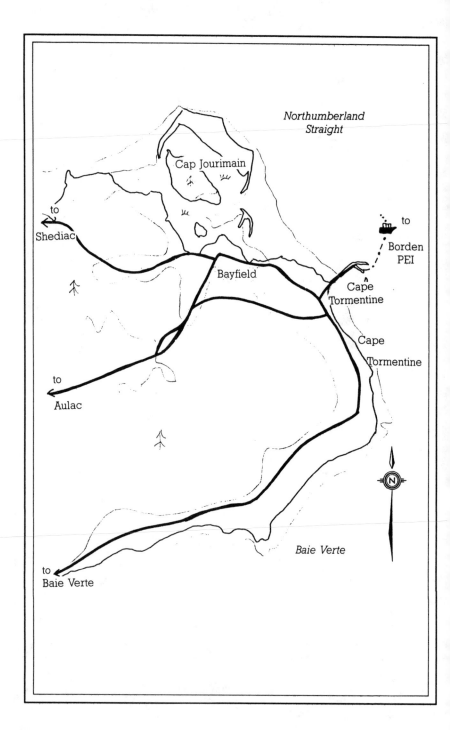

The Northumberland Strait shoreline is composed of two fairly distinct sections — the Shediac-Shemogue shore is an extension of the Acadian fishing settlements that stretch all the way from Lamèque, but the peninsula bounded by the waters of the Northumberland Strait and Baie Verte is more Scottish and pastoral in nature. People rarely visit the region for more than a few hours on their way to and from Prince Edward Island, although Shediac's July Lobster Festival does attract more visitors. Birding is quite good in fall and winter, especially between Cap Jourimain and Cape Tormentine at the northeast tip of the peninsula north of the ferry terminal.

The Cap Jourimain marshes are now part of a wildlife management area and an excellent place to visit in all but the bleakest months of the year. Over 200 bird species have been seen within the 640 hectares of marsh and adjacent waters. They are accessible from Highway 955 or Highway 15 by taking a minor road north of Bayfield to the point. This is just before a bridge and becomes a causeway to the shoreline — it is also the best place to see shorebirds in late summer. Loons, grebes, cormorants, sea ducks, and sometimes **Northern Gannet**, migrate past here in April and May. The marshes inside the crab-shaped island are uncovered at low tide and there are also extensive mudflats. Marshbirds are quite common in spring when there is a good chance of seeing **Great and Snowy Egrets** with the many **Great Blue Heron**, but **Cattle Egret** is less frequent. Cap Jourimain has attracted a **Tri-colored Heron** in spring, when **Little and Common Black-headed Gulls** have also dropped by.

Shorebirds appear in small numbers and may stay to nest, with a count of **14 Willet** in mid May indicating they are quite common. **Ruff** have occured often enough to suggest they might establish the first breeding site in North America, and **Wilson's Phalarope** have also discovered the breeding potential of the marshy ponds. Among the waterfowl, **Northern Shoveler, Gadwall and Redhead** are becoming more frequent in early summer and are a good bet to join the breeding **Black Duck, Northern Pintail, Green- and Blue-winged Teal**. A few **Lesser Scaup** have also been found prospecting for nestsites. A **Red-shouldered Hawk or Snowy Owl** may linger into summer waiting for a mate, but **Osprey** is the most likely summering raptor.

Sharp-tailed Sparrow nest along the edge of the marshes, and the fields and woods support good numbers of other songbirds, especially warblers. There is also a large **Cliff Swallow** colony at the lighthouse. The causeway road provides glimpses of shorebirds and is also good for landbirds — **Osprey and Black-billed Cuckoo** have been noted in summer. Songbirds are quite varied with **Alder Flycatcher, Cliff Swallow, Boreal Chickadee, Hermit Thrush, Ruby-crowned Kinglet, Solitary Vireo, Rose-breasted Grosbeak, Purple Finch, Dark-eyed Junco and Sharp-tailed Sparrow** indicating the variety of habitats. Warblers nesting in the area include **Northern Parula, Magnolia, Cape May, Black-throated Green, Yellow-rumped, Chestnut-sided, Bay-breasted and Canada Warblers, Ovenbird, Northern Waterthrush and American Redstart**.

Shorebirds are very common on fall migration with the first birds already present by mid July. The highest numbers appear in late July-mid August and again in September. As many as **1600 Short-billed Dowitcher, 200+ Greater and 185 Lesser Yellowlegs, Red Knot and Dunlin, and 55 Hudsonian Godwit** have been seen here. Larger shorebirds are, in fact, a feature of the area, and this is one of the best places in Atlantic Canada to see **Hudsonian Godwit. Semipalmated Plover, Least, White-rumped and Semipalmated Sandpipers** are also common. There have also been regular visits from **Ruff, Baird's and Stilt Sandpipers, Long-billed Dowitcher and Red-necked Phalarope** in fall. The fall flocks of **Ring-billed and Bonaparte's Gulls** should be checked for any **Common Black-headed and Little Gulls** — the latter returning as early as the second week of July.

After most of the shorebirds have left, waterfowl take over — an astounding **410 Red-throated Loon** have been counted in late October, although the count is normally far less from late September to late November. Large numbers of **Northern Pintail** migrate with the flocks of dabbling ducks in mid August-late October. Diving ducks are also abundant on fall migration, with **Common Eider and Red-breasted Merganser** joined by transient flocks of **White-winged, Black and Surf Scoters** — small groups of **Greater and Lesser Scaup** have been reported in late October.

An alternative or additional access is over the roadbridge and right about a mile further on along Trenholm Road to the beach. This can be walked at low tide in late summer and fall for good numbers of **Semipalmated and Black-bellied Plovers, Ruddy Turnstone, Greater and Lesser Yellowlegs, Red Knot, Pectoral, White-rumped, Least and Semipalmated Sandpipers, Dunlin, Sanderling, Short-billed Dowitcher and Hudsonian Godwit. Lesser Golden-plover, Whimbrel, Ruff, Wilson's and Red-necked Phalaropes** have also been noted on this beach.

The Christmas Bird Count takes in most of the peninsula and indicates the richness of these waters which rarely freeze. **Common and Red-throated Loons, Horned Grebe and Great Cormorant** winter in small numbers, along with the odd **Great Blue Heron, Northern Gannet and Thick-billed Murre**.

Over **1400 Canada Geese and 500 Black Duck** may be present, along with a few **Brant, Mallard and Northern Pintail** — the majority being located at Cap Jourimain. Diving ducks concentrate inshore, with **Oldsquaw, Common Goldeneye and Red-breasted Merganser** by far the commonest species, although **Greater Scaup, Common Eider, White-winged, Black and Surf Scoters, Bufflehead and Common Merganser** all occur. Most of the wintering gulls, which include fair numbers of **Iceland Gull** and the odd **Glaucous and Ring-billed Gulls**, overwinter in the ferry terminal area. **Purple Sandpiper** flocks sometimes have a **Red Knot** in tow.

Horned Grebes and Common Loon

Landbirds are spread over the peninsula in winter with **Snow Bunting and Common Redpoll** easily outnumbering all other species. **Rough-legged and Red-tailed Hawks** both overwinter, and the resident **Barred Owl** population may be joined by a **Snowy Owl or Northern Hawk Owl**. Wooded areas have **Ruffed** and the odd **Spruce Grouse, Black-backed and Pileated Woodpeckers, Boreal Chickadee, Golden-crowned Kinglet, Pine Siskin and Evening Grosbeak**, and more open areas attract **Mourning Dove, Horned Lark, American Tree Sparrow and Lapland Longspur**. Northern Mockingbird, Loggerhead Shrike, White-throated, Swamp and Field Sparrows, and Brown-headed Cowbird have been reported on the Cape Tormentine Christmas Bird Count but must be considered irregular at best.

The most surprising feature of the area is the large number of sparrows, blackbirds, **Golden-crowned Kinglet and Yellow-rumped Warbler** regularly overwintering—a recent count of **115 Golden-crowned Kinglet and 110 Yellow-rumped Warbler** is astounding when you consider how cold it gets! There were also good numbers of **Red-breasted Nuthatch, White-winged Crossbill, Common Redpoll and American Goldfinch** on the same count, and **365 Black-capped Chickadee** on the 1989 count. **Northern Shrike** do regularly appear in small numbers. Reports of wintering **Loggerhead Shrike** are possible given the slightly warmer temperatures, but the species is fast disappearing from even its summer range.

The windswept point at Cape Tormentine serves as the terminal for the Prince Edward Island ferry. Before the days of fast turnaround, the coastline south of the ferry terminal received visits from birders who had just missed the outbound ferry, but now there is very little wait between ferries. Waterfowl of all kinds stream through the Northumberland Strait. **Pied-billed Grebe** are almost exclusively spring visitors, but **Horned Grebe** are more likely to be seen with the first **Red-throated Loon** parties in late September.

Pelagics generally prefer to pass north of Prince Edward Island, but there are **Northern Gannet and Leach's Storm-petrel** in late fall and a few shearwaters, alcids and jaegers in late summer and early fall. Diving ducks can be quite common in May-June, and a few **White-winged and Surf Scoters** may stay for the summer, but the largest numbers are reserved for fall, when good numbers of **Black and Surf Scoters** stage offshore. The ferry offers an opportunity to see seabirds on a regular basis. **Common and Red-throated Loons** are common in fall, when there may be a few **Red-necked Grebe** among the **Horned Grebe** parties.

Shorebirds are less common here than on the Cap Jourimain marshes, and only **Semipalmated and Black-bellied Plovers, Least, Semipalmated and White-rumped Sandpipers** appear in any numbers. Gull numbers increase in August with **Bonaparte's Gull** flocks leaving with any accompanying **Common Black-headed Gull** before the freeze-up. **Ring-billed Gull** are more likely to winter in sheltered harbours—there have been as many as **61** on the Christmas Bird Count, and flocks of **Glaucous and Iceland Gulls** after late October may contain an **Ivory Gull**.

Oldsquaw are the most abundant wintering ducks, but **Common Eider** occur in good numbers with **White-winged Scoter and Red-breasted Merganser** — other species are regular but found in much smaller numbers. Seaducks are more likely close to Cape Tormentine, especially **Common Eider, White-winged, Black and Surf Scoters**. Gulls hang out at the terminals, and **Sabine's Gull** is possible among **Black-legged Kittiwake and Arctic Tern**. Songbirds do linger into the Christmas period with **Bohemian Waxwing, White-breasted Nuthatch, White-crowned Sparrow, Red-winged and Rusty Blackbirds** attracted to feeders and yards, and **Brown-headed Cowbird** can be quite common.

Other places to visit from this site
The warmer waters of Baie Verte to the south are another staging site for loons and other waterfowl. As many as **70 Common Loon** stay well into June, and **Red-throated Loon** appear in fall. **Barrow's Goldeneye** are regular among the flocks of **Common Goldeneye, Greater Scaup** and scoters in October and November. **Common Eider and Oldsquaw** form the bulk of wintering flocks, and **King Eider, Razorbill, Thick-billed Murre and Dovekie** may join the wintering **Black Guillemot**, but dabbling ducks are rare. **Turkey Vulture** have been seen in summer after the main hawk migration has taken place from mid April to mid May, and there are nesting records of **Willet**—a species showing clear signs of an increase on the Northumberland Strait.

Very few shorebirds drop into the Port Elgin area, but passerines find plenty to attract them and keep them into winter. An astonishing number of **Yellow-rumped Warbler** regularly overwinter around the cabins from Port Elgin to Upper Cape, and there are nearly always a few **Brown Creeper and Ruby-crowned Kinglet** to supply the **Northern Goshawk and Northern Shrike** populations in winter. Flocks of **Common Redpoll and Snow Bunting** spread over the countryside, and there are a few **Lapland Longspur** with them. Other finches and sparrows find less to attract them, but the **American Tree Sparrow** parties have been joined by **American Goldfinch, White-crowned, White-throated and Field Sparrows**.

Shediac is best known for its lobsters and the white sand beach of Parlee Beach Provincial Park, which attracts **Sanderling** and the odd **Piping Plover** in late summer. Very few birders visit the Shediac area, but I found **Ruby-throated Hummingbird and Eastern Meadowlark** to be regular in summer and fall. There are also a few **Gray Partridge** managing to survive winter weather and hunting pressure. The shoreline to Shemogue has rafts of seaducks — with **White-winged, Black and Surf Scoters** abundant in May and October. This is probably the best time to look for other waterfowl as well as there have been **400 Red-breasted Merganser** off Shemogue in mid October.

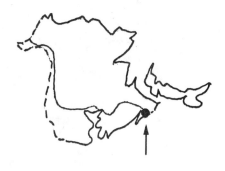

SACKVILLE AREA

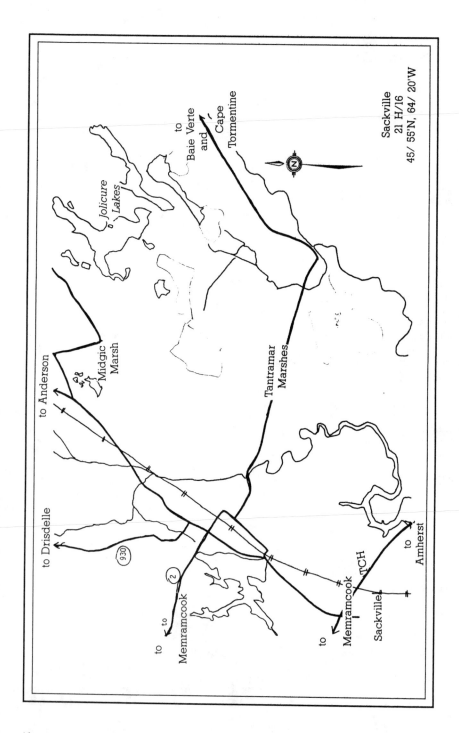

Sackville
21 H/16
45° 55'N, 64° 20'W

to
Baie Verte
and
Cape
Tormentine

Jolicure
Lakes

Midgic
Marsh

Tantramar
Marshes

to Anderson

to Drisdelle

930

2

to
Memramcook

to

TCH

to
Memramcook

Sackville

to
Amherst

The Border Region is steeped in history dating back to the mid 1600s when it was first drained and dyked for farming by Acadian settlers. The British arrived in the middle of the eighteenth century and established Sackville as their main settlement. Now Sackville is the campus of Mount Allison University and the location of the Canadian Wildlife Service Atlantic Region headquarters. While the university is one of the most important employers, CWS, and its joint-venture partner Ducks Unlimited, has the greatest influence on the surrounding area in terms of habitat management. Together with the Town of Sackville they have started the 50-acre Sackville Waterfowl Park which will feature interpretation of the wetland areas created and stabilized. The many marshes and impoundments support a high breeding population of ducks and rails, as well as being very important staging sites for waterfowl and shorebirds in spring and fall.

The Sackville Waterfowl Park supports a variety of dabbling and diving ducks from April to November, including **Wood Duck, Mallard, Green- and Blue-winged Teal, Ring-necked and Ruddy Ducks**. Other birds regularly viewed on the sanctuary are **Pied-billed Grebe, American Bittern, American Coot, Sora and Common Snipe**. Access to the park is off East Main Street by the tourist information centre and from the downtown business centre. A series of trails cross wetland and woodland areas. The park will also be the focus for an annual waterfowl festival started in 1990. **Gadwall** pairs may appear in early May and a few **Mallard, Blue-winged Teal and Red-breasted Merganser** nest close to town.

Sackville lies on the edge of the Border Region, but is very close to a number of excellent birding areas. Spring starts early with the first **Brown-headed Cowbird** flocks in early March and larger numbers with **Rusty Blackbird and American Goldfinch** later in the month. By mid April, **Red-breasted Merganser, Killdeer, Yellow-bellied Sapsucker and Eastern Phoebe** have put in an appearance, and there may sometimes be a northbound **Gyrfalcon**. Large numbers of **Tree Swallow** and a few **Eastern Bluebird, American Pipit, Northern Parula, Eastern Meadowlark and White-crowned Sparrow** follow in early-mid May, when **Snowy Egret, Wilson's Phalarope and Common Black-headed Gull** have been seen. By the end of May, most nesting warblers are in town, and there are usually a few **Black-throated Blue and Blackpoll Warblers** among them. Flocks of **100 Black-bellied Plover** are not uncommon, **Lesser Yellowlegs** may be seen as late as mid June, and **Killdeer** nest close to town.

Among the more interesting summer landbirds, **Common Nighthawk, and Ruby-throated Hummingbird** are both listed as breeding species, and **Great Horned Owl and Whip-poor-will** may well nest, but **Wilson's Phalarope** are still presumably at the exploratory stage. **Yellow-bellied, Least and Olive-sided Flycatchers, Gray Catbird, Cedar Waxwing, Loggerhead Shrike, Solitary Vireo, Northern Parula, Tennessee, Blackburnian, Chestnut-sided and Wilson's Warblers, Ovenbird and Northern Waterthrush** are all relatively rare in summer, although most nest each year. **Brown Creeper and Winter Wren** both nest in the Birch Hill road area, while **Red-eyed Vireo, Bay-breasted and Wilson's Warblers, Common Yellowthroat, Bobolink, Common Grackle, Vesper and Chipping Sparrows** are widespread. **Black-billed Cuckoo and Blue-gray Gnatcatcher** are now rare but regular in late summer and fall. Rarities like **Orchard Oriole** have appeared in June.

Shorebirds are common along the river in fall, with **600 Lesser Yellowlegs** counted in mid July and **1800 Dunlin** in mid November at the two ends of the migration period. **Semipalmated and Least Sandpipers** are both abundant, and fair numbers of **Lesser Golden-plover** arrive with the later waves. A count of **70 Hudsonian Godwit** in August is not considered unusual. **Solitary Sandpiper** drop by in early September, and **Hudsonian Godwit** can be looked for in late October. A stray **Yellow Rail** may wander into Sackville from Midgic in early August, but fall rarely produces many rarities until quite late when an odd **Cattle Egret or Mew Gull** may appear. Late October is a good time to look for any lingering **Snowy Egret** or migrant **Western Kingbird and Lark Sparrow**.

Snow Geese accompany the flocks of **Canada Geese** in early November, but only the latter stay over the winter. **Black Duck and Mallard** are the only common wintering ducks, but there are some **Common Eider and Common Merganser**, and the odd **Great Blue Heron, Green-winged Teal, Ring-necked and Wood Duck** to make the river interesting. A count of **10,000 Common Grackle** has been made in late October. The number of **Lapland Longspur** builds up to **50** or more in late November, and a few stay on with as many as **1700 Snow Bunting** and smaller **Common Redpoll** flocks on wasteground and marshes. Other common winter residents are **Black-capped Chickadee, Red-breasted Nuthatch, American Tree Sparrow, Dark-eyed Junco, White-winged Crossbill, American Goldfinch and Pine Siskin. American Robin** occasionally linger for the Christmas Bird Count, which has also turned up **Yellow-rumped and Pine Warblers, White-throated, Song and Swamp Sparrows, Common Grackle and Brown-headed Cowbird**.

Bald Eagle, Northern Harrier, Northern Goshawk, Red-tailed and Rough-legged Hawks, and Short-eared Owl are all found around town in winter, and there may also be a **Snowy Owl** to compete with any late **Broad-winged Hawk, Gyrfalcon or Merlin**. As many as **230 Ring-necked Pheasant** can be seen out in the open when snow is on the ground — the few **Ruffed Grouse** are much more circumspect.

Woodpeckers are widespread with **Pileated and Black-backed Woodpeckers** occasionally feeding in town. The greatest activity is in early winter when boreal birds such as **Gray Jay and Bohemian Waxwing** arrive to occupy town feeders and bushes. **Snow Bunting, American Tree Sparrow, Dark-eyed Junco and Common Redpoll** are everywhere, which draws **Northern Shrikes**, and these flocks often entertain **Song and White-throated Sparrows, Lapland Longspur** and blackbirds. A few **Boreal Chickadee, Pine and Evening Grosbeaks, Red and White-winged Crossbills** visit feeders in hard winters, and some **Northern Shrike, Red-winged Blackbird and Brown-headed Cowbird** usually overwinter in and around town.

A repeat Boxing Day **Turkey Vulture** at Sackville is unlikely but appropriate given the seasonal fare. A rare **Red-bellied Woodpecker** recently spent early winter, although **Red-headed Woodpecker** is more likely. Some of the more impressive wintering songbirds have included **Great Crested Flycatcher, Brown Thrasher, Northern Mockingbird, Varied Thrush, Ruby-crowned Kinglet, Yellow-rumped Warbler, Common Yellowthroat, Eastern Meadowlark, Northern Cardinal, Dickcissel, Lark and Grasshopper Sparrows**.

Midgic Marsh just to the north of Sackville has a large number of nesting **Northern Pintail, Sora and Virginia Rails** and a few **Pied-billed Grebe, American Bittern, Blue-winged Teal, Northern Shoveler, Wood Duck and American Coot**, but is best known for its summering **Yellow Rail** which are found until mid August. A **Purple Gallinule** at Midgic Marsh in fall was probably a vagrant, and just what an **American Bittern** was doing here in mid January only the bird itself knows.

Waterfowl numbers were much higher in the 1950s when **Mallard** were released, but few pairs now breed—most of the **Wood Duck** are in the White Birch road area where **21 males** have been counted in early July. A few **Short-eared Owl** nest on the marshes, but the **Sedge Wren** colony has disappeared to be replaced by a colony of **Marsh Wren**. Bobolink, Savannah, Sharp-tailed and Swamp Sparrows are all common nesting birds on the marshes and wasteground. As many as **300 Tree, 100 Bank and 250 Cliff Swallows** have been counted in the spring and a few **Purple Martin** may join them in August.

Some **Rough-legged Hawk** reappear in early spring when **Northern Harrier** establish breeding territories, and there are often a few **Snowy Owl** on their way back north when **Barred and Short-eared Owls** are sitting on eggs in late April. A few pairs of **Broad-winged Hawk** find enough cover to nest in the Birch Hill area. **Common Goldeneye, Bufflehead and American Wigeon** pause briefly on the marsh, but they have to watch out for a **Peregrine** which returns each year to get its fill of ducks.

Small numbers of **Greater Yellowlegs and Least Sandpiper** stop by in mid May, and there are sometimes **Black Tern**. Apart from an odd **Upland Sandpiper** and the nesting **Common Snipe and Spotted Sandpiper**, most shorebirds are absent until early August, when **Semipalmated Plover, Lesser Golden-plover, Lesser Yellowlegs, Pectoral Sandpiper and Short-billed Dowitcher** are common. **Whimbrel** follow in early September, when the last of the **Bonaparte's Gull and Black Tern** have left.

Little Blue Heron and Black-crowned Night Heron have both been seen in the area, although **Great Blue Heron** are the most likely birds feeding on the marsh. **Ruddy Duck and Hooded Merganser** stop in with the later waterfowl, and there may be a few late **Virginia Rail** joining them. Large numbers of **Red-winged Blackbird** roost on the marsh from late October to mid November, and these flocks often contain **Eastern Meadowlark and Dickcissel**. Few birds winter on the marsh, although a **Great Horned Owl** has been seen and **Spruce Grouse** are resident.

The Jolicure Marshes and lakes are becoming much better known now that they are receiving management. They are one of the best places to see nesting **Black Tern, Sora and Virginia Rail**, and there are **Common Moorhen and American Coot**, and possibly **Yellow Rail**, in the area. **Wilson's Phalarope** have now discovered the marshes and may soon breed. The ponds are managed more for waterfowl which are very common on migration. A few **Northern Shoveler** nest and parties of **30** or more are not uncommon in late summer.

Oldsquaw, White-winged, Surf and Black Scoters all pause here on their way north, and **Common Loon** find the open water inviting enough to nest. **Horned Grebe, Double-crested Cormorant, Bufflehead and Ruddy Duck** are regular with the scoters in fall, but **Common Goldeneye** are the commonest diving duck species. **Osprey and Northern Saw-whet** both nest in the area, and **Rough-legged Hawk and Northern Harrier** regularly winter. **Sedge Wren** may return here after a long absence, and other interesting passerines nesting at Jolicure include **Olive-sided Flycatcher, Black-and-white, Nashville, Magnolia, Black-throated Green and Wilson's Warblers, and Sharp-tailed Sparrow**.

Sedge Wren

Aulac has recently suffered a major fire which probably destroyed much of the coniferous forest. This would be a pity because **Black-backed and Three-toed Woodpeckers** were often seen here in winter when most birders made their visits. **American Woodcock and Northern Saw-whet** nest, which makes a summer visit more interesting. Most birds of prey arrive for winter with counts of **50 Rough-legged Hawk, 10 Northern Harrier, 8 Short-eared Owl**, and occasional **Snowy Owl and Gyrfalcon** hunt over the marshes. The spruce-larch bog and its ponds have **Common Loon, Black Duck, Blue- and Green-winged Teal, and Ring-necked Duck** nesting, and a new Ducks Unlimited pond at Beausejour may add other ducks. There is an assortment of songbirds, including **Rusty Blackbird and Palm Warbler**.

Other places to visit from this area

The closest point to the Nova Scotia border is occupied by the Tintamarre National Wildlife Area which takes its name from the "racket" caused by geese and ducks on the marshes. This adjoins Missaguash Marsh in Nova Scotia. The farm fields of the Acadians are gone, but some of the old barns remain and are used by birds of prey as hunting perches. The ponds and marshes attract nesting ducks and marshbirds, and an increasing number of shorebirds. **Wood Duck** are common breeders, and both **Mallard and Northern Shoveler** are regular — **Redhead and Ruddy Duck** are expected to nest soon, and so are **Wilson's Phalarope** which are becoming increasingly common. Marshbirds are also common, with **Sora** leading the way and **Virginia Rail** not too far behind. **Yellow Rail** are irregular visitors, and so are **Glossy Ibis and Great Egret** in the spring. Birds of prey also find the marshes to their liking. In summer **Northern Harrier and Short-eared Owl** are the most likely species, with the former more common than anywhere else in North America as far as breeding density goes. **Sharp-tailed Sparrow** is the common nesting sparrow in the wetter areas, with **Savannah Sparrow** replacing it on the drier grasslands — **Bobolink** is another fairly common nesting species. The area is very bleak in winter, but this does not seem to deter the large flocks of **Snow Bunting** — maximum count **8000** in mid December — wheeling around ahead of wintering **Rough-legged Hawk and Snowy Owl** and the odd **Short-eared Owl**.

An amazing visitor was a **Burrowing Owl** which took up temporary residence in the rubble of a collapsed barn at Aulac in late June one year. Late May **Long-eared Owl**, June **Northern Shoveler** and July **Turkey Vulture** were less mind-boggling visitors. Appearances by **Turkey Vulture and Burrowing Owl** indicate that rarer raptors do turn up on the Tintamarre Marshes, but the **Eurasian Kestrel** that stayed from December into late spring was even further off-course.

Tantramar Dam offers a good opportunity to watch shorebirds at close range. Large numbers of **Pectoral Sandpiper** gather in October, and have been joined by several **Long-billed Dowitcher**. **Semipalmated Plover, White-rumped and Semipalmated Sandpipers** are also common. Visits from two different **Eurasian Whimbrel** are the best of the shorebird reports at Tantramar Dam, and an **American Avocet** has been found on two separate occasions. Diving ducks raft in Cumberland Basin and can be studied by telescope, and there are usually a few gulls around.

On the other side of Sackville, Dorchester offers a similar variety of birds in somewhat smaller numbers. The best shorebird sites are found alongside Shepody Bay where saltmarshes and mudflats provide excellent feeding for ducks at high tide and shorebirds at low tide. Counts of **30,000 Semipalmated Sandpiper, 500 Dunlin and 330 Black-bellied Plover** indicate the large numbers that can be found. Dabbling ducks are commonest in September, with **Black Duck** the most abundant species, and there are usually a few diving ducks offshore. A **Cattle Egret** has been seen in early November after any **Great Blue Heron** have left. Flocks of **5000 Common Grackle** in late October and **2500 Snow Bunting** in early December break up by the end of the year, when most birds have left the area. **Ring-necked Pheasant** are possible all year, but **Loggerhead and Northern Shrikes** split the year between them, and an odd **Vesper Sparrow** may linger and even winter. There is an influx of **Canada Geese** and seaducks in March and April.

Upland Sandpiper has nested at Steeves Point, but Grand Anse off Highway 935 is the best spot for shorebirds in fall—with counts of **72,000 Semipalmated Sandpiper** and totals of **300+ Semipalmated and Black-bellied Plovers, 250 Short-billed Dowitcher, and 100+ Lesser Yellowlegs, Red Knot and Sanderling** from late July to early October. **Baird's and Western Sandpipers** tend to migrate in the first wave, but **Wilson's Phalarope** can appear at any time, and flocks of up to **1300 Dunlin and 500 White-rumped Sandpiper** appear in October with a few staying into November. **Killdeer, American Woodcock and Hudsonian Godwit** are also regular. The flocks are best studied at high tide when they gather shoulder-to-shoulder on the shoreline. **Parasitic Jaeger** sometimes stray up Shepody Bay in July, and **Peregrine** are quite often seen in summer. Flocks of **Black Scoter** often gather off Grand Anse in July and August.

Moncton was founded by Germans from Pennsylvania but named after a British commander. The Petitcodiac River sometimes looks like a stream of chocolate milk at low tide, but it is popular with gulls and a few **Lesser Scaup** may stop for a while on the lake to the west. The best year-round birding is over the bridge at Riverview, where **Pileated and Black-backed Woodpeckers** are resident and **Northern Mockingbird and Eastern Meadowlark** regular migrants, and there may be an **Eastern Bluebird** on the fenceposts in spring. A few **Cattle Egret** have wandered to Riverview in late May, but a **Snowy Egret** fishing in a small marshy pond in the middle of a newly-constructed traffic circle in Moncton has to be considered something of an oddity.

Steeves Mountain Provincial Park just west of Moncton is a good place to take in the dawn chorus, which has the songs of **Rose-breasted Grosbeak and Bobolink** to distinguish it. **Common Nighthawk, Ruby-throated Hummingbird, Yellow-bellied Sapsucker, Gray Jay and Pine Siskin** are also present.

A count of **250 Double-crested Cormorant** on the 1988 Christmas Bird Count is extremely high. **Mallard** are becoming increasingly common, with as many as **700** in February 1989, and, together with somewhat fewer **Black Duck**, provide the only regular wintering waterfowl. Flocks of **Horned Lark and Bohemian Waxwing** enliven the winter months and offer more colour to the skittish groups of **Common Redpoll and Snow Bunting** on the fields. **Ring-necked Pheasant, Mourning Dove, Blue Jay, American Tree Sparrow, Dark-eyed Junco, Brown-headed Cowbird, White-winged Crossbill, Pine and Evening Grosbeaks, and American Goldfinch** appear in good numbers around town. **Yellow-bellied Sapsucker, Cedar Waxwing, Pine Warbler, Savannah Sparrow and Red-winged Blackbird** are less regular, and a few **Lapland Longspur** are normal.

The increasing number of feeders have encouraged a few **White-breasted Nuthatch, Northern Mockingbird, American Robin, Ruby-crowned Kinglet, Eastern Meadowlark, Savannah, Chipping, Song and White-throated Sparrows, Red-winged Blackbird, Common Grackle, Purple Finch and Pine Siskin** to remain in town, and **House Finch** can now be added to their number.

This abundance has brought an increase in the number of **Sharp-shinned Hawk, Northern Goshawk and American Kestrel** staying for the winter. There have even been a **Northern Harrier, Gyrfalcon, Barred and Snowy Owl** or two to add to the songbirds' worries. There used to be a fair number of **Gray Partridge** from earlier introductions, but **Ring-necked Pheasant** are much more likely.

Spring is not long after the build up of **Common Merganser** to as many as **350** birds in mid February, when a white **Gyrfalcon** was a welcome recent visitor. An occasional **Boreal Owl, Loggerhead Shrike or Eastern Meadowlark** may arrive in mid April, but the pace quickens towards the end of the month when **73 American Woodcock** have been flushed from the area. The same time period has also produced an unusual flock of **78 Snow Geese**. It is usually May before the last **Snowy Owl** leaves.

Northern Mockingbird are now resident in the city and raise two broods and **Warbling Vireo** are regular summer visitors, but summer birding is usually quite nonproductive, although a **Little Blue Heron and 5 Green-backed Heron** in July suggest local marshes are worth checking. These also produced broods of **Black Duck**, pairs of **Green- and Blue-winged Teal, and Northern Shoveler**, and drake **Mallard and Ring-necked Duck** for Hank Deichmann in early June. The most surprising report I have seen given the location is a count of **2500 Bobolink** in late August.

A few miles to the west of Moncton is the rural community of Salisbury where a breeding colony of **Upland Sandpiper** was established some time in the 1960s. Birds have returned to the same site alongside Highway 2 near the junction with Highway 112 every year since, although sightings now are infrequent. Any breeding birds can be seen from the road. In August the same fields are attractive to flocks of **100+ Lesser Golden-plover**, and it is safe to assume there are **Buff-breasted Sandpiper** among them. The brushy fields are also a perfect site for any **Vesper and Field Sparrows**, and there are sometimes **Great Crested Flycatcher, Indigo Bunting and Northern Oriole** along the Petitcodiac River. **Loggerhead Shrike** have bred in an old orchard, but nesting pairs of **Killdeer, Mourning Dove, Horned Lark, Eastern Meadowlark and Savannah Sparrow** are more likely — the **Brown-headed Cowbirds** are not choosy about which gets a late Easter egg!

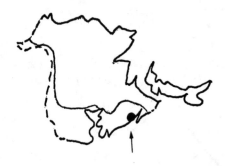

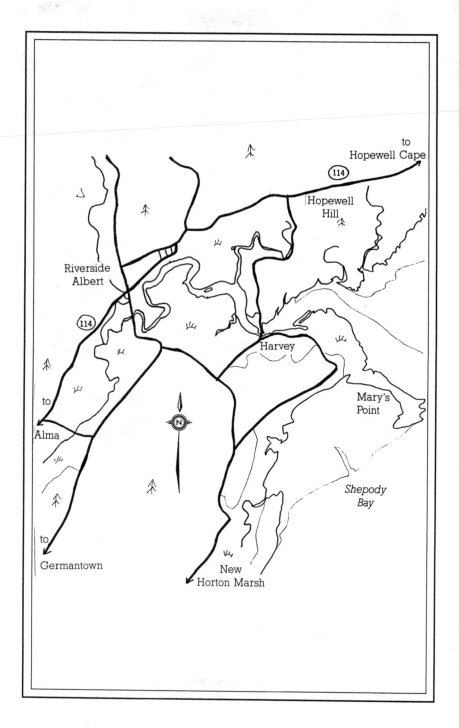

The Riverside-Albert area is part of the Shepody National Wildlife Area, a series of marshes, ponds, dykes and shorelines hosting large numbers of herons, egrets, ducks and shorebirds. The most famous site is Mary's Point, but several other locations are equally rewarding. Now that Rob Walker is an area resident, even the woods and fields are getting extensive coverage and Rob's feeder is working overtime.

If there is one place that is an absolute must for shorebird enthusiasts it has to be Mary's Point, perhaps the best-known shorebird roost in North America. Literally **millions** of southbound Arctic shorebirds use the sand beach and nearby tidal mudflats and salt-marshes over the fall. Access is via private land off Highway 915 south of Riverside-Albert and a mile east on Mary's Point road. The tightly-packed roosting flock tends to spread out over the extensive mudflats at low tide, so the best time to visit is when the tide is rising. Careful protection is necessary as a truck driver drove right through the roosting flock at Dorchester Cape on the other side of Shepody Bay one August and killed over a thousand birds, most of them adult **Semipalmated Sandpiper**. Fortunately, help has arrived in the form of the declaration of the area as Canada's first 'Hemispheric Shorebird Reserve' on August 8, 1987.

As many as **500,000 Semipalmated Sandpiper** have been counted at one time at Mary's Point, but other species are also very common. Over **2500 Least Sandpiper, 2000 Short-billed Dowitcher, 1000 Semipalmated Plover, 850 Black-bellied Plover, 750 Sanderling, 450 Dunlin, 250 Lesser Yellowlegs and White-rumped Sandpiper, and 200 Purple Sandpiper** have been counted. **Piping Plover, Ruddy Turnstone, American Woodcock, Willet, Whimbrel, Hudsonian Godwit, Red Knot and Pectoral Sandpiper** are also regular visitors in fall.

With so many birds present at Mary's Point it is not surprising rarities turn up, and the list is a long one. **Upland, Buff-breasted, Baird's, Western and Curlew Sandpipers, and Ruff** have all appeared in August-September. **Western Sandpiper** have put in appearances in mid June and mid July when few shorebirds were present. As many as four have been found in the mid August-late September period — quite an identification achievement given the huge numbers of "peeps" present. A count of **200 White-rumped Sandpiper** in late October had far fewer relatives for company. Not all shorebirds leave the area. Up to **275 Purple Sandpiper** regularly winter, and a few **Sanderling** were seen in early December recently.

Although shorebirds provide the main interest, the area has a wealth of other birds to offer. Winter is usually a quiet time, but there have been over **1200 Snow Bunting** counted in mid December, when a few late **Great Blue Heron** may be on their last legs. A few **American Tree and White-throated Sparrows, and White-winged Crossbill** are to be expected, but **Bohemian Waxwing and Hoary Redpoll** have been welcome additions. **King Eider and Gadwall** have provided the best spring duck sightings, and **Great Egret** is the most regular of visiting herons and egrets which have included **Snowy and Little Egrets**. A few **Parasitic Jaeger** have flown by Mary's Point in May.

Birds of prey are common on spring migration with a late April count of **60 Sharp-shinned Hawk, 40 Broad-winged Hawk** and single **Bald Eagle, Red-tailed Hawk and Merlin** fairly indicative. **Peregrine** are also regular spring migrants from late March to late May. **Merlin and Peregrine** quite often summer in the area, perhaps attracted by the nesting waterfowl and marshbirds—most **Peregrine** seen are from the nearby release site in Fundy National Park. **Northern Shoveler** have certainly bred, and both **American Coot and Least Bittern** have summered. **Blue-gray Gnatcatcher** is regular in both spring and fall, and **Dickcissel** occasionally appears in fall.

The period of shorebird migration brings the most birders, so an increase in the number of records at this time is inevitable. In recent years, the point has attracted an occasional **Lesser Black-backed Gull** in early fall, perhaps the over-wintering bird from Digby, Nova Scotia. Fewer birds of prey put in an appearance, but **Peregrine** are often seen in September and October, and a few **Cooper's Hawk and Gyrfalcon** are seen on fall migration, too. **Red-throated Loon, Red-necked Grebe, Canada Goose, Mallard, Bufflehead and Black Scoter** occur offshore in small numbers, and a count of **900+ Double-crested Cormorant** in early October is extremely high. There are usually several parties of **Purple Sandpiper** on the rocks, which may shelter a **Red Knot or Dunlin** through the early winter, when **Pine Grosbeak** are often common in the area.

Birds of prey occasionally overwinter—**Bald Eagle, Northern Goshawk, Rough-legged Hawk and Great Horned Owl** are all fairly regular, but **Golden Eagle** in December and **Northern Hawk Owl** from early January to mid April would have to be considered unusual. The Riverside-Albert Christmas Bird Count is distinguished for its high numbers of **Black Duck, Red-breasted Nuthatch, American Tree Sparrow, Common Redpoll, White-winged Crossbill and Snow Bunting**, and its total of 80+ species in good years, although 40+ is more typical.

The woods yield a few **Gray Jay, Brown Creeper, Golden-crowned Kinglet and American Robin**, while the fields and feeders provide food and cover for **Mourning Dove and Horned Lark** and the usual range of blackbirds, finches and sparrows, including **White-throated and Song Sparrows** and the occasional **Northern Shrike, Savannah and Swamp Sparrows, Dickcissel and Eastern Meadowlark**.

Coverage of the Riverside-Albert area has previously been greatest in winter, so **Pine Warbler** in mid January and **Belted Kingfisher** in mid February are to be expected. **Great Blue Heron, American Bittern and Tundra Swan** in the count period are very surprising given the bleakness of the landscape. A **Common Yellowthroat** on the 1988 count was a major surprise. **Gyrfalcon** in mid April and late May, and occasional spring

Bobwhite make a case for visiting later. There has also been a rare summer **Western Kingbird**, a **Turkey Vulture** in mid October, and a **Pine Warbler** in mid November as rewards for visitors in other seasons. An even more surprising mid-October discovery was a **Great-tailed Grackle**, one of very few Canadian records.

The Harvey area is very attractive to late shorebird flocks and sometimes gets larger numbers than nearby Mary's Point. A few **Short-billed Dowitcher** may stay until mid September, but maximum counts of **4000 Semipalmated Sandpiper, 500 Sanderling, 400 White-rumped Sandpiper and 300 Dunlin** are typical of late September-October visits. Ducks are also plentiful in fall and may linger on into winter as a December count of **450 Black Duck** shows.

Spring and summer visitors have included **Cattle Egret and Northern Mockingbird**, which now nests. Midwinter **Long- and Short-eared Owls** are possible around Harvey, and early winter **Barrow's Goldeneye, Red-headed Woodpecker and Western Kingbird** have also been reported. **Least Bittern, Black-crowned Night Heron**, and some uncommon raptors like **Turkey Vulture, Golden Eagle and Short-eared Owl** have provided variety at Harvey. **Blue-gray Gnatcatcher, Indigo Bunting and Dickcissel** are fairly regular at Harvey Bank in fall. **Sedge Wren, Loggerhead Shrike and Bohemian Waxwing** have been among the more unusual spring and summer vagrants, and **Varied Thrush and Blue Grosbeak** are the best fall vagrants so far. The same location assumed international importance in late March, 1987, when a male **Common Chaffinch** appeared at Rob Walker's feeder, where a **Lincoln's Sparrow** recently spent part of the late winter.

New Horton Marsh is close to Mary's Point and is rapidly becoming one of the better places to find **Least Bittern and Common Moorhen** in summer. An odd **Golden Eagle** or white phase **Gyrfalcon** may zip by in December and April. The most interesting records at New Horton have been of summer **Scissor-tailed and Great Crested Flycatchers**. **Lesser Black-backed and Common Black-headed Gulls, and White-winged Dove** are the best of the late summer sightings, while **Red-headed Woodpecker, Townsend's Solitaire, Blue-gray Gnatcatcher, Prairie and Pine Warblers, Yellow-breasted Chat, Blue Grosbeak and Dickcissel** are the best of the later migrants. Other unusual visitors have been **Marbled Godwit and Brewer's Blackbird** at the beginning of October, **Tundra Swan** in mid December, and **Golden Eagle** from the end of January into early February.

Other places to visit from this site
The closest unit to Alma of the Shepody National Wildlife Area is Germantown Marsh which covers an area of 665 hectares. As many as **2000 Canada Geese** stage in spring on this and adjoining units. **Black Duck, Blue-winged Teal and Ring-necked Duck** all nest in the natural marsh and impoundment, and **American Wigeon, Gadwall and Northern Shoveler** are likely to join them — **Lesser Scaup and Redhead** have also appeared in May.

Marshbirds are another early summer feature with **American Bittern, Sora and Virginia Rail** staying on to breed. The first broods of **Common Moorhen** were also found in the summer of 1987. A **Red-shouldered Hawk** in late April was probably a migrant, but **Black Tern, Short-eared Owl, Eastern Bluebird, Marsh Wren and Swamp Sparrow** all nest at Germantown, which is best approached on foot by way of dykes from the eastern end of the Midway road.

Daniel's Marsh by the community of Hopewell attracts **Great and Snowy Egrets** in mid April-mid May, and small flocks of northbound **Bohemian Waxwing, Rusty and Red-winged Blackbirds** in late March-mid April. For the last three winters, its most prestigious resident has been an adult **Golden Eagle**, which was joined by a subadult in February 1989. There was a flock of **25 Snow Geese** at Hopewell in early April, and a pair of **Eastern Bluebird** have nested at Hopewell Hill. I have visited the area in mid November, when I found flocks of **American Goldfinch, Pine Siskin and Common Redpoll**. Hopewell Cape to the north has nothing of the variety of Mary's Point, but it has attracted **Glossy Ibis** in April, **Turkey Vulture** in early July, **Wilson's Storm-petrel** in mid September, **Blue-gray Gnatcatcher** in late September, and **Western Kingbird and Pine Warbler** in November.

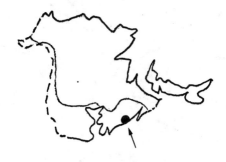

ALMA AREA

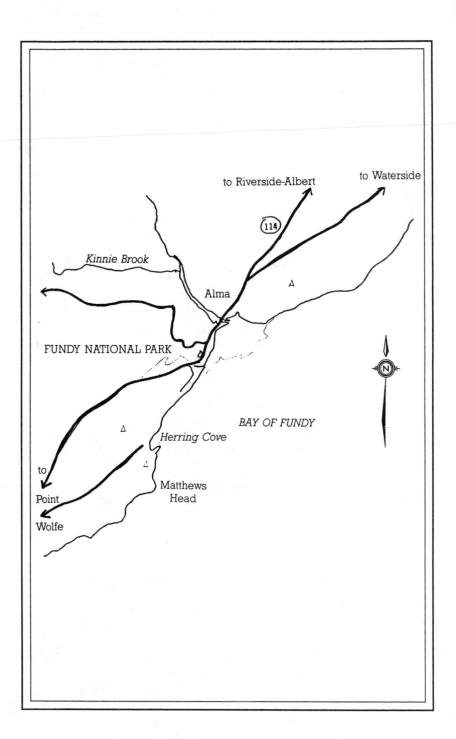

to Riverside-Albert

to Waterside

(114)

Kinnie Brook

Alma

FUNDY NATIONAL PARK

BAY OF FUNDY

Herring Cove

to
Point
Wolfe

Matthews
Head

The Chignecto Bay section of New Brunswick's coastline is occupied by Albert and Westmoreland counties. The outer bay gets the majority of birding attention year round because its coast is part of Fundy National Park, although the majority of fall shorebirds stage and feed in the marshes and along the headlands of the inner bay. Fundy can be approached from the west by driving southeast from Penobquis on Highway 114, but most visitors arrive by taking the same highway south from Moncton. The small section along the coast from Waterside to Alma is the most productive area.

Alma was a major logging and shipbuilding town in the mid 1800s, but it shows few signs of its past — tourism is now more important than fishing for most residents, especially since the national park was established. The coastal bluffs overlook sand and mudflats inundated twice daily by the highest tides in the world, and inland areas are characterized by deep valleys cut by torrential streams. Much of the park area is covered by coniferous forests and bogs, but there are extensive areas of mixed and hardwood forests. The park checklist contains over 200 bird species, about half of which breed, and the best birding is close to Alma.

The coastal community of Alma relies on the lobster and scallop fishery and tourism, but it has recently become better known for some excellent birds. The community always comes up with a few birds on the park Christmas Count, but **Western Kingbird and Gray Catbird** may appear in early December and leave before they can be counted in with any **Common Grackle, Brown-headed Cowbird and Fox Sparrow** at the feeders. **Lapland Longspur** is another winter possibility, although **Dark-eyed Junco** provide the highest numbers of wintering sparrows. The only regular wintering sparrow is the **White-throated Sparrow**, of which the highest count I have seen is 13, but there are usually some **American Tree and Song Sparrows**.

The 1988 count produced record numbers of **Red-breasted Nuthatch, Golden-crowned Kinglet, Dark-eyed Junco, White-winged Crossbill and Pine Siskin. Brown Thrasher, Northern Oriole, Eastern Meadowlark, Dickcissel and Rufous-sided Towhee** have all stayed late enough to be counted, and a **Northern Cardinal** made the count week in 1989. The usual feeder birds at Alma have been supplemented by **Vesper, White-crowned and Field Sparrows**. Few spring migrants appear in Alma before May, although **Cooper's Hawk and House Finch** have been noted in mid April. The cliffs have been graced by vagrant, but possibly increasing, **Golden and Bald Eagles, and Red-shouldered Hawk**. Rarer summer visitors have included **Northern Oriole, Scarlet Tanager, Northern Cardinal, Indigo Bunting and Grasshopper Sparrow**.

Fall tends to be more productive in Alma itself — **Red-headed Woodpecker, Western Kingbird, Northern Mockingbird, Brown Thrasher, Yellow-breasted Chat and Dickcissel** are all irregular fall migrants. One of the most productive areas is along the saltmarsh margins of the Upper Salmon (Alma) River and by the small pond nestled under the roadside cliff. **Pied-billed Grebe and Green-backed Heron** are irregular in late May and June, when **Cattle Egret** may also be seen. **Brown Thrasher, Eastern Bluebird and Blue-gray Gnatcatcher** are often seen on spring migration. The best time to visit the saltmarsh is at low tide, when I have seen **Common Black-headed Gull** among the flock of **Ring-billed Gull** there. I can also add **Mew Gull** to the **Thayer's and Bonaparte's Gulls** reported for the rivermouth.

This is one of the few places in the park where shorebirds have been numerous. There may be as many as **3000+ Semipalmated Sandpiper, 400 Greater Yellowlegs and 100 Least Sandpiper** in the height of fall migration, when two dozen or so **Semipalmated Plover, Lesser Yellowlegs and Short-billed Dowitcher** are present. **Killdeer, Black-bellied Plover, Ruddy Turnstone, Whimbrel, Willet, Pectoral Sandpiper, Dunlin and Sanderling** arrive in fall with one or other of the waves of **White-rumped Sandpiper** in August and October.

The small beach pond was a good place to look for marshbirds, and it obliged with regular **Sora** and occasional **Green-backed Heron and Cattle Egret**. A **Virginia Rail** was a rare addition to the park list in mid September, and other species could be expected. The pond often attracts dabbling ducks when its level is high, but most birds prefer to use the Alma River marshes between tides. **Black Duck, Green- and Blue-winged Teal** offer the highest counts, but **Mallard** are regular and **Gadwall, Northern Pintail and American Wigeon** somewhat less reliable. The beach edge is also popular with newly-arrived warblers in spring, and has attracted a few **Marsh Wren and Seaside Sparrow** among the more usual **Sharp-tailed Sparrow** migrants.

Loons occur in reasonable numbers offshore, with **95 Common and 75 Red-throated Loons** very respectable maxima, and there have also been counts of **40 Great and 100 Double-crested Cormorants**. In the winter an icy spell may bring in **Razorbill, Thick-billed Murre and Dovekie**, but alcids and jaegers are not common — a few **Parasitic Jaeger** in July and August being the exception rather than the rule. Few waterfowl and gulls winter. Diving ducks are almost always present offshore at high tide and can reach good numbers in spring, when **400 Common Eider, 130 Black and 30 White-winged Scoter, and 800 Red-breasted Merganser** have been counted. The fall totals are as high, and in some cases higher, with counts of **220 Common Eider, 140 Common Goldeneye** and good totals of **Bufflehead, White-winged, Black and Surf Scoters, and Common Merganser**. **Canada Geese** are fairly common, and sightings of **Snow Geese** in early May, October and December, and **Barrow's Goldeneye** in late winter, offer an indication that flocks should be carefully checked.

One of the most productive sites anywhere in Fundy National Park is the small pond in a natural hollow below park headquarters. MacLaren Pond attracts a large number of migrants in spring and fall, and the surrounding bushes and copse are probably the best places to search for rarer species if time is very limited. The pond itself is interesting, having sustained an injured **Canada Goose** for a number of weeks as well as attracting **Green- and Blue-winged Teal, and Hooded Merganser** in spring and fall.

Swallows are a major summer feature, with **Cliff Swallow** often found among the **Tree and Barn Swallows**, and there is the likelihood of a **Purple Martin** in early June. I have counted over 50 songbird species in a half-hour stroll around the pond in the last week of May. All the park's warblers find their way here, including small numbers of **Nashville, Blackburnian, Canada and Black-throated Blue Warblers**. **Warbling and Philadelphia Vireos** are regular in spring, when **Blue-gray Gnatcatcher** is guaranteed to appear at some time. **Northern Mockingbird, Brown Thrasher and Gray Catbird** are also regular late spring migrants, along with the odd **Great Crested Flycatcher** among the small numbers of **Eastern Kingbird**. **Cedar Waxwing and Bobolink** are present among the blackbirds, and there is always the chance of flushing a **Whip-poor-will** in late May-early June. As many as **20 Ruby-throated Hummingbird** have been counted in this area in early June, when 13 warblers noted included an **Orange-crowned Warbler**.

There have also been fall visits to MacLaren Pond from **Northern Pintail, Sora, American Coot, Stilt and Solitary Sandpipers, and Short-billed Dowitcher**. Fewer people visit the park in fall when shorebirds attract them to other locations, but it's worth a look for **Nashville Warbler** in August, and **Blue-gray Gnatcatcher and Indigo Bunting** in October. **Yellow-billed Cuckoo, Eastern Meadowlark, Rufous-sided Towhee and Seaside Sparrow** have all passed through in mid-late fall. A **Lark Sparrow** has also been seen in August, and **Rose-breasted and Blue Grosbeaks** have appeared in October.

The most conspicuous wildlife on the golfcourse at dawn are the many whitetailed deer which come out to feed before the golfers start out. A winter carcass also attracted five **Bald Eagles** recently. The open country and bushes are good for songbirds, and a few larger landbirds such as **Black- and Yellow-billed Cuckoos**, and an **Upland Sandpiper** on the way to the Fredericton or Salisbury areas. There are often good numbers of **American Robin** on migration, as a mid October flock of **200** indicates. **American Pipit** is common at this time, long after the nesting **Bobolink** have left. The Point Wolfe road has **Alder Flycatcher, Gray Catbird, Nashville Warbler and Chipping Sparrow** as regular nesting species, and **Sharp-shinned Hawk and Ruby-throated Hummingbird** often enough to suggest they, too, may nest. Swallows are very common on migration, and so are blackbirds in late fall and early spring.

The Chignecto campground area above MacLaren Pond has a similar variety of songbirds, plus a number of boreal species in early winter, when **Common Redpoll and Pine Siskin** flocks have reached over **100**—there is also a good chance of finding **Bohemian Waxwing and Red Crossbill**. An exhaustive search of the secondgrowth and hardwoods around the campground will often turn up **Philadelphia and Warbling Vireos** in early summer. The manicured lawns are also used by parties of migrant **American Robin, American Pipit, Common Grackle, Brown-headed Cowbird and American Goldfinch**. **Brown-headed Cowbird** are very common in early winter with counts of **300** in early December and **1000** in early January not too unusual.

The Kinnie Brook trail starts beyond the campground on top of the steep hill opposite a small day use area. It leads through typical Acadian forest, along a ridge, and back through the woods. Kinnie Brook goes underground near the east end of the flood-plain for about 800 feet and then re-emerges close to a flat-topped cliff that provides a good view of the coastline. The coniferous forest has good numbers of mixed and boreal forest species, including **Gray Jay, Red-breasted Nuthatch and Black-throated Green Warbler**, and the deep ravine is a good place to listen for the songs of **Olive-sided Flycatcher and Winter Wren** among the thrushes and warblers. A **Field Sparrow** has been noted on the first field in summer.

The first short trail southwest of the Headquarters area is named after one of the first settlers — the Dickson Falls trail is one of the better trails for warblers. There has been a fairly drastic change in the forest cover following logging and farming, and balsam fir may well replace the previously dominant red spruce. Although most of the trail leads through spruce-fir forest, where **Black-backed Woodpecker** is possible, the best birding is in the hardwood sections before the leaves are fully out. **Magnolia, Black-burnian, Blackpoll and Bay-breasted Warblers** are common at this time, but harder to find later in the summer when the canopy is closed. Nearby Maple Grove trail has fewer softwood trees and a lusher growth of ferns than on the coastal trail. Sugar maple is dominant and favoured by **White-breasted Nuthatch**. This is also a good place to look for **American Woodcock, Ruby-throated Hummingbird, Yellow-bellied Sapsucker, Gray and Blue Jays and Wood Thrush**, although the commonest breeding species are **Least Flycatcher, Eastern Wood-pewee, Red-eyed Vireo and Ovenbird**.

A recent study of the park indicated that the commonest breeding songbirds are **Bay-breasted, Blackburnian and Tennessee Warblers, Yellow-bellied Flycatcher, Black-throated Green Warbler, American Redstart, Magnolia Warbler, Swainson's Thrush, Yellow-rumped Warbler and Ovenbird**. This shows the mixed nature of the forests. **Veery** are becoming more regular in summer, and a total of 26 or more eastern warblers have been recorded — 22 have bred on a fairly regular basis.

Both **Three-toed and Black-backed Woodpeckers** sometimes stray into the Alma area, although both are more often seen in the deeper coniferous woods, and **Pileated Woodpecker** can be expected at times. The fields outside the park are often taken over by large flocks of migrant blackbirds, which could contain some vagrants.

Christmas Bird Counts usually have a few **Red-throated and Common Loons, Canada Goose, Common Goldeneye, Ruffed Grouse, Ring-billed Gull, Hairy and Downy Woodpeckers**, plus an odd **Horned Grebe, Great Blue Heron, Mallard, Barrow's Goldeneye, Common Eider, White-winged Scoter**, several birds of prey and a good selection of songbirds. **Black-capped and Boreal Chickadees** are common in winter, as are **Red-breasted Nuthatch, Golden-crowned Kinglet, American Tree Sparrow, White-winged Crossbill, Common Redpoll, American Goldfinch and Evening Grosbeak**. **Northern Goshawk, Red-tailed and Rough-legged Hawks, and Great Horned Owl** are all possible, and there are usually a few **Mourning Doves**.

Other places to visit from this area
Waterside has a popular sandy beach and a scenic point known as Cape Enrage. Large numbers of waterfowl use the area in early spring, when counts of **2000 Canada Geese**

and 3000 Black Scoter have been made. The marshes are also popular with marshbirds — the first returning **Great Blue Heron** may be joined by **Little Blue Heron, Snowy and Great Egrets**. Spring sightings of **Dunlin, Short-billed Dowitcher and Peregrine** show that waterbirds are not the only spring attraction. **Northern Gannet** also stray into Chignecto Bay from late March, and larids are worth checking out as **Caspian Tern** arrive here in spring, and wintering **Glaucous and Iceland Gulls** linger into June.

Summer is usually fairly quiet, although **Piping Plover** have nested, and a pair of **Eastern Bluebird or Loggerhead Shrike** may check out the fields in June. The Waterside beach has also attracted the attention of **Semipalmated Plover** which have nested at least once. By early August small numbers of shorebirds have started to arrive, although there are nothing like the numbers found in Shepody Bay. **Piping Plover, Solitary Sandpiper and Red Knot** leave early in the migration period, when an occasional **Stilt Sandpiper** might also be found.

By September **Pectoral, Stilt, Baird's and Buff-breasted Sandpipers** are occasionally present in small numbers, and both **Wilson's and Red-necked Phalaropes** can be looked for. **Marbled Godwit** has been recorded at Waterside in September. Once winter starts to close in, the first flocks of **Purple Sandpiper** appear at Cape Enrage. Marshbirds are fairly regular in fall, and late-leavers include an early September **Little Blue Heron** and mid-October **Great Egret**, while an early October **Clapper Rail** drew some applause.

A few birds of prey can be seen after the nesting **Northern Harrier and Short-eared Owl** have left, and a mid November **Golden Eagle** was one of the better raptors. The close proximity of the Bay of Fundy is demonstrated by the occasional appearance of **Greater Shearwater** and other pelagics in October, and the more regular arrival of **Thick-billed Murre and Dovekie** in November.

Hawks are well represented between Cape Enrage and the eastern edge of the national park. The steep cliffs provide the necessary updraft for migrating **Red-tailed and Broad-winged Hawks**, and **Merlin and American Kestrel** can be seen chasing migrant songbirds and shorebirds, although **Sharp-shinned Hawk and Great Horned Owl** are relatively scarce. Songbirds can be found feeding in the alders, cherries, maples and scrubby conifers at the base of the cliffs, especially warblers and finches in spring and fall. **Western Kingbird** are regular, as are **Northern Mockingbird, Brown Thrasher, Gray Catbird and Northern Oriole**.

The Point Wolfe coastline was an important logging area in the 1800s, and the mill pond created at that time provided a temporary home for fall shorebirds and occasional **Snowy Egret and American Coot**. The dam was removed in 1984 to allow salmon to return to the river. **Red-throated Loon** are quite common offshore in spring and fall, together with parties of **White-winged Scoter and Bufflehead** and the odd **Barrow's Goldeneye or Dovekie**. The deep ravines and coastal bluffs are attractive to a variety of breeding songbirds, and there are usually a pair of cliff-nesting **Common Raven**.

Vagrants are commonest at Point Wolfe in spring and summer, when **Great Crested Flycatcher, Northern Mockingbird, Gray Catbird, Brown Thrasher and Yellow-breasted Chat** have all been noted. A whole series of trails start out from Point Wolfe campground. The Marven Lake trail provides access to places over 6 miles away, including the lake itself which has a primitive campsite for overnight hikes. Marven Lake is surrounded by red spruce and yellow birch, and is a good place to look for **Yellow-bellied Flycatcher, Brown Creeper, Bay-breasted, Blackburnian and Tennessee Warblers**. There are also nesting **Ring-necked Duck** and rarer park birds like **Northern Goshawk, Great Horned Owl, Pileated Woodpecker, Gray-cheeked Thrush and White-winged Crossbill** in the area. The Coppermine trail, which is a three-mile loop, is excellent for boreal warblers, and has had **Gray-cheeked Thrush** in summer and **Gyrfalcon** in winter. The more strenuous Foster Brook trail offers nesting **Red-tailed Hawk and Red-breasted Nuthatch**.

Herring Cove is certainly worth a visit—it can be reached by taking a two mile trail through spruce-fir forest or by following the Herring Cove road. The beach is a good place to study the Fundy marine life, but be very careful not to get trapped by the tide, especially if you decide to explore the caves. **White-winged and Surf Scoters** are common on migration, and there have also been **Brant and Mallard** at Herring Cove.

Shorebirds are regular in fall but numbers are small except for **Greater Yellowlegs and White-rumped Sandpiper**. Migrants often use the cove as a resting place in spring and fall, and the vagrants have included **Western Kingbird, Great Crested Flycatcher, Blue-gray Gnatcatcher, Eastern Meadowlark, Northern Oriole, Indigo Bunting and Field Sparrow**.

Matthews Head can be reached from the cove and offers the best location for a seawatch. Parties of seaducks stream by in spring, when up to **250 White-winged and Surf Scoters, and 70 Oldsquaw** are present for a month from early April. These flocks have included some **Mallard and Black Scoter** and the only **Greater Scaup and King Eider** noted in the park. **Peregrine** nested here in the 1940s and now do so again as a result of a release program. The budworm-damaged spruce-fir and white birch forests are a good place to look for **Black-backed Woodpecker, Bay-breasted, Blackburnian and Tennessee Warblers, and White-winged Crossbill**. Rarer vagrants at Matthews Head have included **Great Crested Flycatcher, Yellow-breasted Chat, Northern Cardinal and Lark Sparrow** in recent years.

The two mile-long Caribou Plains trail is an easy introduction to boreal habitats, including a beaver pond, raised bog and coniferous woods. Deer rather than caribou now use the area and have increased as secondgrowth invades the bog. Mixed wood cover has already brought **Nashville, Black-throated Blue and Blackburnian Warblers, and Rose-breasted Grosbeak** to the area which has a rich fern cover. Close to the parking lot, **Ruby-throated Hummingbird and Yellow-bellied Sapsucker** appear regularly, and the bog has **Cedar Waxwing and Rusty Blackbird** alongside **Common Yellowthroat, Yellow-rumped Warbler, Swamp and Lincoln's Sparrows**. Anyone travelling on this trail should come prepared for a change in weather, as I found out in an early June snowstorm! **Northern Harrier, Spruce Grouse** and a few pairs of **Pine Grosbeak** are adequate compensation for getting wet.

Wolfe Lake near the park's northern entrance is surrounded by a spruce forest populated by **Yellow-bellied Flycatcher, Tennessee, Magnolia and Canada Warblers**. There are also **Eastern Kingbird, Eastern Phoebe, Chestnut-sided Warbler, Rose-breasted**

Grosbeak, Field and Swamp Sparrows in the secondgrowth around the lake. **Spotted Sandpiper and Belted Kingfisher** both nest, and there are **Barn Swallow** among the commoner **Bank Swallow** parties hawking over the lake. Wolfe Lake is quite popular with diving ducks, especially **White-winged and Surf Scoters** in spring, and **Oldsquaw, White-winged, Surf and Black Scoters, Hooded and Common Mergansers** in late fall. A few **Mallard** can be looked for among the **Black Duck**, and two fall sightings of **Snow Geese** suggest that **Canada Geese** are probably as regular as **Double-crested Cormorant**. **Lesser Yellowlegs and Solitary Sandpiper** feed along the muddy margins in fall after the **Northern Harrier and Broad-winged Hawk** broods have taken to wing.

The park's interior can be reached by driving the Old Shepody road and taking one or more of the trails off it. Bennett Lake is very popular with waterfowl and attracts **Black Scoter, Hooded and Common Mergansers** and occasional **Mallard and Great Blue Heron**. **Red-tailed Hawk** have nested along Bennett Brook, and **Northern Goshawk and Broad-winged Hawk** are regular breeders — this is also one of the best areas in the park to find **Great Horned and Barred Owls**. A brood of **Northern Hawk Owl** just outside the park boundaries in mid August suggest that this species could also be looked for in treed bogs. The lakeside forests have a high summer population of warblers, and there is a good chance of finding **Mourning Dove, Ruby-throated Hummingbird, Black-backed and Pileated Woodpeckers, Red-breasted Nuthatch, Brown Creeper, Veery, Solitary Vireo and Rose-breasted Grosbeak**.

Tracey Lake is surrounded by softwood forest, although the northern section of the trail leading to it passes through hardwoods. **Double-crested Cormorant** visit the lake, which has nesting **Common Merganser** and fall **Bufflehead and Hooded Merganser**. **Spruce Grouse** are a regular attraction in the woods by the lake, and **Three-toed Woodpecker** has nested. The Laverty Lake trail winds through a beech-maple stand, offering a chance to see **Sharp-shinned Hawk, Black-billed Cuckoo and Ruby-throated Hummingbird**, but is best known for its **Gray-cheeked Thrush** population in the black spruce. Warblers are common along the trail and the lake sometimes has **Surf Scoter** in summer.

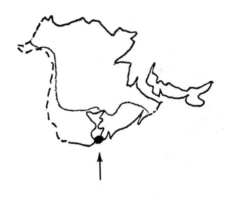

SAINT JOHN

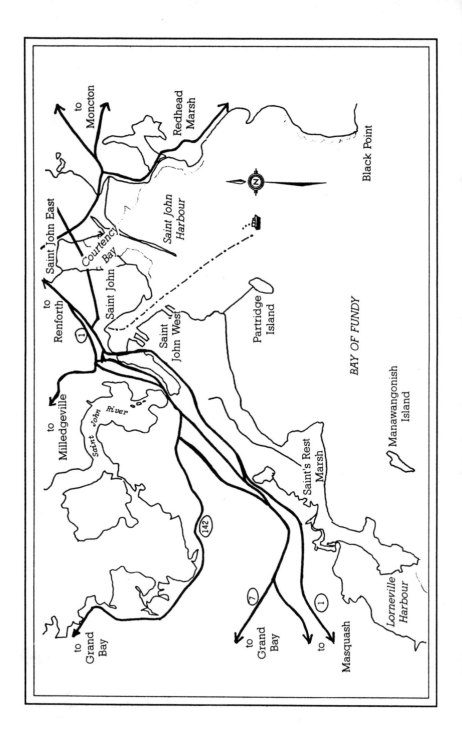

The estuary of the St. John River was discovered by Samuel de Champlain on Saint John the Baptist's Day in 1604, and the town has kept the name. While the river can be spelled St. John, the town retains the full name of Saint John—and woe betide anyone foolish enough to forget it! Many historic sites are within walking distance of the city centre, and the birding is also very productive as the excellent guide "Finding Birds Around Saint John" indicates. The museum is situated in a parkland area where songbirds are very evident year round, and the bay shore is very attractive to ducks and waterfowl. Two of the best birding sites in New Brunswick are found either side of Saint John at Saints Rest Marsh and Red Head Marsh, which attract almost every marshbird known to occur in Atlantic Canada.

Red Head Marsh is located at the eastern limits of Saint John beyond Bayside Drive. This cattail marsh and expanse of open water is an excellent place to go birding from late May to October, although **Great and Snowy Egrets** may appear as early as April. **Pied-billed Grebe, Green-backed Heron and Least Bittern** are fairly regular, and the nesting waterfowl may include **Gadwall and Common Moorhen. Blue-winged Teal, American Wigeon and Ring-necked Duck** are also nesting species, and both **Northern Shoveler and Ruddy Duck** appear often enough in early summer to offer hopes of eventual breeding.

Hazen Creek sewage lagoon at the upper end of the marsh off Black River road is good for dabbling ducks and swallows, while the adjoining marsh is well used by **Sora** and other marshbirds. A few **Marsh Wren** have re-established themselves and have young in the nest by mid July. It's best to park by the seawall and walk alongside the marsh shore by following a trail starting in the southeast field and skirting the shore through spruce-fir woods. Don't do what I did at dusk and land up in a ditch trying to park on a now-closed road off Red Head road. The nesting **Killdeer** by the sewage works got the last laugh!

Glossy Ibis and Snowy Egret are seen each year from mid April to late May, and other herons and egrets are also possible. Rare spring visitors to Red Head Marsh include **Snow Goose, Common Teal, Garganey, Lesser Scaup, Purple Gallinule, American Avocet, Red-shouldered Hawk and Gyfalcon**, and there have been rare winter visits by **Northern Lapwing**. By early June a **Little Blue Heron** may share the marsh with nesting **Green-backed Heron and Black-crowned Night Heron**. Any summering **Tri-colored Heron, Yellow-crowned Night Heron, Common Moorhen, Wilson's Phalarope, Caspian and Gull-billed Tern** are dependent on the level of the marsh.

The erosion of cliffs at Red Head has caused a deterioration in the quality of the local mudflats, but good numbers of shorebirds still appear from mid July to October, and **Stilt and Western Sandpipers** are seen most years. There have been visits by **Marbled Godwit** in mid September. As many as **250 American Wigeon** have staged here in mid September when most of the dabbling ducks reach their peak. Songbirds are not a major attraction of the area, but **100 Black-capped Chickadee** in mid September suggests it must have something to offer.

The bay shore east of town is another area of sand and mudflats popular with gulls and shorebirds. The site is best known for its roosting **Double-crested Cormorants** at midtide on Shag Rock. The freight marshalling yard reached from Lancaster Avenue and Dufferin Row is often closed off, so an approach from Seaside Park on Argyle Street is better. Courtenay Bay has mudflats popular with shorebirds in fall and gulls in the winter months. **Glaucous, Iceland, Ring-billed and Common Black-headed Gulls** are all regular wintering species congregating at low or mid tide off the east ends of King Street East and Elliot Row or along the waterfronts of Crown Street. A few **Bonaparte's Gull** also appear in winter, and early spring and small parties of **Purple Sandpiper** are often seen. As many as **500 Semipalmated Plover and Semipalmated Sandpiper, 100 Least Sandpiper and 50 Lesser Yellowlegs** have been counted in fall.

Stopping on the causeway is forbidden but you can walk from a parking spot on Hanover Street. The south end of Sydney Street is also recommended as a good vantage point for cormorants, ducks and gulls—over **5000 Double-crested Cormorant** have been counted in the harbour in late April, and a few **Ring-billed and Common Black-headed Gull** regularly winter with the **Great Black-backed, Herring, Glaucous and Iceland Gulls**, and are supplemented by new arrivals in mid April.

Courtenay Bay has produced good counts of **Black Duck, Common Goldeneye, Bufflehead, Common and Red-breasted Mergansers** in winter, and smaller numbers of **Common and Red-throated Loons, Great Cormorant, Mallard, Green-winged Teal and Greater Scaup**. Other winter visitors have included **Great and Double-crested Cormorants, Great Blue Heron, Northern Pintail, Gadwall and Barrow's Goldeneye**. **Bald Eagle** are often seen, and there are usually one or two **Northern Goshawk, Sharp-shinned, Red-tailed and Rough-legged Hawks, Northern Harrier, Gyrfalcon, American Kestrel and Snowy Owl** around town.

Saint John itself deserves to be known for more than its Reversing Falls caused by the tidal surges and river flow. The safe confines of the restaurant or the more open location of the Falls View lookout offer the best places to watch the phenomenon. **Great Black-backed Gull** nest on Goat Island and **Common Merganser** winter in the area. The New Brunswick Museum parking lot is close to wintering **Common Goldeneye, Bufflehead** and rarer **Barrow's Goldeneye**. By mid March there may also be good numbers of **Greater Scaup** on the river.

Winter counts often produce large numbers of **Mourning Dove, American Robin, American Goldfinch, Common Redpoll and Evening Grosbeak**, and reasonable counts of **Hairy and Downy Woodpeckers, Northern Mockingbird, White- and Red-breasted Nuthatches, Brown Creeper, Bohemian Waxwing, Common Grackle, Brown-headed Cowbird, Northern Cardinal, Pine Grosbeak, Pine Siskin, American Tree, White-throated, Fox and Song Sparrows**. An amazing 17 species of ducks appeared one Christmas Bird Count, including **Green-winged Teal, Northern Pintail, Gadwall, Canvasback, Ring-necked Duck, Greater and Lesser Scaups, and Hooded Merganser** — the only common species, however, was the **Common Merganser** with 238 tallied.

Some of the more interesting late December visitors have included **Pied-billed Grebe, Northern Harrier, Peregrine, American Kestrel, Short-eared Owl, Red-headed and Black-backed Woodpeckers, Yellow-bellied Sapsucker, Brown Thrasher, Winter Wren, Northern Cardinal, White-crowned Sparrow, Northern Oriole, Red-winged Blackbird and Dickcissel**.

Rockwood Park in the north of the city has interesting walking trails and several small lake habitats dotted among the forest of scrubby birch, cedar and spruce. A few waterfowl and shorebirds can be seen in summer and fall, but the main attraction is the park's songbirds. **Wilson's Warbler** are relatively common breeders, and summer may also bring a **Rough-winged Swallow or House Wren** around the ponds. In winter the shrubbery and secondgrowth are popular with **Common Redpoll, American Goldfinch and American Tree Sparrow**, and there is always the chance of adding **Northern Mockingbird, Bohemian Waxwing, Northern Cardinal and Fox Sparrow**. The local zoo even has a regular **Eurasian Wigeon** in spring.

The western city limits are quite productive during migration periods. **Indigo Bunting** regularly arrive in mid April. Several birds are persuaded to stay into winter — notably **Northern Mockingbird, Ruby-crowned Kinglet and Pine Warbler**. Some of the better fall migrants have been in the western sections of Saint John, and have included **Yellow-billed Cuckoo, Marsh Wren, Northern Mockingbird, Yellow-breasted Chat, Prairie and Pine Warblers, Rufous-sided Towhee and Dickcissel**.

Perhaps the best wetland area within a major city in Atlantic Canada, Saints Rest Marsh has attracted 232 species at last count — an astounding amount for a site within city limits. The extensive marsh, lagoon and wasteland area is productive year round, but especially from late March to mid November. Waterfowl use the marsh ponds, lagoon and creek from late March to mid May, with **American Wigeon and Green-winged Teal** quite common and **Northern Shoveler** a local speciality. The lagoon area favoured by ducks can be reached from the gravel pits to the north or from the eastbound lane of the Trans-Canada Highway.

A sewage lagoon at the north end is always worth a look. The marsh itself attracts wandering herons and egrets from mid April to late May. **Snowy Egret** appear every spring, and so do **Glossy Ibis** which have now occured in sufficient numbers to allow nearby nesting — the first in New Brunswick. **Great Egret** arrivals are more irregular. Small numbers of rails also occur in spring, although late summer and fall provide more records.

Wilson's Phalarope

Shorebirds are not prominent in spring, but a few commoner species do occur and there have been sightings of **Upland Sandpiper** in mid April, **Wilson's Phalarope** from mid May, and even a pair of **American Avocet** in mid May. The phalaropes stay on to attempt nesting, and are often joined by **Gadwall** or put to flight by a **Peregrine**. Exceptional visitors to Saints Rest Marsh have been **Yellow-crowned Night Heron and Tri-colored Heron** and the region's first **White Ibis** for many years. Large numbers of **Double-crested Cormorant** overfly the marsh and hills on their route between the nesting island and river feeding areas. **Common Moorhen and Least Bittern** have both been seen here in summer and may nest, and **Virginia Rail** are regular enough in August to suggest they also breed. **Sharp-tailed Sparrow** songs wheeze out a greeting from mid June, and there are usually good numbers of migrant songbirds in the surrounding fields and woods. I found three **Rough-winged Swallows** around the 100-nest **Bank Swallow** colony on the mound in June.

The arrival of the fall shorebirds is a major feature from late July to mid October — most birds use the marsh at high tide when neighbouring mudflats and beaches are unavailable. Maximum counts include **20,000+ Semipalmated Sandpiper, 2000 Semi-palmated Plover, 500 Least Sandpiper, 350 Short-billed Dowitcher, 300 Lesser Yellowlegs, and 100 Pectoral Sandpiper and Dunlin**. Smaller numbers of **Piping Plover, Killdeer, Red Knot and Red-necked Phalarope** also appear. A mid July **Long-billed Curlew** was obviously somewhat off-course, but an odd **Western Sandpiper** might be expected in September. Mid-late August **Baird's, Stilt and Buff-breasted Sandpipers** are normal, and **Wilson's Phalarope** remain in the area until September. When the **Pectoral Sandpiper** numbers build to **100+** in mid October most shorebirds have left, but an early November **American Avocet** did not.

Most of the regular dabbling ducks start to reappear in August, when **Golden Eagle and Peregrine** have both been noted, and September migrants may have to dodge the attentions of **Cooper's Hawk**. A few **Snowy Egret, Virginia Rail and Glossy Ibis** linger until mid September or rarely October, and rarities such as **Common Moorhen and American Coot** can be looked for—the latter has totalled over **50** in early November.

Songbirds also use the area from mid August with fairly regular sightings of **Marsh Wren** in October, when flocks of **125 Lapland Longspur** are not unusual. **Prairie Warbler and Lark Sparrow** at Saints Rest Marsh in early September represent rare sightings in New Brunswick. By mid November the wintering flocks of **Snow Bunting** are in residence and may contain a windblown waif or two avoiding the attention of an occasional **Gyrfalcon**.

Neighbouring Manawangonish has excellent marshes which are very extensive at low tide. Although the variety is lower, the shorebird numbers are usually higher and are impressive even by Bay of Fundy standards. Some typical high counts would be **9000 Semipalmated Sandpiper, 3100 Least Sandpiper, 950 Short-billed Dowitcher, 600 White-rumped Sandpiper, 300 Semipalmated Plover, 215 Lesser Yellowlegs, 120 Greater Yellowlegs and 70 Black-bellied Plover. Killdeer and Spotted Sandpiper** reach good relative numbers, and there is an excellent chance of seeing **Wilson's Phalarope** in late July and early August. However, access is limited and some roads have been closed.

The last site on the western limits of Saint John is Lorneville, where the harbour mudflats attract good numbers of shorebirds at low tide. A walk out to the points at Black Beach and Lorneville is worthwhile in winter when waterfowl can be seen close inshore. There may be as many as **300 Black Scoter** in early January, and other species are equally common. Larger numbers occur in spring. Nesting colonies of **Great Blue Heron, Double-crested Cormorant, Common Eider, Great Black-backed and Herring Gulls** on Manawangonish Island can be reached by chartering a boat from the docks at Lorneville or West Saint John—the best time to visit would be early June-mid July when the birds are on their nests, but the birds should not be disturbed. This location also produced the first confirmed Canadian nest of **Glossy Ibis**.

Musquash lies just to the west of Saint John beside the Trans-Canada Highway. The dyked and drained marshlands controlled by Ducks Unlimited have been reflooded by Highway 1 and attract large numbers of dabbling ducks, including as many as **50 Wood Duck** in late summer. **Pied-billed Grebe and Ring-necked Duck** are also present in summer. There are also good numbers of shorebirds, especially **Greater Yellowlegs, Black-bellied Plover and Lesser Golden-plover**, which are joined by a few **Upland Sandpiper** in late summer and early fall. Among marshbirds, **Great Egret** have appeared in both spring and fall. **Gadwall** have settled at Musquash in mid May and early October, and a male **Hooded Merganser** has been seen sitting on a muskrat house in early June, but the best return visitor is a **Red-headed Woodpecker** which has made two visits in early winter.

Other places to visit from this site
The Fundy coast east of Saint John is characterized by steep coastal slopes and 300-ft cliffs. Small bays behind barrier beaches at rivermouths, deltas and interior saltmarshes are all popular with migrant shorebirds. The cliffs are rapidly eroding and forming

beaches and intertidal ledges—cobble beaches in the area are very popular with **Semi-palmated Plover**. The first section of coastline is easily accessible with headlands providing good lookouts for loons and seaducks. In addition, the broad coastal barrens provide unexpected habitat for boreal songbirds including **Palm Warbler and Lincoln's Sparrow**.

The best-studied section of the coast is between West Quaco and St. Martins. Highway 111 offers access to some excellent beach and mudflat habitats, and the area has been proposed for special reserve status. Quaco Head is a good place to look for **Purple Sandpiper** in winter, when loons, grebes and scoters are also common. The northbound flocks of **Canada Goose and Brant** all leave by early June. St. Martins has a cobble beach, seacaves and enough cover for migrant songbirds. As many as **100 Brant** have appeared in early October, although this species is now largely confined to spring visits. Spring brings small flocks of **Cedar Waxwing**, and somewhat larger numbers of **White-throated and Fox Sparrows**. **Broad-winged and Rough-legged Hawks, and Merlin** are regular in late September, when **Caspian Tern and Yellow-billed Cuckoo** are likely, and **Mourning Dove** are common in early November.

The Quaco Bay coast is best visited in spring and fall when migrants are most in evidence—**Sharp-tailed Sparrow** stay to nest but most birders are checking out the shorebird flocks from mid July to October. Counts of **1500-2500 Semi-palmated Plover, Least and Semi-palmated Sandpipers, and Sanderling** are quite impressive, and there are usually some **Willet, Lesser Yellowlegs and Short-billed Dowitcher** early on. The later flocks have some early-arriving **Purple Sandpiper** and an occasional **Red-necked Phalarope**.

The Black River area has a wider range of habitats including a small saltmarsh and mudflats at the Emerson Creek roadbridge on Highway 825. The Black River area is not as productive as it was when there were larger marshes—the area's best bird was a **Northern Hawk Owl** over a century ago. Similar habitat at Gardner Creek has migrant shorebirds and occasional herons and rails. There is another good-looking saltmarsh and beach behind a sandspit at Tynemouth Creek.

The section of Fundy coastline west of Saint John around Maces Bay is one of the most popular with summer tourists because of the many white sand beaches, especially that at New River Beach. The first stop at Seely Cove rates a walk out to the headland where migrants and inshore ducks and cormorants might be expected. The Maces Bay shoreline is an excellent place to watch shorebirds in fall. Peeps provide the largest counts, but other species are also well represented. Counts of **6500 Semipalmated Sandpiper, 3000 Least Sandpiper, 2000 Semipalmated Plover, 300+ Ruddy Turnstone, Short-billed Dowitcher, White-rumped Sandpiper and Sanderling, and 150 Greater Yellowlegs** are normal, and **30 Lesser Yellowlegs and 40 Purple Sandpiper** quite respectable.

Other species seen here regularly include **Black-bellied and Piping Plovers, Killdeer, Whimbrel, Solitary Sandpiper and Red-necked Phalarope**. **Ruddy Turnstone** have also overwintered with the flock of **Purple Sandpiper**. Other birds in winter have included **Brant**, which start to reappear in good numbers as early as mid February, although the usual peak is in late March. **Dovekie** are also possible in winter, when loons, grebes, cormorants, ducks and gulls can all be found. Further up the bay the wintering ducks of Little Lepreau Basin include **Bufflehead**, which are probably attracted by the strong tidal current close to the Trans-Canada Highway roadbridge. A few **Bald Eagle** take up temporary residence in fall.

Point Lepreau is the site of a nuclear power station which explains the number of wintering waterfowl drawn by the warm water. This has been the only place to attract **Dovekie** in recent years—arrangements to visit the point must be made in advance with New Brunswick Hydro. Little Lepreau is a good place to check out the gulls as a **Franklin's Gull** has been recorded in late May.

As the most southerly point in the region, Point Lepreau is a good place to see large numbers of pelagics as well as flocks of up to **300 Purple Sandpiper** in winter when there may be as many as **60 Red-necked Grebe** and a few **Horned Grebe**. **Razorbill** are common, and **Common and Thick-billed Murres, and Black-legged Kittiwake** regular, and there may be a few **Greater Scaup, Bufflehead and Harlequin** among the early winter flocks of **Common Eider** and all three scoters. Strong westerly winds tend to keep the duck flocks inshore.

A **Great Blue Heron** has tried to overwinter in the Point Lepreau area, and early February reports of **Spruce Grouse** are interesting given the location. Other winter visitors have included **Bald Eagle, Rough-legged Hawk, Bonaparte's and Ring-billed Gulls**. Songbirds are a scarce commodity in winter, but a few **Mourning Dove and Red-breasted Nuthatch** find enough food to stay.

In spring and fall, large numbers of ducks stream by the point and there is a good chance of **King Eider** in late March and early April—by the end of April, **500 White-winged Scoter** can be counted. A mid May **Lark Bunting** and summering **Marsh Wren and Eastern Bluebird** are unusual sightings. Pelagics are occasionally driven inshore, but the only regular migrants are **Northern Gannet** in October.

The area is less productive than the inner beaches of Maces May for shorebirds, but counts of over **600 Semipalmated Plover, 1000 Semipalmated Sandpiper and 250 Least Sandpiper** indicate there is suitable habitat for the commoner species. **Solitary Sandpiper** are also seen fairly often in fall, and **Piping Plover** sometimes appear during the shorebird migration. Songbirds are not a major feature of the point, but several fall **Northern Parula and Sharp-tailed Sparrow** and a late October **Northern Cardinal** show it is worth checking out. A mid September **King Rail** arrived by choice, but a **Least Tern** at the same time of year came courtesy of a hurricane.

The Dipper Harbour-Chance Harbour coastline contains a number of harbours and saltmarshes alongside Highway 790. These provide good birding year round. Dipper Harbour has a variety of diving ducks, including regular fall and winter parties of **Bufflehead**, and a few shorebirds are regular. Similar habitats at Round Meadow Cove and Little Dipper Harbour off the highway are more productive in terms of shorebirds, herons and dabbling ducks, including spring and late summer **Little Blue Heron**, and the small island at the end of a breakwater is a good lookout point for diving ducks. The commonest shorebirds in late July are **Short-billed Dowitcher**, and this species is surprisingly common in spring when nearly **600** were counted in late May. Dipper Harbour has had a **Stilt Sandpiper** in mid April and **Willet** lingering into late October as out-of-season shorebirds.

There have also been spring records of **Common Teal and Tri-colored Heron** and late fall **Laughing Gull**. The small saltmarsh at Chance Harbour attracts small numbers of shorebirds, especially **Least Sandpiper**, early and a few **Whimbrel and Purple Sandpiper** later. The Chance Harbour marsh has also turned up a possible **King Rail** in mid April and **Tundra Swan** in mid December.

The next major birding site is Pocologan Harbour, where a strong tidal current and extensive mudflats bring in good numbers of waterfowl and shorebirds, as well as feeding parties of gulls and terns. A walk around Pocologan Point would produce **Common Eider** year round. In winter grebes and loons are quite common, while non-breeding **Black and Surf Scoters** may stay in the area long after the spring rafts have left. Sightings of **Ruddy Duck and Common Black-headed Gull** in late October suggest that shorebirds are not the only fall attraction at Pocologan Harbour. The only land-bird I have seen reported was a **Western Kingbird** in September.

New River Beach to the west has two nature trails leading to rocky cliffs and sheltered inlets. The Chittick's Beach trail goes through a coastal forest and along a beach to four small coves, while the Barnaby Head trail winds out to the headland and along a low cliff to a bog. **Common Eider** are indeed common inshore. Large flocks of **Double-crested Cormorant** are not as frequent as they used to be, but **Black Scoter** are common in late April, when a few **Willet** may appear. Some of the more interesting vagrants at New River Beach have been **Golden Eagle and Field Sparrow** in April and **Franklin's Gull** in mid August. **King Eider** are a possibility in winter, and an early January **Short-eared Owl** and mid September **Loggerhead Shrike** extoll the merits of visiting year round.

GRAND MANAN

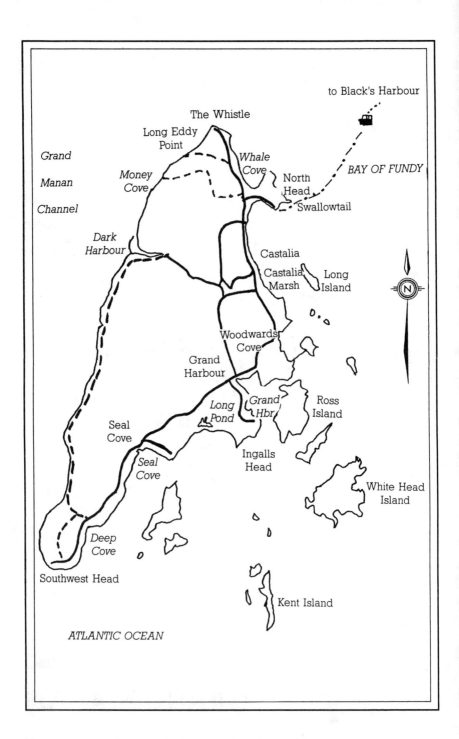

to Black's Harbour

The Whistle

Long Eddy
Point

Whale
Cove

North
Head

BAY OF FUNDY

Grand

Manan

Channel

Money
Cove

Swallowtail

Dark
Harbour

Castalia

Castalia
Marsh

Long
Island

N

Woodwards
Cove

Grand
Harbour

Long
Pond

Grand
Hbr

Ross
Island

Seal
Cove

Seal
Cove

Ingalls
Head

White Head
Island

Deep
Cove

Southwest Head

Kent Island

ATLANTIC OCEAN

The Bay of Fundy is one of North America's most important feeding areas for pelagics and shorebirds and it also serves as a wintering area for waterfowl. The outer bay provides a perfect habitat for pelagic birds, whales, sharks and fish, while the inner bay offers intertidal zones favoured by geese, diving ducks and shorebirds. The cool summer temperatures extend the southern breeding range of **Leach's Storm-petrel, Atlantic Puffin and Arctic Tern**, while warm winters encourage **Brant and Razorbill** to linger north of their normal wintering zone.

The whole region can be enjoyed if there is time, but a visit to one or more of the Fundy Isles provides a glimpse of the Bay of Fundy without the need to travel far. This is a maritime world in miniature in a marvellous setting. A few words in the right ear and you can catch a ride with a fisherman, but even the ferry ride from Black's Harbour may provide a number of pelagic species. **Atlantic Puffin** have already been successfully returned to their former colonies in Maine, and there is every indication **Razorbill and Common Murre** will follow on their own. Another imminent immigrant is certainly the **Manx Shearwater** which summers in larger numbers every year. **Northern Gannet and Great Cormorant**, however, have not shown any inclination to reoccupy old breeding sites.

The largest of the Fundy Isles is Grand Manan itself. The first settlement was on Ross Island which is reachable at low tide, but now only Grand Manan and White Head Island are inhabited year round. The heavy ocean swell often precipitates rockfalls, especially on the southeast coast, and the 300-ft. basalt cliffs on the north coast are unique. The climate is pleasant year round, and the birding is outstanding as John James Audubon found out on a visit in 1831. You can explore the island quite easily by road, but it cries out to be walked.

The Christmas Bird Counts give a good indication of the island's possibilities. As many as 71 species have been counted here, which makes it more productive than the Saint John area which receives far more coverage. Several birds rare in winter elsewhere in Atlantic Canada occur here on a regular basis and in fair numbers, as maximum counts of **125 Red-necked Grebe, 330 Great Cormorant, 160 Brant, 540 Black Duck, 50 Mallard, 110 Common Goldeneye, 140 Bufflehead, 50 Greater Scaup, 140 Oldsquaw, 3800 Dovekie, 2500 Thick-billed Murre, 750+ Razorbill, 2500 Great Black-backed Gull, 7500 Herring Gull, 7500 Black-legged Kittiwake, 430 Purple Sandpiper, 175**

Mourning Dove, 100 Common Raven, 195 Evening Grosbeak, 270 White-winged Crossbill and 120 American Goldfinch indicate.

The commonest wintering ducks are **Black Duck, Common Eider, Oldsquaw, Common Goldeneye and Red-breasted Merganser**. Birds of prey are fairly common, with **Red-tailed and Rough-legged Hawks** joined by **Northern Harrier, Northern Goshawk, Bald and Golden Eagles, Peregrine, Merlin, American Kestrel, Snowy Owl and Northern Saw-whet**— 10 of the last-named appeared on the 1989 count, which also included three of the recently-introduced **Wild Turkey**. Other species found in winter in somewhat smaller numbers include **Red-throated Loon, Horned Grebe, Northern Gannet, Common Eider, Harlequin, Sanderling, Red-breasted Nuthatch, Brown Creeper, American Robin, Northern Mockingbird, Northern Shrike, Song and American Tree Sparrows, Common Grackle, Red-winged Blackbird, Brown-headed Cowbird and American Goldfinch**.

Most of the wintering songbirds are found at feeders in the main community of Grand Harbour. They have included **Winter Wren, Northern Mockingbird, Savannah, Song and White-throated Sparrows**. A few rarer waterbirds have been seen close to the community of Grand Harbour, including **Yellow-crowned Night Heron, Green-backed Heron, Ruddy Duck, Common Moorhen and Yellow Rail**, and a **Little Blue Heron** was picked up dead in early May. The rarer shorebirds are found mainly at Castalia, but a **Marbled Godwit** has turned up at Grand Harbour.

The commonest birds on an early spring visit are the **10,000+ Brant** staging here in late March-May—especially at Grand Harbour. The Wolves, islands off Black's Harbour, have **Common Eider** all year and as many as **90 Harlequin** in early April. Very few people visit the island in spring, so records of **Golden Eagle, Green-backed, Little Blue and Tri-colored Herons, Cattle Egret, Curlew Sandpiper, Red-headed Woodpecker, Varied Thrush, Yellow-throated Warbler and Lark Sparrow** are probably only part of the story.

Most Grand Manan visitors in summer are tourists, but birders do make visits outside the peak fall season—as three summering records of **Golden Eagle** and a mid July **Great Skua** clearly indicate. **40 Wild Turkey** were released in 1987 and will provide an interesting experience for visitors if they survive. A **Black Skimmer** seen from the ferry at the end of July is another example of a rare summer vagrant. **Laughing Gull** is, perhaps, more regular in spring and early summer, and I saw **Red-necked Phalarope and Black-legged Kittiwake** on my only visit in mid June.

The fall certainly offers the greatest variety and numbers of birds. The ferry crossing has yielded good numbers of **Wilson's Storm-petrel and Manx Shearwater** in August and early September, which is a good time to look for as many as **20 Parasitic Jaeger** and a few **Pomarine Jaeger**. A count of **150 Northern Gannet** at the end of the month, **hundreds** of **Black-legged Kittiwake**, small numbers of **Greater and Sooty Shearwaters**, and a few **Leach's Storm-petrel and Manx Shearwater** in October round out the season. An occasional **Snow Goose** may also drop by in October. By November few pelagics remain, but there are more **Razorbill and Dovekie**. **Bonaparte's Gull** are also common on migration with a few staying into January. An odd **Long-tailed Jaeger or Great**

Skua in mid September, and inshore **Northern Fulmar** are possible from the ferry. And an occasional **Sabine's Gull or Roseate Tern** or a late **Piping Plover or Stilt Sandpiper** may pass by in mid-fall.

Shorebirds are concentrated at one or two main beaches, but **Baird's and Buff-breasted Sandpipers** prefer habitats away from the shoreline. Larger landbirds are well represented on Grand Manan, especially around the larger communities where gardens provide a ready supply of insect food and fruits. **Yellow-billed Cuckoo** is irregular in September and October, when a few **Western Kingbird** also turn up. The wires are more likely to yield **Eastern Kingbird** early in September, when as many as **150 Northern Flicker** have been counted passing through. **Red-headed Woodpecker** regularly appear late September-mid October.

Counts of **5000 Yellow-rumped and 250 Palm Warblers** during October are matched by **500 Dark-eyed Junco**. This naturally attracts predators, especially **Merlin**, which are very common in late September, but **Peregrine** are more likely in October. Another regular fall migrant is the **Yellow-billed Cuckoo** which passes through in small numbers in early October. **Northern Cardinal** stays year round, and the feeders persuade **Mourning Dove, Red-breasted Nuthatch, American Robin, Song Sparrow and Red-winged Blackbird** to overwinter in small numbers each year.

A prime birding spot at the northern tip of Grand Manan is The Whistle, which can be as productive in spring as fall. This is a good viewpoint for **Northern Gannet**, gulls and marine mammals. Very few reports from the Whistle in May and June have included **Scissor-tailed Flycatcher, Orchard Oriole and Field Sparrow** — plenty to whistle about! Good numbers of southbound hawks may be seen from late August to the last week of October, and the bushes may be filled with songbird migrants in May and September. **Red-breasted Nuthatch** also make their own tin whistle sound in mid September — when over **100** have been counted. Notable fall finds have been **Red-headed Woodpecker, House Wren, Blue-gray Gnatcatcher, Warbling Vireo, Yellow-breasted Chat and Clay-colored Sparrow**.

Western Kingbird

RB
1987

The point is also a good place to look for seabirds. **Manx Shearwater, Parasitic and Pomarine Jaegers** are present until late September. **Little and Common Black-headed Gulls** have also been reported in September.

Whale Cove has attracted spring **Snowy Egret and Upland Sandpiper** and fall **Forster's Tern, Western Kingbird and Yellow-headed Blackbird**. A trail leads from the Anglican Church at Whale Cove by Hole-in-the-Wall to the Swallowtail Light, where the lightkeepers were keen observers of migrant and nesting songbirds. I walked most of this trail in mid June — it took three hours and I saw **Green-winged Teal, Chimney Swift, Cliff Swallow, Veery, Blackburnian and Canada Warblers** among commoner species. **Red-eyed, Philadelphia, Solitary and Warbling Vireos** are all regularly seen in spring. The Swallowtail has produced **Blue-gray Gnatcatcher and Prairie Warbler** in mid May, and **Pine Warbler and Brewer's Blackbird** in September. Rarer visitors in the third week of May one year were both **Yellow-throated and White-eyed Vireos**. A mid September **Sabine's Gull** and early October **Turkey Vulture** are the best of larger birds.

Flocks of **Great Cormorant** can be seen flying by North Head in early February, and migrant **American Woodcock** can be looked for in early April. Songbirds are abundant in late May and some, including **Northern Mockingbird**, stay to nest. North Head recently turned up mid May **White-winged Dove, Rufous-sided Towhee and Orchard Oriole**, early June **House Finch** and the first confirmed nesting of **Northern Cardinal** with 2 juveniles flying by early August.

Its greatest concentration of birds is, however, in fall, when parties of **Common Nighthawk and Eastern Kingbird** find different ways of catching flying insects in late August and set the tone for the season. The next month sees another wave of migrants pausing briefly in the scrubby growth at North Head. **Lesser Black-backed Gull, Gull-billed Tern, House Wren, Prothonotary Warbler and Lark Sparrow** have all been seen in late August. **Red-headed Woodpecker, Clay-colored Sparrow, Yellow-breasted Chat, Yellow-throated and Connecticut Warblers** have been the best of the early-mid September vagrants. **House Wren, Pine Warbler, Rufous-sided Towhee, Dickcissel and Brewer's Blackbird** have enlivened birding visits, but the best bird was a nonpasserine — a **Curlew Sandpiper** in mid month. Even as late as mid November the cold weather birder can hope for a rarity — most likely a **Dickcissel**, but sometimes a **Yellow-breasted Chat**. By the end of the month, a **Snowy Owl** may be in residence.

The prime birding spot on Grand Manan — at least for shorebirds — has to be Castalia just south of North Head. The most surprising winter report was of a mid January **Clapper Rail**, a rare visitor to the province any time of year. Spring shorebirds may drop in and include true vagrants — **Wilson's Phalarope, American Oystercatcher, Ruff, Curlew Sandpiper and Little Stint** providing birds from three different regions in late May and June. An **American Avocet** has been seen at Castalia, and an adult **Little Stint** southbound in early August was likely one of two seen northbound the previous June. As many as **250 Purple Sandpiper** have been counted in May, but the marshy ponds are more likely to support herons and egrets. **Great and Snowy Egrets** are regular from late April, and **Tri-colored Heron** can be looked for in May.

This mixture of marshes, saltflats and sandy beaches rarely fails to produce high counts of the commoner species, and more **Long-billed Dowitcher and Stilt Sandpiper** than anywhere else on the Bay of Fundy. Any time from mid July to mid October will see over two dozen shorebird species if a movement is on. Counts of **6400 Semipalmated Sandpiper, 1500 Least Sandpiper, 1000 Semipalmated Plover and Short-billed Dowitcher, 400 Black-bellied Plover** and three-figure totals of **Ruddy Turnstone, Lesser Yellowlegs, White-rumped Sandpiper, Dunlin and Sanderling** are as good as anywhere on the mainland away from Shepody Bay. In addition, there are small parties of **Killdeer, Lesser Golden-plover, American Woodcock, Whimbrel, Greater Yellowlegs, Red Knot, Pectoral, Purple and Spotted Sandpipers** for variety. Rarer species like **Hudsonian Godwit, Willet, Baird's, Buff-breasted, Stilt and Upland Sandpipers, Long-billed Dowitcher and Wilson's Phalarope** occur on a regular basis. There are up to **10,000 Red-necked Phalarope** just offshore. Most of the **Stilt Sandpiper** pass through in late August, and **American Avocet, Marbled Godwit and Curlew Sandpiper** have all appeared in fall.

Little Blue Heron are possible, but rare, at Castalia marsh in late summer, but **Snowy Egret** are regular visitors in late summer and fall. The parties of **40+ Black-crowned Night Heron** may contain a **Yellow-crowned Night Heron** or two in early September, and a few birds will hang around until November. There have even been a **Sandhill Crane** in mid September and a **Tri-colored Heron** from mid September to mid October one year. **Gull-billed Tern** is a possibility in late August, and both **Black Skimmer and Forster's Tern** have also been noted at this time. **Caspian Tern** wait until September and early October to put in an appearance.

Cooper's Hawk and Peregrine can both be looked for when shorebirds and songbirds are on the move, but the first **Snowy Owl and Northern Shrike** arrive in November long after the majority have left. **American Pipit** flocks may total over **120** in mid October. Early October was the time for the amazing visit of a Siberian **Stonechat**. Other good landbirds seen in fall include **Red-headed Woodpecker, Willow Flycatcher, Northern Wheatear, Golden-and Blue-winged, Prothonotary, Pine and Orange-crowned Warblers, Grasshopper and Seaside Sparrows, and Yellow-headed Blackbird.**

A family of **Roseate Tern** have been noted in mid August at Long Island, where the most regular attraction is a lingering **Red-necked Grebe** in summer, and Nantucket Island has nesting **Black-crowned Night Heron**. The action really heats up in fall with a good movement of swallows early on and sparrows later. Most of the rarities have been noted late in fall after Castalia slows down. **Cooper's Hawk, Black-billed Cuckoo, and Rufous-sided Towhee** are fairly regular, and the main movement is from late September-early October, when **Gray Catbird** are common and up to **175 White-throated Sparrow** crowd the bushes at Bancroft Point, where **Purple Martin** have appeared as early as late April and **American Kestrel** have summered.

White Head and its island may not have quite the quantity of birds, but they do have the quality. Among summering birds, **Red-headed Woodpecker** are fairly regular and **Eastern Bluebird** have double-brooded. Pelagics are sometimes seen, including a **Manx Shearwater** that appeared in late August. September is usually marked by a small passage of **Brant**, which may stay well into January, but a party of **10 Tundra Swan** seen in mid November moved on. There have also been a few **Northern Saw-whets** in early May at Ingall's Head.

Apart from Castalia, the only place favoured by waterfowl is Long Pond. **Gadwall** are often seen among the **750+ Black Duck** in late September-early October, and **Harlequin, Greater Scaup, White-winged, Black and Surf Scoters** are all part of the late October-mid November passage. A pair of **Harlequin** have also been found off the beach in late May. Some of the higher shorebird counts have included **850 Semipalmated Sandpiper, 375 Semipalmated Plover and 300 Sanderling**, with smaller numbers of **Ruddy Turnstone, Least and White-rumped Sandpipers** in attendance. **Cooper's Hawk** has chosen this location several times in spring. The west coast of the island is much harder to reach, although several **Northern Saw-whets** were noted along the Dark Harbour road in mid May. Southern Head has also been productive in spring with a late May **Summer Tanager** and a mid June **Willow Flycatcher**, plus a **Blue Grosbeak** in early September. Another waterfowl location is Great Pond, which attracts occasional fall **Ruddy Duck**.

Other places to visit from this site
One of the best nesting seabird sites is tiny 15-acre Machias Seal Island very close to the coast of Maine. This can be reached by boat by contacting the Grand Manan Tourist Association. It's possible the constant fog hid it from early settlers and allowed New Brunswick to claim it for Canada. Huge numbers of nesting seabirds now call it home, and there are always alcids, terns and gulls in the surrounding waters. **Greater, Sooty and Manx Shearwaters, Northern Fulmar, Wilson's Storm-petrel, Parasitic Jaeger, Red and Red-necked Phalaropes** are all possible on this trip.

The small colony of **Atlantic Puffin** needed little help to survive and grow — partly because **2000 pairs of Arctic and 600 pairs of Common Terns** are a sizeable alternative to would-be gull predators. A single pair of **Roseate Tern** have joined the birds near the landing spot. There are now over **1600 Atlantic Puffin** safely sharing the island with **200+ Razorbill**, and the colony of **200+ Leach's Storm-petrel** may also have benefitted from this — with a vanguard of **Manx Shearwater** looking like they might take advantage, too. There are also an increasing number of **Common Murre** nesting here, and every likelihood **Thick-billed Murre** will follow. Such a concentration of seabirds means plentiful food supplies for **Greater and Sooty Shearwaters, and Black-legged Kittiwake**, which have to endure the unwelcome attentions of **Great Skua, Pomarine and Parasitic Jaegers**. Rarer visitors to Machias Seal Island waters such as **Cory's Shearwater, South Polar Skua and Long-tailed Jaeger** are eclipsed by the sighting of a **Black-capped Petrel** following the Gulf Stream north — a **Sooty Tern** stayed from late June until mid August.

Infrequent reports of **House Wren, Yellow-throated, Prairie and Hooded Warblers, and Yellow-headed Blackbird** suggest the island provides the same kind of migrant trap as Grand Manan. Protection of the islands is in good hands, but disputes over sovereignty have caused friction — I hope the few summering **Laughing Gull** get the last laugh. I don't know if Elsie Mitchell's comment that visitors are strictly limited to 13 Canadian and 12 from the USA was made tongue-in-cheek, but it ties in with the past history — David Clark reports that the current party limit is 30 a day with no nationality breakdown! Other nesting species include **Least Sandpiper, Barn, Tree and Cliff Swallows, and Savannah Sparrow**. Other songbirds are obviously not here by choice, but regular sightings of **Seaside Sparrow** indicate some do arrive anyway.

Kent Island is close to Grand Manan and has a **Leach's Storm-petrel** colony in residence from late April to August — **Northern Gannet** have attempted to nest. Kent Island is another good place to look for shorebirds in fall. The maximum counts of **5000 Red-necked Phalarope, 3500 Semipalmated Sandpiper, 1000 Semipalmated Plover and Least Sandpiper, 500 Short-billed Dowitcher** and several hundred **Black-bellied Plover, Ruddy Turnstone, and White-rumped Sandpiper** are very impressive, but I am intrigued by the record of **200 Spotted Sandpiper** — a species not given to such concentrations anywhere else. There are also regular parties of **Whimbrel, Greater and Lesser Yellowlegs, Willet, Stilt and Solitary Sandpipers**, and occasional visits from **Upland, Baird's and Western Sandpipers**.

A movement of **300 White-crowned Sparrow** in mid May was obviously on the right track. Summer brings a few **King Eider** and songbird vagrants blown here in storms. There is a more obvious songbird migration in August, and a **Lesser Black-backed Gull** has made it in mid September. Spring has produced **Sandhill Crane** way off their normal migration corridor at Kent Island, and a **Clapper Rail** made an unscheduled visit in early April. **Yellow-throated and Connecticut Warblers** are good examples of summer vagrants, while **Prothonotary, Golden- and Blue-winged, Pine and Prairie Warblers** have all appeared in fall. Rather more off course were **50 Black Skimmer** in mid September.

One of the closest islands to Maine is Campobello Island — a favourite summer home of Franklin D. Roosevelt for many years as the international roadbridge bearing his name indicates. It would be nice to report **Franklin's Gull** summers here, but, in fact, only the closely-related **Laughing Gull** usually represents the black-headed gull group — they nest in nearby Maine. The winter months see huge numbers of birds here, as the Christmas Bird Count shared with Eastport, Maine shows. Some of the better counts produced have been **14,000 Black-legged Kittiwake, 4500 Herring Gull, 925 Oldsquaw, 727 Black Duck, 465 Razorbill and 440 Bonaparte's Gull**. There have also been three-figure totals of **Great Cormorant, Bufflehead, Common Eider, White-winged Scoter, Red-breasted Merganser, Purple Sandpiper, Black Guillemot and Common Redpoll. Common Loon, Horned and Red-necked Grebes** reach double figures on some counts.

Other birds seen regularly in small numbers include **Red-throated Loon, Mallard, Greater Scaup, Surf and Black Scoters, Bald Eagle, Red-tailed Hawk, Ring-billed, Iceland and Glaucous Gulls, Mourning Dove, Red-breasted Nuthatch, Northern Shrike, Cedar Waxwing, American Tree, White-throated and Song Sparrows, Evening and Pine Grosbeaks, and Brown-headed Cowbird**. The highest recent count produced 59 species. **Common Black-headed Gull and Common Murre** have both been reported as overwintering species on Campobello Island, and **Blue-gray Gnatcatcher** was a recent early May migrant.

Upper and Lower Duckponds are actually saltwater coves opening to the Grand Manan Channel. They are very popular with migrating waterfowl, including **thousands** of **Brant, Black Duck, White-winged and Black Scoters, and Common Eider**, and smaller numbers of **Surf Scoter and Black Guillemot**. Shorebirds are a strong possibility around the barrier beach and barachois pond — but the water level changes from year to year.

Flood tides sometimes deposit hundreds of sea trout in the ponds to provide a feast for waterfowl and gulls. The best seawatches are often conducted from the northern end of the island between Wilson's Beach and East Quoddy Head.

The closest island to the New Brunswick coast is Deer Island—another stepping stone to the Maine coast. The turbulent waters of Head Harbour Passage between Campobello and Deer Islands are home to huge numbers of phalaropes, gulls and terns from August to October, and the summer ferry is worth taking for seabirds. A peak count of **300,000 Red-necked Phalarope** is as good a reason as any to make the trip in late summer. Flocks of **100,000 Red Phalarope** are also common in late August and can be seen from the ferry. **Great Skua, Common and Thick-billed Murres** appear in summer, when the resident **Black Guillemot** are quite conspicuous. The free ferry from Letete on Highway 772 takes birders close to the feeding location of **2 million Red-necked Phalarope and 30,000 Bonaparte's Gull**—both taking advantage of the churning tides which bring tiny euphrasid shrimp to the surface in August.

The south end of Deer Island, at the Deer Island Point park, provides the best viewpoint from the land. The park is favoured by gulls from late August to late October— With a few **thousand Bonaparte's Gull** at peak periods. **Black-legged Kittiwake** also appear in large numbers and over **8000** have been counted in late December. With so many gulls around, it's not surprising to find **Franklin's Gull** irregular from mid September to the end of October, **Sabine's Gull** possible any time from late August to early November, and **Little Gull** here each year in October. Good numbers of **Common and Arctic Terns** also pass through this area in fall. Other birds seen in August include **Common Eider, Black Guillemot, Broad-winged Hawk, Cape May Warbler, Scarlet Tanager and Rose-breasted Grosbeak**.

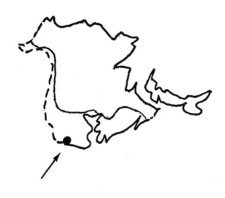

PASSAMAQUODDY BAY

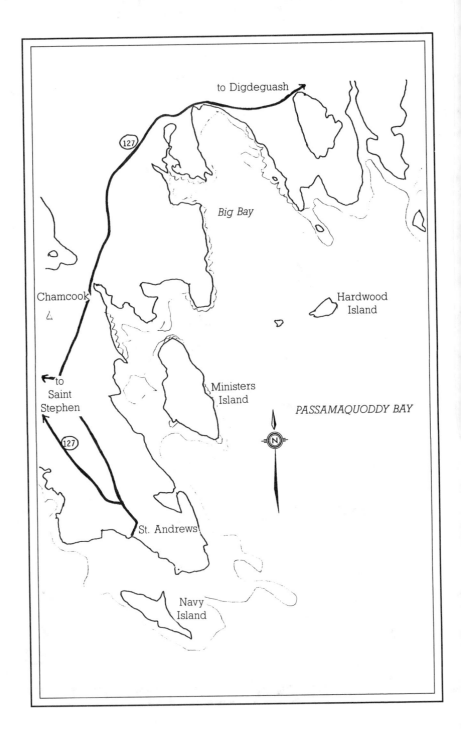

Rural Charlotte County is known as a holiday area and the home of several biological research and natural history interpretation facilities. Many of the early settlers were Scots, and this heritage is reflected in St. Andrews which is the most visited of the small towns in Charlotte County. The waters of Passamaquoddy Bay are very rich in marine life which ensures a concentration of waterfowl, gulls and shorebirds year round. Areas by the Maine border cater more to the tourist trade, but the coastal region to the east of St. Andrews is still very much involved with the fishery.

The setting of St. Andrews makes it ideal for birdwatching, although most of the original forest has been cleared which restricts the number of nesting birds. The town is best visited in spring and fall migration periods when large numbers of migrants gather on the shores of Passamaquoddy Bay to feed. The coastline provides a feeding and staging area for ducks, geese, shorebirds and gulls, and attracts a number of **Osprey** and a few **Bald Eagle**.

Winter is a good time to visit St. Andrews. Waterfowl find enough food in Passamaquoddy Bay to overwinter. The local Christmas Bird Count has good numbers of **Black Duck, Common Eider, White-winged and Surf Scoters, Greater Scaup and Bufflehead**, and smaller numbers of **Common and Red-throated Loons, Horned and Red-necked Grebes, Canada Goose, Mallard, Common Goldeneye, Oldsquaw, Red-breasted Merganser and Black Guillemot. King Eider** are seen most winters, **Blue-winged Teal** have also appeared in December, and there have been reports of **Lesser Scaup** in mid February, but whether these are overwintering birds or returning migrants is not clear. There are usually a few wintering **Great Cormorant**.

Few hawks winter in the area, although **Bald Eagle** are regular and **Cooper's and Red-tailed Hawks, and Gyrfalcon** have made rare appearances. The only regular wintering shorebirds are **Purple Sandpiper**, but **Dunlin** have overwintered at times. **Mourning Dove** are very common in late fall and winter, and **Red-breasted Nuthatch, Northern Cardinal and Song Sparrow** are all regular feeder birds. Some of the more unusual winter vagrants on the Passamaquoddy Bay count include **Northern Saw-whet, Western Kingbird, Northern Mockingbird, Ruby-crowned Kinglet, Yellow-breasted Chat, Rufous-sided Towhee, Chipping and Field Sparrows, Dickcissel, Common Grackle and Rusty Blackbird**.

Spring is less productive here than on other parts of the Fundy coast because most songbirds tend to use offshore islands as stepping stones north, but there are occasional falls — over **300 Yellow-rumped Warbler** have been noted at St. Andrews in early May.

There have been some outstanding finds in spring. A late March **Loggerhead Shrike** may have been a little early for its own good, and a mid April **Black-billed Magpie** was obviously lost, but **Great Crested Flycatcher, Blue-gray Gnatcatcher, Prothonotary and Cerulean Warblers** in mid-late May, and **Orchard Oriole** in early June were all on cue. A **Glossy Ibis** in late April is a possibility now that the species is nesting along the Fundy coast, and **Hooded Merganser** can also appear in spring. Among migrants at the Rossmount Inn, two male **Brewer's Blackbirds** reported in early April are outstanding.

St. Andrews offers few larger landbirds in the summer months, although small islands in Passamaquoddy Bay have **Great Black-backed and Herring Gulls, Double-crested Cormorant, Great Blue Heron and Common Eider** colonies. These colonies should not be disturbed, but birds from the colonies can be seen quite easily. **White-winged Scoters** often stay well into summer. **Bald Eagle and Osprey** also nest in the area. The first provincial nest of a **Wood Thrush** at the end of May and a June **Red-bellied Woodpecker** suggest the grounds of the Algonquin Hotel do persuade some migrants to stay.

The woods in and around St. Andrews, especially on the way to Brandy Cove, are an excellent place to look for songbirds, particularly flycatchers and warblers. In three days in June I tallied five flycatchers and 14 warblers plus **Gray Catbird, Gray-cheeked Thrush, Veery and Rose-breasted Grosbeak**. I also saw **Willow Flycatcher, House Wren, and Indigo Bunting** in the Brandy Cove area in early summer.

Fall is as likely to turn up migrants, as regular sightings of **Gray Catbird and Rose-breasted Grosbeak** indicate, and **Dickcissel** are irregular winter residents. Large flocks of **Bonaparte's Gull** build up from early August into October. Counts of **300 Semipalmated Plover and 1600 Semipalmated Sandpiper** in fall indicate good shorebird habitat close to town. **Hooded Merganser** regularly arrive in mid October, and **Sora** may pause briefly in September. The coastline has been proposed for ecological reserve status which would provide some measure of protection. **Seaside Sparrow** is rare, but has been appearing with increasing frequency in mid fall. A few rarities can be expected, as September records of **Bewick's Wren, Orchard Oriole and Grasshopper Sparrow**, October **Bay-breasted Warbler and Indigo Bunting**, and an early November **Prairie Warbler** indicate. A **Cattle Egret** in mid November left things a little later than usual.

The waters of Passamaquoddy Bay offer an opportunity to watch marine seabirds feeding. Around **1000 Red-necked and 200 Red Phalaropes** are normal concentrations close to shore in late August, when **Ring-billed and Bonaparte's Gulls** are common. **Black Duck** reach a January peak of **2500** and then leave for open waters before returning in March. Diving ducks show a similar pattern with a mid winter peak and a March influx of over **1000**.

The more pelagic seaducks reach a December peak of **1200**, but are largely absent from the area until the late March-early April movements bring concentations of **7500** or more. At this time both **Canada Goose and Brant** are likely. A large number of ducks, geese, shorebirds and gulls feed in the St. Croix River estuary, including **300 Bufflehead, 150 Surf Scoter and 30+ Barrow's Goldeneye** in late February-early March. A few **Bald Eagle and a number of Osprey** are present in spring—these birds may roost west of the community.

Fishing is also excellent in Chamcook Lake if birds are not the only holiday focus. A large number of ducks, geese, shorebirds and gulls feed and stage in Chamcook harbour, and **Bald Eagle and Osprey** fish it during the summer. A small marsh to the east just north of Glebe Road is worth checking in spring and late summer.

Chamcook Mountain is owned by Bob and Lynda Estes of the Rossmount Inn. They bought the property from the previous owners in the mid 1980s and have maintained the trail up the mountain and through the old-growth conifers to the highway. This is an excellent trail system to look for breeding songbirds. In early June I found **Eastern Wood-pewee, Red-breasted Nuthatch, Gray Catbird, Winter Wren, Warbling Vireo**, 17 species of warbler, including **Nashville, Black-throated Blue, Bay-breasted, Blackburnian, Wilson's, Canada and Mourning Warblers, Northern Parula and Northern Waterthrush, and Rose-breasted Grosbeak**. The view from the summit is also worth the hour-long ramble.

The coastal strip to the north of St. Andrews has had both **House Wren and Grasshopper Sparrow** in summer, both species beginning to appear regularly enough in Charlotte County to indicate that breeding may be imminent, and Chamcook Lake produced a **Golden-winged Warbler** in mid May one year. There has also been a **Mew Gull** among the smaller gulls in late summer. A **Carolina Wren** also found enough to overwinter one year. Some of the best mudflats and saltmarshes are located a little further along Highway 127 at Bocabec and Digdeguash. The small saltmarsh at Bocabec is one of the better places to look for herons and egrets, especially in May and August. There is also a major passage of **Common Nighthawk** in late August, when as many as **500** have been counted. Two male **Rufous-sided Towhees** have been found in summer at Bocabec. An **Eastern Screech Owl** at Holt's Point, Bocabec, in July has no ready explanation.

The Digdeguash Harbour mudflats are used by herons, gulls and shorebirds at low tide, and the river is a feeding and minor staging area for an array of ducks, including **Common Eider and Red-breasted Merganser**, shorebirds and gulls. This is also a good place to look for **Bald Eagle and Osprey**. The mudflats are close to Highway 1, and there are access points at several places off Highway 127. The Digdeguash Harbour area has also supported a **Glossy Ibis** in mid April.

Other places to visit from this area
The Pennfield Dragway east of St. George was being used for police cruiser training when Anne Bardou and I drove out one evening in June, but we tallied an impressive 26 species, including four swallows, three flycatchers, **Ruby-throated Hummingbird, Gray Catbird**, four warblers and four sparrows, including **Lincoln's Sparrow**. The

second-growth strips and boggy patches between runways are surprisingly well-populated and have enabled at least **four pairs** of **Eastern Bluebird** to attempt nesting. A **Brown Thrasher** and summering **Field Sparrows** have enlivened a June visit to the Pennfield Dragway, the same time as a **Western Kingbird** at Pennfield.

The St. George-Pennfield area has extensive mudflats along the Magaguadavic River estuary—these attract good numbers of shorebirds at low tide, and waterfowl and alcids at other times in season. **Bald Eagle, Osprey and Northern Harrier** may all appear along the river in fall.

The Pennfield Christmas Bird Count has a good selection of birds although numbers are much lower than those at St. Andrews and Grand Manan. **Great Cormorant, Black Duck, Greater Scaup, Common Eider, Oldsquaw, White-winged and Surf Scoters, Common Goldeneye, Bufflehead, Common and Red-breasted Mergansers** are the commonest waterfowl, with **Common Loon, Horned, Red-necked and Pied-billed Grebes, Mallard, Harlequin, White-winged, Surf and Black Scoters, Barrow's Goldeneye and Black Guillemot** also present. As many as **60 Purple Sandpiper and 55 Bonaparte's Gull** may winter, but **Black-legged Kittiwake** is the winter gull, along with a few **Iceland Gull**. A **Great Blue Heron** was one of many reported on the 1988 New Brunswick counts. **Bald Eagle** sightings include as many as five or six birds, and **Rough-legged Hawk, American Kestrel, Great Horned and Short-eared Owls** have all been noted in winter.

The Black's Harbour count features good numbers of **Common Eider, Oldsquaw and White-winged Scoter**, along with a few dozen **Common Loon, Great Cormorant, Surf Scoter, Common Goldeneye, Bufflehead, Common and Red-breasted Mergansers**. The 1989 count also had **Horned and Red-necked Grebes, Mallard, Greater Scaup** and yet another **Great Blue Heron**. A few hawks are usually seen on the count. Woodpeckers are not common on the Pennfield or Black's Harbour Christmas Bird Counts, but winter lists have included **Northern Flicker, Three-toed, Black-backed and Pileated Woodpeckers**. **Boreal Chickadee, Red-breasted Nuthatch, Cedar Waxwing, Common Redpoll and White-winged Crossbill** numbers indicate a boreal component in local woodlands. There have also been a few **American Tree Sparrow, Lapland Longspur, American Goldfinch, Common Grackle and Brown-headed Cowbird** and a **Northern Mockingbird** to add variety.

Continuing west leads to Black's Harbour—the terminal for the Grand Manan ferry—and Beaver Harbour. If the conditions are right, as many as **400 Red-necked Phalarope** may gather off Black's Harbour in mid May.

Red-necked Phalarope

Small numbers of wintering waterfowl are a regular feature here, with **Common Loon, Horned and Red-necked Grebes, Great Cormorant, Black Duck, Common Eider, Old-squaw, White-winged, Surf and Black Scoters, Common Goldeneye, Bufflehead, Common and Red-breasted Margansers** straying inshore and joined by an occasional wintering **Dovekie or Black Guillemot**. A year-end visit by an **Osprey** resulted from the fishplant in Beaver Harbour, but **Bald Eagle** is more likely.

The Letete Peninsula provides the access to the Deer Island ferry, but it also worth visiting in its own right because the waters here are among the most productive in Passamaquoddy Bay in respect of shellfish and birds. Strong currents and upwelling concentrate planktonic food in the Letete Passage-Western Passage area, and this attracts large numbers of pelagics, loons, cormorants, **Great Blue Heron, Brant,** ducks, shorebirds, phalaropes, gulls, terns and alcids to the waters and mudflats off McMaster Island which lies just west of the ferry route. Back Bay and Letang Harbour suffer from fishplant and pulpmill pollution but there are major scallop grounds and a good number of ducks in winter and during migration periods.

The St. Croix River estuary east of St. Stephen can be reached by taking a minor road east for a few miles. St. Stephen has had as many as **20 Cattle Egret** on migration in late April. Oak Bay a little further east off the Trans-Canada Highway has a provincial park and mudflats, where **Great Blue Heron** is regular at low tide. The constant mixing of salt and freshwater by Cookson Island makes that area of Oak Bay very popular with waterfowl and shorebirds at high and low tides. Small parties of **Lesser Scaup** gather in spring.

A most interesting recent happening is the appearance of a breeding colony of **15 pairs** of **Pine Warbler** in white pines at a cemetery outside St. Stephen. The successful rearing of a brood of **House Finch** as early as late March in the town indicates the benefits of overwintering. A pair of **Red-shouldered Hawk** near St. Stephen in early May was an encouraging recent sign of an increase — six pairs have been located in Charlotte County. Notable vagrants at St. Stephen have included **Eastern Meadowlark** in February, **House Wren** in late May and summer, **Grasshopper Sparrow** in summer, **Harris's Sparrow** in late August, and **Northern Cardinal** in late fall.

A local Christmas Bird Count (shared with Calais, Maine) recently produced 45 species, including **Double-crested Cormorant, Bonaparte's Gull, Pileated Woodpecker, White-breasted Nuthatch, Northern Cardinal, House Finch** and a **White-crowned Sparrow**. The commonest species were **148 Mourning Dove, 40 Red-breasted Nuthatch, 200 Bohemian Waxwing, 235 American Tree Sparrow and 55 Pine Grosbeak**.

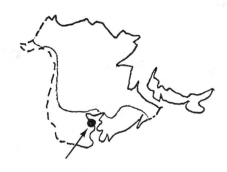

GAGETOWN—
McGOWAN'S CORNER

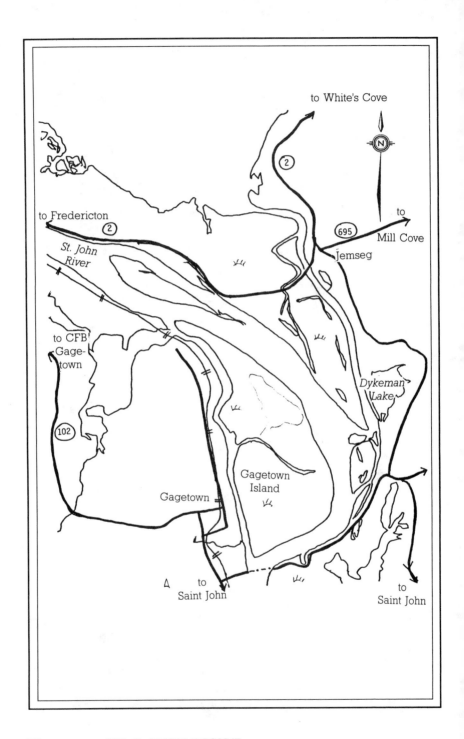

to White's Cove

to Fredericton

St. John
River

to Mill Cove

Jemseg

to CFB
Gage-
town

Dykeman
Lake

Gagetown
Island

Gagetown

to
Saint John

to
Saint John

The St. John River opens up into another large flooded river valley east of Fredericton — Grand Lake is the largest inland lake in the province. A smaller flooded valley known as Washademoak Lake can be explored by canoe from Cambridge-Narrows east, but the open expanses of Grand Lake are best avoided. Ferries cross Washademoak Lake and the St. John River at several points, providing plenty of chances to check out all shorelines. Many of the roads are closed in winter, although Christmas Bird Counts at Cambridge-Narrows and Jemseg are generally very successful.

Waterfowl are well represented with **Redhead** turning up more regularly, but the most interesting nesting species is the **Black Tern** with several colonies. Many Fredericton naturalists make this their premier birding destination during spring migration. Habitats in the area include fields, pastures, wet meadows, freshwater marshes and ponds, wet riverine forests and the river itself. The area is particularly wet during the spring floods in April and May, making it an ideal place to see waterfowl, marshbirds and shorebirds.

Gagetown and Jemseg are situated on opposite sides of the St. John River, but they are connected by a seasonal ferry service which provides access to good waterbird sites both sides of the river, although I suspect Lower Jemseg has the most variety. Hank Deichmann's visit to the area at the end of March turned up **200 Canada Geese, 50 Black Duck,** and a few **Wood Duck, Ring-necked Duck, Green-winged Teal and American Wigeon**, suggesting that migration starts early.

Snow Geese, Greater Scaup and Bufflehead are regularly found heading north in April, when **Barrow's Goldeneye and Oldsquaw** have all been seen, and there have been a number of spring **Redhead** to suggest that breeding is not far away. **Cattle Egret and Glossy Ibis** appear most years in May, and **Black Tern** are nearly always around, along with some **Common Tern**. **Great Cormorant, American Wigeon, Blue-winged Teal, Ring-necked Duck and Surf Scoter** all arrive by early May, and **Gadwall and Eurasian Wigeon** are becoming quite regular in spring. By the end of May, a dozen or so **Northern Shoveler,** and a few **Redhead, Sora and Virginia Rail,** may be sharing the marshes with as many as **150 Black Tern** and some **Pied-billed Grebe, Great Blue Heron and American Bittern**. Jemseg is more productive in spring, with **Peregrine and Indigo Bunting** recorded in April, although Gagetown has added **Golden Eagle** in mid April and **Green-backed Heron** in mid May.

A few shorebirds can be expected in spring. There has been a **Ruff** at Lower Jemseg in mid April, when other rare visitors have included **Upland Sandpiper**. **Red and Red-necked Phalaropes** appear in mid-late May, and **Upland Sandpiper** is a spring and summer possibility. The parties of **Bonaparte's Gull** heading north in mid-late May have attracted **Laughing Gull** in late spring. Jemseg has also had **Caspian Tern** in May. **Mallard, Northern Shoveler and Wood Duck** are quite often seen in summer, along with good numbers of nesting **Black Duck, Northern Pintail, Green- and Blue-winged Teal, American Wigeon, Common Goldeneye and Common Merganser**. During high-water conditions a canoe is the best way to explore the area, but later in the summer dirt roads provide access to most areas. Interesting songbirds include **Nashville Warbler** in late April, **Loggerhead Shrike** in early May, and **Indigo Bunting** in mid May.

Osprey are particularly common in the area, several nesting in very strange locations at Lower Jemseg, including an electrical substation and an elm stump in an open field. On my only visit in mid June, I saw a **Bald Eagle** and a pair of **American Kestrel**. **Northern Harrier** and possibly **Short-eared Owl** also nest in the Lower Jemseg area. **Killdeer, Greater and Lesser Yellowlegs and Common Snipe** are the most likely species in summer. **Wilson's Phalarope** is a future breeder with pairs found from late May.

The nesting songbirds include **Veery, Yellow Warbler, Northern Waterthrush and American Redstart** in the woods, and **Bobolink, Red-winged Blackbird and Swamp Sparrow** widespread in fields and wetter wooded areas. Small colonies of **Marsh Wren and Sharp-tailed Sparrow** parcel out the grassy marshes, while a variety of swallows, warblers, **Gray Catbird, Bobolink, Rose-breasted Grosbeak, American Goldfinch**, blackbirds and sparrows share the highway borders. On my visit to Lower Jemseg in mid June, I found **Alder Flycatcher, Cedar Waxwing, Red-eyed Vireo, Common Yellowthroat and Song Sparrow** equally common, and added **Ruby-throated Hummingbird, Northern Parula, Chestnut-sided, Magnolia and Canada Warblers**. A mid July **Scarlet Tanager**, and August sightings of **Yellow Rail, Great Crested Flycatcher and Brown Thrasher** indicate the area's potential. Roadside ponds and flooded fields attract rather more shorebirds in fall, and a **White-winged Dove** was discovered at Lower Jemseg in mid November.

On the other side of the river, at Gagetown I added small colonies of **Purple Martin**, a few **Cliff Swallow, Eastern Wood-pewee and Eastern Kingbird** and a fine selection of warblers. Some mixed woods with old-growth elms, cedars and pines north of the community provided sightings of **Pileated Woodpecker, Yellow-bellied Sapsucker, Least Flycatcher, Red-breasted Nuthatch, Gray Catbird and Philadelphia Vireo**, three thrushes and a total of 12 warbler species, including **Nashville and Bay-breasted Warblers**.

The woods and riverside marshes south of Gagetown are similar to those to the north and east. A good number of **Bobolink** nest in the pastures, along with a few **Brown-headed Cowbird**. Ducks Unlimited are developing a duck breeding area between Queenstown and Hampstead, and I saw **Double-crested Cormorant, Great Blue Heron, Black Duck, Blue-winged Teal, American Wigeon, Common Goldeneye and Killdeer** on my late June visit. There are also small numbers of **Purple Martin and Cliff Swallow** along with the commoner **Tree, Bank and Barn Swallows**, and **Eastern Kingbird** were very common. Fall tends to be a little quieter.

Late October **Prairie Warbler**, and early November records of **Yellow-billed Cuckoo, Orange-crowned Warbler and Blue Grosbeak** are all good sightings for the Gagetown area, and Queenstown has had a **Yellow-breasted Chat** in November. The action picks up again in winter when Fredericton birders are more sedentary. The limited amount of open water restricts waterfowl and **Common Goldeneye** are the only common wintering ducks, but **Great Blue Heron** and a number of birds of prey are to be found. The most common raptor is the **Rough-legged Hawk** with as many as **21** counted, but **Bald Eagle, Northern Goshawk, Sharp-shinned and Red-tailed Hawks, Great Horned and Barred Owls** are all possible. There have also been winter visits by **Northern Harrier, Red-shouldered Hawk, Gyrfalcon, Northern Hawk Owl and Snowy Owl**.

Hairy Woodpecker outnumber all other woodpecker species, but **Black-backed and Pileated Woodpeckers** can almost be guaranteed in winter. Boreal songbirds are perhaps commoner here than elsewhere along the lower St. John River, with **Gray Jay, Red-breasted Nuthatch, Brown Creeper, Bohemian Waxwing, American Tree Sparrow, Snow Bunting, Pine Grosbeak, Common Redpoll, American Goldfinch and Evening Grosbeak** all relatively common. Apart from **Mourning Dove, Golden-crowned Kinglet, Northern Shrike, Bohemian Waxwing, Common Grackle, Rusty Blackbird and Brown-headed Cowbird**, most other species are largely absent in winter. Single **White-crowned Sparrow and Red-winged Blackbird** were lured by local feeders.

Closer to Fredericton, the McGowan's Corner-Scotchtown area is an excellent place to see waterfowl and marshbirds. Access by canoe is possible from Highway 690 bordering Portobello Creek National Wildlife Area. **Snow Geese** are regular migrants in spring, but less so in fall. **Northern Shoveler** are also present in spring, when **American Wigeon** are common, and there have been **Lesser Scaup** in late October. Shorebirds are perhaps more common here than elsewhere in spring—with **Lesser Golden-plover and Upland Sandpiper** fairly regular from late April to early May. **Killdeer and Common Snipe** both nest in the area. **Wilson's Phalarope, Willet, Ruff and Lesser Black-backed Gull** have appeared at MacGowan's Corner in spring, but mid June **White-rumped and Semipalmated Sandpipers, and American Avocet** are more unusual.

Other places to visit from this area

Cambridge-Narrows to the east of Jemseg has a huge **Purple Martin** roost with over **10,000** counted in late August, and it has attracted breeding **Indigo Bunting**, a late April **Eastern Bluebird**, early May **Common Teal**, and summer **Western Kingbird and Northern Mockingbird**. Four more out-of-season sightings have been a late October **Ruby-throated Hummingbird**, early November **Rufous-sided Towhee**, and December **Ruby-crowned Kinglet and Common Grackle**.

The only recent reports I have seen have been from the Christmas Count period. Very few waterfowl winter, although **Common Goldeneye and Common Merganser** are regular, but several birds of prey do remain, including an occasional **Barred Owl** and an **American Kestrel** which returned for years. **Great Horned and Barred Owls** are resident, and so are **Ring-necked Pheasant, Ruffed and Spruce Grouse**. This count also reports one of the highest counts of **Pileated Woodpecker and Gray Jay** each year. Songbirds, while much less numerous than in urban areas, usually include good counts of **American Tree Sparrow, Snow Bunting, Evening and Pine Grosbeaks, Common Redpoll, American Goldfinch and Evening Grosbeak**. This is also a good count for **Red-breasted Nuthatch, Brown Creeper, Golden-crowned Kinglet, Dark-eyed Junco and White-winged Crossbill**, which appear each year in small numbers.

Grand Lake itself has large numbers of **Greater** and occasional **Lesser Scaup** in fall, and there are sometimes **Caspian Tern** among the parties of **Black Tern** in midsummer. The Minto-Gaspereau Forks area has been improved by a mine reclamation project where more than 40 ponds stocked with trout attract waterfowl and perhaps a few marshbirds. **Spruce Grouse** has been seen on the local Christmas Bird Count, which also reported **Brown Creeper and Brown-headed Cowbird**.

French Lake to the north of McGowan's Corner has good counts of waterfowl in fall — **200 American Wigeon, 200 Wood Duck and 20 Ruddy Duck** are indicative of late September-late October visits. Numbers are much lower in spring, when **Ruddy Duck and Surf Scoter** are fairly regular. A few **Canvasback and Common Moorhen** highlighted late September-late October visits to French Lake. Big Timber Lake to the east has **50 pairs** of **Black Tern**. This colony has tallied **Mew and Franklin's Gulls** in early May and **White-winged Tern** in summer.

Black Tern

The St. John River to the west of McGowans Corner is excellent for migrating geese and ducks in spring and fall. Rarer species in the Sheffield-Maugerville area have included **Mallard, Gadwall, Eurasian Wigeon and Common Teal** among the more regular **Surf and Black Scoters**. Sheffield has also attracted **Cattle Egret, Glossy Ibis, Upland Sandpiper, Wilson's Phalarope, Mew Gull, Black and White-winged Terns** in May. **American Wigeon, Northern Shoveler, Redhead and Sora** nest around Sheffield, and a summer roost of **Double-crested Cormorant** is found 11 miles east of Fredericton.

A few raptors pass through the area in spring, including occasional **Gyrfalcon**, but the most numerous birds are often **Brown-headed Cowbird**, which have totalled **500** in late March, and **Tree Swallow**. Maugervile also has large flocks of blackbirds in the fall—**1500 Rusty Blackbird** have been counted in late September, and **Upland Sandpiper** have bred.

One of the newest wildlife sanctuaries is the Portobello Creek National Wildlife Area designed to protect and manage an outstanding example of a flood plain forest and marsh ecosystem. Situated north of Maugerville and west of French Lake and accessible by driving on Highway 690 three miles east to Lakeville, this is one of the most productive wetlands in Atlantic Canada and supports the highest breeding density of cavity-nesting **Common Goldeneye, Common and Hooded Mergansers** known to occur. The marsh is covered by three meters of water in the spring flood but becomes exposed by early June. The main attraction at Portobello Creek is certainly waterfowl, especially in fall. All the common eastern species nest, including **American Wigeon and Northern Shoveler**, and there are good numbers of nesting **Pied-billed Grebe**, as well as **Great Blue Heron, Wood Duck, Black Duck, Blue- and Green-winged Teal, and Ring-necked Duck. Least Bittern** are also present in summer, although a **Sora or Virginia Rail** is much more likely.

As many as **10 Osprey** nests are present in summer when **Red-shouldered Hawk** may be found. A fine grove of mature red oaks and a small pocket of old red cedars are unique. The roadside hardwoods have a good number of **Warbling Vireo**—their song can be directly compared with that of the many **Purple Finch** nesting in the area. Shrubby swamps and wooded swales are also common, and **Sharp-tailed Sparrow** have one of their few interior colonies. One of the most interesting features is its **Black Tern** colony, which has hosted a **White-winged Tern** in early July. **Canada Geese** are common on fall migration and **Snow Geese** in October-November.

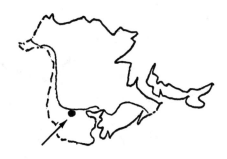

FREDERICTON AREA

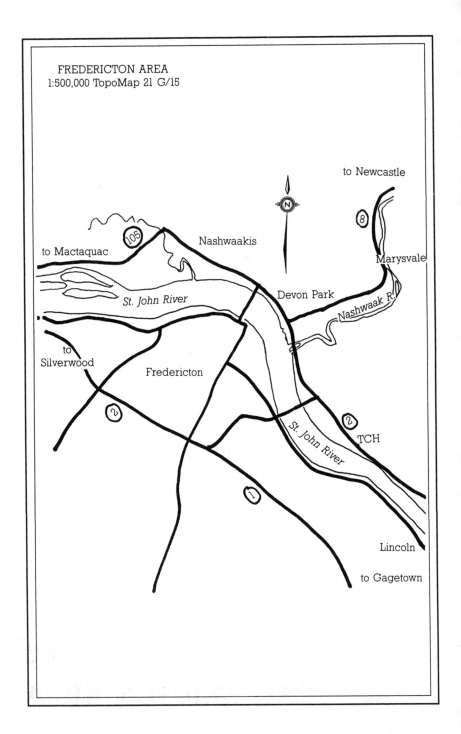

FREDERICTON AREA
1:500,000 TopoMap 21 G/15

to Newcastle

Nashwaakis

Marysvale

to Mactaquac

Devon Park

St. John River

Nashwaak R.

to
Silverwood

Fredericton

St. John River

TCH

Lincoln

to Gagetown

Fredericton is a very productive birding area year round, and its merits have been very thoroughly covered in the Fredericton Nature Club's "Guide to Fredericton and Vicinity". One of the region's most celebrated parks is found in Fredericton, and many rare species nest within a few minutes walk of downtown. Odell Park's 120 hectares was purchased by city council in 1942 but did not receive a complete reprieve from logging until 1954.

The eastern side of the city has been made into the Fredericton Wildlife Management Area which comprises 120 hectares from the mouth of the Nashwaak River to the Princess Margaret Bridge. Habitats include the river, sandbar, muddy shores, riverine woods, fields and gardens. The treed area in the southwest is mostly natural hardwoods but there has been some landscaping and ornamental planting. Over 200 bird species have been recorded, and another ten have appeared just outside the boundary.

An excellent place to watch birds is at the mouth of the Nashwaak River, where numbers of shorebirds are influenced by the river level. The last three miles of the floodplain forms a rich delta and a canoe provides the best means of exploration, with access at the Marysville bridge or downstream by Devon Park. Foot access to the northwest shore is possible from Gibson Street which becomes Canada Street in Marysville. There are access points at the end of Barker Street, off Canada Street just past the railway crossing, and beside Dodona Place in Marysville. An abandoned railway right-of-way parallels the southwest shore and follows the river through fields, pastures, gardens, mixed forest and wet hardwoods. An area of flooded sandpits provide one of very few locations for the gray treefrog whose flute-like trill can be heard in early summer.

Common Merganser often fish below the Marysville rapids, and **Great Blue Heron** are also regular along the riverbanks. Loons, grebes, ducks, shorebirds and gulls are seen in fall, but the cleaning up of the river has ironically reduced numbers. A trip up the Nashwaak River might also be worthwhile as **Laughing Gull and Cattle Egret** have been reported in fall. Both **Red-tailed and Rough-legged Hawks** winter in the area. Devon Park to the northeast is now more productive. The completion of the Mactaquac Dam does not seem to have affected summer and fall water levels. **Greater Scaup, Bufflehead and Oldsquaw** reappear in October. **Lesser Golden-plover, Pectoral Sandpiper and Dunlin** are all seen in October, when **Eastern Bluebird, Prairie Warbler and Yellow-breasted Chat** can be expected.

Spring starts with the passage of large numbers of **Greater Scaup, White-winged, Surf and Black Scoters**, and occasional **Gadwall, Canvasback and Lesser Scaup** from mid April to early May. A few pairs of **Scarlet Tanager, Northern Oriole and Rose-breasted Grosbeak** nest in town, and there are usually several pairs of **Eastern Phoebe, Eastern Wood-pewee, Blackburnian and Chestnut-sided Warblers**.

The floodplain and delta of the Nashwaakis Stream on the north bank of the St. John River has on its east bank small areas of woodland in a natural state that can be reached from behind the Memorial School ballpark, the end of Terra Nova Street or from Hill-court Drive. The floodplain extends on the north side of the St. John River a mile west to Clements Island and can be reached by taking a private road beside 150 Sunset Drive. The road is bordered by oak and pine stands, a small cattail marsh and alder thickets. Other access points include a dirt road by the Burpee Street ballpark and another road on Sunset Drive which leads towards the Wilkins airstrip and is not flooded in spring.

A visit in late spring turns up **Wood and Black Ducks, Great Blue Heron and Great Black-backed Gull**. The cattail marsh is especially favoured by **Red-winged Black-bird**, but **Upland Sandpiper** can no longer be expected as in the past. Nashwaakis has had nesting **Northern Mockingbird** and a pair of **Indigo Bunting** in early July.

Wood Duck

Odell Park is a 120 hectare hardwood oasis in the centre of the city maintained by the City of Fredericton, and includes a provincial arboretum opened in 1985. The main entrance is at Rookwood Avenue off Waggoner's Lane, but there are several other access points for pedestrians. The New Brunswick Species collection of nearly 50 different native trees has its own posted trail and there are other hiking trails through the varie-ty of forest habitats, which include a rare stand of 400-year-old eastern hemlock. Many of the older trees were planted by the earliest Loyalist settlers. Hardwood stands in-clude white ash, yellow birch, hop-hornbeam, basswood and butternut among the dominant sugar maples and beeches. Red spruce, balsam fir, red maple and white birch are also common, and a few white pine, red oak and white cedar also occur. The upper levels of the park are mainly wooded, and the park's wilderness area has sandstone ledges, where most of the rarer plants are found, and a number of intermittent springs.

This is an excellent place to see and hear **Great Crested Flycatcher, Wood Thrush, Black-throated Blue and Mourning Warblers, Scarlet Tanager and Northern Oriole** among the regular **Red-eyed Vireo, Ovenbird and Rose-breasted Grosbeak**. The conifer stands also have **Boreal Chickadee, Ruby-crowned Kinglet and Pine Grosbeak** in among the usual boreal warblers which include **Cape May Warbler**. **Barred Owl** may sometimes be seen, especially in early winter, and **Great Horned Owl and Common Raven** have also nested. There is also at least one resident pair of **Pileated Woodpecker** which were in full voice when I visited in late June.

Unusual spring and early summer visitors I know of in Fredericton have been **Sand-hill Crane, Red-shouldered Hawk, American Avocet, Purple Sandpiper, Great Crested Flycatcher, Loggerhead Shrike, Pine Warbler, Clay-colored Sparrow and Blue Grosbeak**, but coverage by local birders is excellent and more may have been noted recently. **Three-toed Woodpecker** have bred in Fredericton, which indicates the wide variety of habitats.

Another excellent birding location is the UNB Woodlot alongside Highway 101 south of Regent Mall and Vanier Highway around Corbett Brook. This contains a wide array of habitats, including bogs, marsh, pond, streams, softwoods, hardwoods, mixed woodws, secondgrowth, clearcuts and a gravel pit. The bogs either side of Highway 101 are best known for their flowers but may reveal a **Spruce Grouse, Boreal Chickadee or Lincoln's Sparrow** if you're lucky. Corbett Marsh has **American Bittern, Sora, Virginia Rail, Black Duck and Blue-winged Teal**, but the Ducks Unlimited nest boxes have attracted **Tree Swallow** rather than the **Wood Duck** they were put up for. Beavers have transformed the habitat of Corbett Pond to the east, but people have had more to do with the changes in the adjoining sandstone caves.

The varied wooded habitats can be driven, walked or cycled on many roads. **Barred Owl, Pileated Woodpecker, Yellow-bellied Sapsucker, Winter Wren** and an assortment of thrushes and warblers are readily seen in summer, and over 100 bird species have already been recorded within the woodlot boundaries. Plantations of various conifers have nesting **Great Horned Owl**, and the logpiles have raised broods of **Mourning Dove, Blue and Gray Jays**.

In town, the UNB Forest Research Centre chimney welcomes up to **2200 Chimney Swift** in late May, and another notable gathering takes place in late August when **5000 Purple Martin** have been counted along the river. The UNB campus also hosts as many as **2000 American Crow** to a roost in October. Sugar Island on the Keswick Ridge has breeding **Sharp-tailed Sparrow** and one or two rare nesting **Willow Flycatcher**. This area is best visited by canoe with a launching point at the end of Crocks Point Road east of Highway 616.

Fredericton has a very productive Christmas Bird Count, which regularly totals over 50 species — not bad for an interior count in Atlantic Canada. **Canada Goose, Black Duck, Common Goldeneye, Common Merganser, Mourning Dove, Blue Jay, Black-capped Chickadee, Bohemian Waxwing, American Tree Sparrow, Snow Bunting, Pine Grosbeak, Common Redpoll, Pine Siskin, American Goldfinch and Evening Grosbeak** are abundant and reach three figures. High counts of **Greater Scaup, Ruffed Grouse, Hairy and Downy Woodpeckers, Horned Lark, Gray Jay, White- and Red-breasted Nuthatches, Golden-crowned Kinglet, Brown-headed Cowbird and Purple Finch** are equally interesting.

18 Pileated Woodpecker, 7 White-throated Sparrow, five birds of prey, **Iceland and Glaucous Gulls**, six sparrows and three icterids among 54 species in 1987 were also noteworthy. The importance of mature trees is also indicated by the 1988 totals of **60 Downy, 54 Hairy, 7 Pileated and 3 Black-backed Woodpeckers, 800 Black-capped Chickadee, 94 Red- and 8 White-breasted Nuthatches, and 7 Brown Creeper**. The count also had **Great Blue Heron, Bald Eagle, Northern Goshawk, Red-tailed and Rough-legged Hawks, and Barred Owl**.

The songbird totals included **Horned Lark, Ruby-crowned Kinglet, Northern Mockingbird, Pine Warbler, Northern Cardinal, Chipping, Song and White-crowned Sparrows, and House Finch** — a fine collection considering Fredericton's distance from the coast. Winter vagrants such as **Gyrfalcon, Eastern Phoebe, Tufted Tit, Loggerhead Shrike, Brown Thrasher, Northern Cardinal, Field Sparrow and Indigo Bunting** are unexpected given the location. A little later in the winter, birders added **27 Mallard** on upriver islands, a **Northern Hawk Owl** and a very tardy **Hermit Thrush** on the UNB campus in early February.

The Fredericton Wildlife Management Area is less than a mile from the city centre and lies between the railway bridge and Princess Margaret Bridge. Its 120 hectares were first set aside as a sanctuary in 1962 and cover a wide variety of habitats, including the river, sand bar, muddy shore, tangles, bottomland hardwoods, fields and gardens. Landscaping has introduced many ornamental species and there is a historic Loyalist cemetery. The area may be flooded in spring but is usually completely accessible from Waterloo Row. The river attracts spring groups of **Oldsquaw, White-winged and Surf Scoters**, and **Black Duck and Common Goldeneye** are joined by other waterfowl in October and remain until freeze-up. A pair of **Cinnamon Teal** have also been seen in the Fredericton Wildlife Management Area in late April, around the time to look for **Golden Eagle and Gyrfalcon**. A **Field Sparrow** has also summered several times in the last 15 years. Five singing **Willow Flycatcher** in June indicate a local stronghold. **Common Nighthawk and Chimney Swift** are common sights in summer.

Both gulls and shorebirds are common on migration. **Semipalmated Plover, Greater Yellowlegs and Least Sandpiper** are all quite common in August and September, and gulls are common year round. **Laughing Gull** is more likely from late August to September. Some of the better birds found in and around the sanctuary area in fall have been **Leach's Storm-petrel, Cattle Egret, Canvasback, Barrow's Goldeneye, Sandhill Crane, Virginia Rail, Hudsonian Godwit, Long-billed Dowitcher, Baird's** and Buff-breasted Sandpipers, Sabine's, Laughing and Common Black-headed Gulls, Black-legged Kittiwake and Dovekie. A party of **17 Snow Geese** spent the first part of the winter in the area one year.

The last clearly-defined site in this section of the St. John River is Mactaquac Provincial Park overlooking the headpond of the Mactaquac Dam. Here **Double-crested Cormorant, Canada Geese, Common Goldeneye and Common Merganser** winter in reasonable numbers, and there are a few **Great Cormorant, Mallard, Barrow's Goldeneye and Hooded Merganser**, too. Inland sightings of **Glaucous and Iceland Gulls**, and even more surprisingly, **Purple Sandpiper** indicate the nature of the St. John River. Good counts of **Red-breasted Nuthatch and Pine Grosbeak** and the occasional **Black-backed Woodpecker or Northern Shrike** show that boreal habitat is plentiful enough to support them through the winter. **Brown Thrasher and Song Sparrow** were more surprising 1988-89 winter sightings.

There are 10 miles of walking trails in the park and an international bass-fishing tournament in early July, but information was sadly lacking on the birdlife despite an interpretive program until Gerry Bennett pulled in on his Trans-Canada birding trek.

We now know **Ruffed Grouse, American Woodcock, Barred Owl, Pileated Woodpecker, Gray Catbird, Brown Thrasher, Wood Thrush, Veery, Philadelphia and Solitary Vireos, Northern Oriole, Rose-breasted Grosbeak, Rufous-sided Towhee, Vesper Sparrow** and over 20 warbler species, including **Black-throated Blue Warbler**, nest.

There are also enough interior conifers to sustain **Spruce Grouse, Black-backed and Three-toed Woodpeckers, Gray Jay, Common Raven, Boreal Chickadee, Blackpoll and Palm Warblers, and Red Crossbill**. Mactaquac also has eight nesting flycatchers — **Eastern Kingbird, Great Crested Flycatcher, Eastern Phoebe, Eastern Wood-pewee, Least, Alder, Yellow-bellied and Olive-sided Flycatchers**, which would suggest an effective insect repellent is a good idea when visiting. A count of **12 Nashville Warbler** in mid October provides an interesting commentary on warbler migration. Very little has been written of the area upriver, but the rural nature would suggest open-country birds are widespread. Birds of prey are certainly common in early winter, with **Bald Eagle and Red-tailed Hawk** seen in December and January.

Other places to visit from this site

The river north of Oromocto also has large numbers of **Double-crested Cormorant** in April and May. **Lesser Golden-plover** are common on migration, while **Buff-breasted Sandpiper, Wilson's and Red-necked Phalaropes** are infrequent visitors. Oromocto also has good blackbird counts in fall — with **3000 Red-winged Blackbird** in late October, and raptors have included **Great Horned Owl and Peregrine** in early winter.

The upper St. John River valley does not have the broad expanses of water found east of Nackawic, but the river and its floodplain have played very important roles in the development of the region. Many of the communities retain the look of the early years of settlement when farming was very important, but the logging and river transportation of the 1800s have largely disappeared. Hardwoods and wet secondgrowth occupy much of the riverine floodplain and the network of country roads gives access to most good birding spots.

Stops alongside the main road are likely to yield **Yellow-bellied Sapsucker, Least Flycatcher, Eastern Wood-pewee, Gray Catbird, Veery, Red-eyed Vireo, Cedar Waxwing, Black-and-white Warbler, Ovenbird, American Redstart, Rose-breasted Grosbeak and Purple Finch**. A late evening visit will turn up **Common Nighthawk, Whip-poor-will** and a selection of swallows, likely including a few **Cliff and Rough-winged Swallows**. Local farmers have been very supportive of the protection of habitats for both breeding and migrating birds, and it's a good idea to talk to them—not only to get permission to enter their land but to find out what birds are around.

The tree-lined streets and stately private homes of Woodstock are a reminder of its historic past—it was the first incorporated town in the province. A bridge linking up with Maine Interstate 95 crosses the river, which has a typical floodplain combination of flats, mixed woodlands, pastures, meadows and hayfields close to town. Connell Park has some campsites and is a good starting point.

The floodplain itself offers nesting **Great Blue Heron, Black Duck, Common Merganser and Spotted Sandpiper**, and the surrounding pastures have **Ring-necked Pheasant and Mourning Dove** and a number of **Cliff Swallow and Vesper Sparrow**. **Hooded Merganser** have also raised young in the area, which has **Purple Martin, Rough-winged Swallow and Warbling Vireo** populations on the increase rather than in decline as elsewhere in the Maritimes. **Bank Swallow** colonies are also expanding, and the more heavily wooded sections have **Broad-winged Hawk, Wood Thrush, Solitary Vireo, Northern Parula and Blackburnian Warbler**.

The local Christmas Bird Count generally nets around 30 species and rarely has large numbers of anything except **Blue Jay, Black-capped Chickadee, Snow Bunting, Evening Grosbeak, and Common Redpoll**, with **Pine Grosbeak and American Tree Sparrow** the next in line. **Ring-necked Pheasant** are common year round, and so are **Red-breasted Nuthatch**, and woodpeckers, especially **Downy Woodpecker**—**Black-backed and Pileated Woodpeckers** are both present. **White-breasted Nuthatch, American Robin and Common Grackle** can also be looked for. **Red-tailed Hawk** is the commonest winter raptor, but **Bald Eagle, Northern Goshawk, Rough-legged Hawk and Great Horned Owl** are regularly seen.

Migration periods may turn up some unusual species in the Woodstock area, although there are few local observers. A few **Green-backed Heron** may summer, which indicates likely nesting, but a **Little Blue Heron** in mid July was more likely to have been a non-breeding bird. The only spring reports of note have been **Cooper's Hawk** in late March and mid April, **3 Black-necked Stilt** at the end of April, **Cliff Swallow** at the end of the month, **Green-backed Heron** in early May, and a **Turkey Vulture** in late May. Fall reports are scanty, with **Great Crested Flycatcher** in early September the best.

Hartland has a similar combination of habitats, but its mixed woodlands tend to offer more cover to birds of the deeper woods. These include **Red-tailed Hawk, Barred Owl, Boreal Chickadee, Veery, Scarlet Tanager and Black-throated Blue Warbler**. Typical floodplain nesters such as **Green-winged Teal, Common Goldeneye, Osprey and Red-winged Blackbird** begin nesting early, and are complemented by the later-arriving **Purple Martin, Rough-winged Swallow, Bobolink and American Goldfinch** of the farmlands.

Raptors, including **Barred Owl**, can be looked for along wood edges. Most of the waterfowl leave and **Snowy Owl** may have just arrived by late November. Birds of prey are quite well represented in winter, with **Bald Eagle, Northern Goshawk, Sharp-shinned, Red-tailed and Rough-legged Hawks, Great Horned, Barred and Snowy Owls** all accounted for. **Ring-necked Pheasant, Mourning Dove and Common Grackle** are common on the farmlands, but the dominance of **Blue Jay, American Tree Sparrow, Snow Bunting, Evening and Pine Grosbeaks, and White-winged Crossbill** underlines normal winter conditions.

Black-backed Woodpecker, Red-breasted Nuthatch, Brown Creeper, Golden-crowned Kinglet and Bohemian Waxwing point out the boreal nature of the woodlands. Both **Turkey Vulture and Northern Hawk Owl** have turned up at Hartland on spring migration, when **Red-headed Woodpecker and Eastern Bluebird** are also possible.

Florenceville is the heart of New Brunswick's potato farming, and its nesting birds reflect the agricultural bias. **Mourning Dove, Purple Martin and Rough-winged Swallow** are fairly common, and there are **Ruby-throated Hummingbird** here and in nearby Oakland. Spring arrives early with **Northern Saw-whet, American Robin, Red-winged Blackbird and House Finch** all recorded by mid March when the last of the wintering **Snowy Owl and Lapland Longspur** leave.

Williamstown Lake to the west has a notable nesting and staging population of **Ring-necked Duck—American Coot** have also raised two broods of young in June and August. Water levels may restrict numbers some years. The best time to visit is in spring with many ducks arriving in early April and most warblers waiting until May. It has attracted occasional **Yellow-crowned Night Heron, Least Bittern and Marsh Wren** in summer.

The Florenceville Christmas Bird Count is an interesting one—not least because it has the second highest count of **Rock Dove** after Fredericton and the highest **Common Raven** total. **Mourning Dove, Hairy and Downy Woodpeckers** are also extremely common in winter, along with **Blue Jay, Black-capped Chickadee, American Tree Sparrow, Snow Bunting, Pine and Evening Grosbeaks. Canada Goose, Common Goldeneye and Common Merganser** are the commonest wintering waterfowl, and both **Mallard and Bufflehead** have been recorded. Raptors are also well represented, and **Pileated and Black-backed Woodpeckers** have rounded out family representation, but the selection of songbirds is relatively low.

KOUCHIBOUGUAC LAGOON

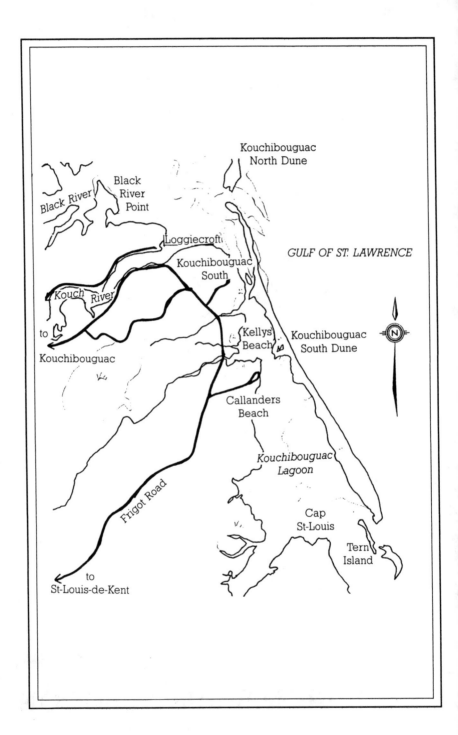

Kouchibouguac
North Dune

Black
River
Point

Black River

GULF OF ST. LAWRENCE

Loggiecroft

Kouchibouguac
South

Kouch River

to
Kouchibouguac

Kellys
Beach

Kouchibouguac
South Dune

N

Callanders
Beach

Kouchibouguac
Lagoon

Frigot Road

Cap
St-Louis

Tern
Island

to
St-Louis-de-Kent

Kouchibouguac National Park has been in the news for two decades for its politics and land ownership disputes, but it deserves to be recognized for its habitats and birdlife. Covering 370 sq. kms. in the northeast corner of Kent County it has a wide variety of unique and representative habitats unmatched anywhere else in New Brunswick. Included in the park are extensive bogs, sand beaches, dunes, saltwater lagoons, saltmarshes, major rivers, boreal forest and hardwoods. Over a third of the park is bogland and this largely birdless habitat plays a very important role in water conservation. There are a few freshwater ponds, but the majority of open water is brackish. A canoe offers the best way to explore the park since access to some places is very restricted or time-consuming on foot.

Forests vary from secondgrowth hardwoods to stands of jack pine and large areas of mixed and boreal forest. This all adds up to a bird list of well over 230 species, and the list is growing as the park becomes better known to birders. The developed portion of the park is also the most accessible, so a high proportion of bird sightings are in the area from the estuary of the Black River to Cap de St-Louis. I did, however, spend a fair amount of time in the Portage River area and can recommend it, especially during spring and fall migration. Some species reach their northern nesting limits in the park, while boreal birds are also quite widespread.

One place not to be missed is Kelly's Beach. Despite its proximity to the park campground and bathing beach, the saltmarshes, dunes and sand beaches regularly produce huge numbers of ducks, shorebirds and terns. The boardwalk from the beach parking area leads over two shallow bays to South Kouchibouguac Dune which stretches about five miles north and south. The section to the north of Kelly's Beach leads to Little Gully where roosting parties of shorebirds may be higher than anywhere else in the park. **Semipalmated and Black-bellied Plovers, Ruddy Turnstone, Red Knot, Dunlin and White-rumped Sandpiper** are particularly common in the second half of shorebird migration, and the southbound **Peregrine and Merlin** are apparently aware of this—**Northern Harrier** are not a threat but scatter the flocks.

The marshes fringing the lagoon are best checked on an incoming or low tide when **Lesser Yellowlegs, Pectoral Sandpiper and Short-billed Dowitcher** are much in evidence. Waterfowl are common at mid and high tide, with a few **Brant** accompanying the northbound **Canada Geese** in spring. A large roosting flock of **300 Double-crested** and a few **Great Cormorants** gathers on the northern tip of the dune in September. **American Wigeon** are plentiful in fall with **Northern Pintail**, and the huge **Black Duck** flocks are containing more **Gadwall, Mallard** and hybrids. Later in the fall, **Common Goldeneye, White-winged Scoter and Red-breasted Merganser** move into the lagoon in good numbers, along with a few **Barrow's Goldeneye and Lesser Scaup**, to be joined by **Common Eider, Greater Scaup and Oldsquaw** in early winter. The later flocks of **Canada Geese** are worth checking for accompanying vagrant waterfowl. I am convinced I saw a **Barnacle Goose** among the goose flocks one chilly November.

The park's Christmas Bird Count is rarely too productive except for **Oldsquaw**, but birds of prey are a specialty. The 1988 count had small numbers of **Northern Harrier, Red-tailed and Rough-legged Hawks, Snowy and Short-eared Owls**, and there were also single **Bald Eagle, Northern Goshawk and Great Horned Owl**. The 1989 count was notable for single **Surf Scoter and Spruce Grouse**. Most of the shallow water freezes, which means just a few overwintering gulls, including **Glaucous Gull**.

Landbirds are few and far between compared to other counts, although **Mourning Dove, Gray Jay, Black-capped Chickadee and Red-breasted Nuthatch** are widespread, and **White-breasted Nuthatch, Golden-crowned Kinglet, Northern Shrike, Song Sparrow and American Goldfinch** more local. The commonest winter songbird is usually the **Snow Bunting**, although irruptions of boreal finches, especially **Common Redpoll**, boost their numbers some years. The 1989 count also had a **Bohemian Waxwing and Red-winged Blackbird**.

The parking lot woods are a good place to look for **Common Nighthawk** in summer, when songbirds are very common. **Spruce Grouse** broods occasionally wander from the deeper woods to feed with the more widespread **Ruffed Grouse**. Most breeding thrushes and warblers find their way here, and there are sometimes **Brown Thrasher and Vesper Sparrow** in the area. I have seen what looked like an **Acadian Flycatcher** by the start of the Kelly's Beach boardwalk in late August.

Spring is a good time for **Snowy Egret**, and there are sometimes a few **Red Knot, Short-billed Dowitcher and Dunlin** in summer plumage in June. The boardwalk to the beach starts by the parking lot and the best route to follow is over the first short bridge, by a small sandspit on the left where **Hudsonian Godwit and Red Knot** feed in the shallows. The godwit parties should be checked out as a **Marbled Godwit** has joined them on several occasions in fall. I have also seen a **Stilt Sandpiper** in the first section of marsh, and other rarities can be expected to occur. This area also has **Piping Plover** and a few **Arctic Tern**. **Willet** are now regular in August, when an occasional **Baird's Sandpiper** can be expected. A few **Common Black-headed Gull and Black-legged Kittiwake** also join the **Ring-billed Gull** parties.

Just after the second bridge take a sharp right along the beach skirting the marshy areas, where **Sharp-tailed Sparrow** breed and **Northern Harrier** is a regular visitor. The first sandspit you reach is favoured by shorebirds and terns, especially if birds have been disturbed from the lagoon beaches closer to the boardwalk. **Hudsonian Godwit, Ruddy Turnstone, Short-billed Dowitcher and White-rumped Sandpiper** are particularly common.

These birds all feed in the shallow muddy water on the east side until low tide allows them to spread out over the spit. Smaller spits run out further along the South Kouchibouguac Lagoon and attract **Piping Plover, Ruddy Turnstone, Red Knot, Lesser Yellowlegs and Least Sandpiper** from July to early September—**White-rumped Sandpiper, Dunlin and Sanderling** are commoner later on. Recent reports include a **Curlew Sandpiper** in late May and **Ruff** in mid August.

The ridge of saltmarsh beyond is a favourite place for roosting **Great Blue Heron** and a few **Lesser Golden-plover and Semipalmated Plover. Pectoral Sandpiper** are common on the spartina-glasswort flats where they are joined by **Buff-breasted Sandpiper**. My best bird in the more distant marshes has been **Long-billed Dowitcher**, but **Western Sandpiper** has appeared.

The Kelly's Beach marshes are also a good place to look for migrant passerines, and **Eastern Meadowlark and Seaside Sparrow** have been noted on the saltmarshes in fall. Early September flocks of **Horned Lark** should be checked for **Lapland Longspur** which occur until early November. The parties of **Savannah Sparrow** later on may attract some other species until the **Snow Bunting** flocks take over the marshes and dunes in November. A **Snowy Owl** found the area appealing enough to stay to mid June one year.

Just beyond the beach is a wide expanse of mudflats where large numbers of **Semipalmated Plover, Least, Semipalmated and White-rumped Sandpipers** can be seen well into September. **Lesser Yellowlegs and Red Knot** are quite common, and a few **Dunlin** can be looked for later. **Piping Plover** are numerous early on when I have counted as many as **20** on several occasions—about the same number of **Pectoral Sandpiper** can be expected. **Glossy Ibis** are regular in both spring and fall.

Waterfowl are also common on the lagoon from mid September, with **Canada Goose, Black Duck and Green-winged Teal** particularly plentiful. **Lesser Scaup and Barrow's Goldeneye** sometimes appear, but diving ducks are scarcer than in the northern section of the lagoon where the water is deeper.

The flats at the southern edge of South Kouchibouguac Dune join Tern Island where the largest tern colony in eastern Canada is located—over **7000 pairs** of **Common Tern** are joined by a few **Arctic Tern** each summer. There have been infrequent reports of both **Roseate and Least Terns** in the tern colony. A return can be made along the Gulf shore of South Kouchibouguac Dune, which is a good place to study **Sanderling** and a few pairs of nesting **Piping Plover**.

Piping Plover

Other shorebirds also use the beach at high tide and after storms when seaweed debris may bring a welcome feast of sandhoppers and other food. **Semipalmated and Black-bellied Plovers, Ruddy Turnstone, Lesser Yellowlegs, Least and Semipalmated Sandpipers** are common, and **Red Phalarope** are sometimes driven inshore by storms.

King Eider at the end of August are likely non-breeding birds summering offshore. After most of the shorebirds have left, attention is switched to offshore where there are usually good numbers of **Common and Red-throated Loons**. The loons offshore have contained a **Pacific Loon** in late September. By October **Northern Gannet** are likely to be blown inshore, but my highest count was of **225** in mid July. **White-winged, Black and Surf Scoters** also appear in large numbers in early October, and mixed flocks of **200** are normal. Skeins of **Double-crested and Great Cormorants** stream by, and I have seen **Leach's and Wilson's Storm-petrels** in the peak passage.

While Kelly's Beach offers the greatest variety, Callander's Beach a little further to the south is worth a visit. **Osprey** fish the shallow water, and there is a good chance of finding a **Cliff Swallow** among the myriads of **Barn, Tree and Bank Swallows**. Ducks and shorebirds are also frequent visitors, especially early in the morning before tourists are up and about, and female **Red-breasted Merganser** quite often steer their young out into the open water from the muddy shore. A walk along the adjoining Cedar trail could add some interesting warblers such as **Canada, Black-throated Blue and Blackburnian Warblers** during spring and fall migration. The trail's white cedars also attract feeding **Red-breasted Nuthatch and Brown Creeper**.

The Rankin's Brook trail along the south shore of the Black River estuary connects with the Loggiecroft road, and is productive in fall when **Solitary and Baird's Sandpipers** may be present. Swallows are very common in spring when **Purple Martin** are regular. Loggiecroft at the mouth of the Kouchibouguac River is accessible by this trail and by road. It is a popular location for shorebirds and gulls. All common shorebirds stop here, and the sandy beach north of the wharf is a good spot for both **Piping Plover and Ruddy Turnstone**. **Spotted Sandpiper** prefer the muddy river shoreline, where **Black-crowned Night Heron** might be expected to join the usual **Great Blue Herons**. It's worth stopping a while to check for **Common Black-headed and Bonaparte's Gulls** in late summer and early fall, when a few **Black and Caspian Terns** feed in the lagoon. The quiet backwater by Highway 117 is a good place to look for summering **Wood Duck** and occasional **Mourning Dove**. Over half of the park's nesting **Piping Plover** are found on North Kouchibouguac Dune.

The last birding site within the developed section of the park is the estuary of the Black River. This is part of the Kouchibouguac Lagoon, but it is best visited by walking along trails from the roadbridges at Fontaine and Black River. It is close to the area under dispute, so a check should be made with park authorities before planning a visit. Large flocks of **Canada Goose, Black Duck, Northern Pintail, American Wigeon and Green-winged Teal** find this an acceptable staging area, and there is a good chance of finding **Blue-winged Teal and Greater Scaup** in spring and fall. It is also the best location for **Hooded Merganser**, and I discovered **60** along one of the brooks by the trail in late fall.

Hooded Merganser

Other places to visit from this site

The Cocagne area is best known for its annual speedboat races, but the bridge over the Cocagne River is a good place to stop in midwinter — flocks of **Common Goldeneye and Common Merganser** usually contain as many as **40 Barrow's Goldeneye**, and a **Great Cormorant** may stray up the river in mid January. Offshore flocks of **1300 Common Eider** in early October and **340 Oldsquaw** in mid November indicate that a heavy passage is underway somewhat earlier. Marshbirds are also quite common — with counts of **32 Great Blue Heron** late in September and a **Great Egret** in June. Parties of **Lapland Longspur** are found in winter, and huge flocks of **1000+ Horned Lark** in late fall and early spring indicate that visits don't have to be in summer or winter, either. An **Eastern Screech Owl** by Cocagne in May and a **Northern Cardinal** in June at Cap des Caissie suggest that more visits are needed.

Buctouche is the home of an old folklore character, "La Sangouine", and a centre for lobsters and oysters. A **Green-backed Heron** made a brief stopover in early September. There are usually a few **Piping Plover and Willet** in summer, when **Eastern Meadowlark** can be found alongside the roads. A mid July visit produced **90 Short-billed Dowitcher, 30 Greater Yellowlegs, 15 Willet, 25 Semipalmated Sandpiper** and smaller numbers of **Piping and Semipalmated Plovers, Ruddy Turnstone, Spotted and Least Sandpipers**, and **135 Short-billed Dowitcher** have been counted in mid August. Shorebirds stay here into early November, when I have seen **Black-bellied Plover, Greater Yellowlegs and White-rumped Sandpiper**.

Black Scoter are common inshore in fall. I have also noted a mid November **Gyrfalcon** disputing feeding territory with a **Northern Goshawk**. **60 Bobolink** have been counted in the fields in mid August, but fall migration is nearing an end when flocks of **Chipping Sparrow** pass through in late October. An early January **Rufous-sided Towhee** obviously missed its cue.

Although Richibucto and Rexton share a boundary on the Richibucto River, they offer completely different characters—Richibucto is Acadian and bustling with activity, while Rexton is British and more laid back. Flocks of **Common Redpoll** feed in the local fields in April, when **Eastern Meadowlark and Bobolink** may first appear. **Caspian Tern** stop by in June and August, and shorebirds are quite common in fall—there is a good chance of finding large roosting flocks off Indian and Richibucto Islands in the outer bay. **Leach's Storm-petrel, Common Murre and Dovekie** follow them in early and late winter but usually don't winter in any numbers. More unusual early summer reports from the Richibucto area include **Warbling Vireo and Field Sparrow**, and nearby Ste-Marie-de-Kent has had breeding **Upland Sandpiper**.

Rexton often attracts marshbirds in spring, especially **Great and Cattle Egrets**, and there has even been a **Cattle Egret** in early November. **Northern Goshawk and Sharp-shinned Hawk** pay dearly for their raids on local chickenhouses, but **Mourning Dove** flocks are allowed to take grain. A late July concentration of **5000+ Bank Swallow** is worth checking out for other hirundines, including **Rough-winged Swallow and Purple Martin**. Kent County's Caines River also provided the first nesting record of **Solitary Sandpiper** when a pair with two young were found in late July.

The best birding site in the southern section of the park is found at Cap de St-Louis which lies at the end of a fire road from St. Louis de Kent. A count of **14 Wilson's Phalarope** in mid May indicates that this species concurs. Waterproof boots are recommended for the wet secondgrowth and hardwoods lining the road and trail. **Whip-poor-will** nest in small numbers, and I saw **Gray Catbird, Veery and Rose-breasted Grosbeak** on all my visits. Other species noted in late spring were likely migrants—I saw **Northern Mockingbird, Brown Thrasher, Wood Thrush, Orange-crowned and Black-throated Blue Warblers, and Field Sparrow**. **Chipping Sparrow** are very common along the beaches in late October. You can park beyond the fishing community and return along the edge of the saltmarshes which have breeding **Sharp-tailed Sparrow**. The end of the trail offers a good view of the tern colony if you have a telescope handy.

The area around the village of Kouchibouguac is an excellent place for birds. The combination of hardwoods, secondgrowth and the river make it particularly attractive to swallows—both **Cliff and Rough-winged Swallows** should be looked for among the regular nesting species. **Osprey** can also be counted on by the roadbridge, and **Killdeer, Spotted Sandpiper and Belted Kingfisher** all nest nearby. The best birding is above the bridge, where I have seen **Northern Oriole and Scarlet Tanager** among the migrating warblers, vireos and sparrows. **Brown-headed Cowbird** occur with sparrows on fields to the north of the river. I have also noted **Eastern Bluebird and Indigo Bunting** to the east of Kouchibouguac along Highway 117, and added my only **House Finch** for the province along the riverside trail. The road and trail along the river's south bank have flocks of finches and sparrows. Nesting **Gray Catbird** are joined by migrant **Northern Mockingbird and Northern Shrike**, and there have also been a few **Rufous-sided Towhee** by this three hour-long trail.

You can walk along both shores, but a canoe is the best way to enjoy the Kouchibouguac River. Late in summer the river level drops and care must be taken to avoid the shoals and sawmill debris. Large flocks of ducks gather in the fall, including parties of **American Wigeon and Northern Shoveler**, and there are often one or two **Double-crested Cormorant, Great Blue Heron** and shorebirds for variety. **Black-crowned Night Heron** may well be regular in late summer and fall, and there is a good chance **Wood Duck and Hooded Merganser** will appear on a September or October list.

During the spring and summer of 1976 my work took me to Portage River at the north end of Kouchibouguac National Park. This small river and its estuary had not been visited all that often, so it was quite a surprise to me to find such a good variety of migrant and breeding birds. It's best to park your vehicle by the first saltmarsh on the right and walk a mile to the beach—the potholes and washouts along the road have mired many a fisherman's truck! The secondgrowth lining the road is a summer home to nesting thrushes and warblers, including several pairs of **Chestnut-sided Warbler**, and there are **Winter Wren and Ruby-crowned Kinglet** adding their songs from the backing conifers. **Brown Thrasher and Philadelphia Vireo** have also been noted along the roadside and at the road entrance, and the wet growth by the river has a few roding **American Woodcock**.

As the bordering forest thins out, a view of the large bog on the left provides a lasting impression of northern Kent County. **Palm Warbler, Common Yellowthroat and Lincoln's Sparrow** are common nesting species, with **Yellow and Wilson's Warblers** along the edges. A little further on, boreal species are more likely, with **Purple Finch** in the poplar groves and all kinds of warblers in the tamaracks and spruces. Right at the end of the trail north of the rivermouth is a stand of pines and secondgrowth, where migrants can be quite plentiful. Sparrows are also common in the shrubs and heaths.

The water areas are excellent for waterfowl of all kinds, and any flocks should be carefully studied. Apart from the many **Great and Double-crested Cormorants** feeding in early summer, there have been early summer and fall reports of **Red-throated Loon and Black-crowned Night Heron** in the estuary. **American Wigeon and Surf Scoter** are also regular on the brackish water, while large mixed flocks of **White-winged, Black and Surf Scoters, Common Eider, Common and Red-breasted Mergansers** are regular in spring and fall. **Bufflehead, King Eider and Harlequin** have all been seen inshore or on the marshy ponds to the north in May, and **Hooded Merganser** are frequent visitors to the quieter stretches of the river in fall. **Lesser Scaup and Redhead** should also be looked for when waterfowl reach their spring and fall peaks.

Birds of prey also breed in the area, with pairs of **Osprey and Northern Harrier** almost certain to be seen—**Northern Goshawk and Barred Owl** nest in the neighbouring woods and make regular sallies over the river. Wintering flocks of **Common Redpoll** may sometimes include a **Hoary Redpoll**. I was lucky enough to find a male **Hooded Warbler** in the spring in the copse at the mouth of Portage River.

For those with the taste for a little adventure, you can wade out at low tide and cross to the other shore on the delta sandbar—but check the tide before you attempt it. You avoid a long walk along the south bank of the river and around the marshes this way— there are usually some **Vesper and Savannah Sparrows**. I was rewarded for my wade across the delta by a male **Chestnut-collared Longspur** in full summer plumage among the sparrows in the sand dunes.

The shoreline to the south by the ponds of the Northern Barachois has nesting **Piping Plover, Bobolink and Red-winged Blackbird**, as well as occasional **Black- and Yellow-billed Cuckoos** and summering **Semipalmated Plover**. Peregrine is also likely when the shorebird flocks start to peak around the time **Hudsonian Godwit and Wilson's Phalarope** can be looked for among the small flocks of other species.

The long route back to Highway 117 will flush **Common Snipe and Sharp-tailed Sparrow** from the saltmarsh, which often has **Mallard, American Wigeon, Gadwall and Blue-winged Teal** along its narrow channels in fall. This trail is hard to follow until the south bank of the river is reached, but there are **Bobolink** on the saltmarshes and a good selection of breeding songbirds, including **Magnolia Warbler and Common Yellowthroat**, in the bordering woods. **Philadelphia Vireo, Scarlet Tanager and Rose-breasted Grosbeak** are all possible in the hardwoods, and a **Solitary Sandpiper** sometimes provides a welcome change from the nesting **Spotted Sandpiper** in the wet marshes by the river. The trip takes three hours.

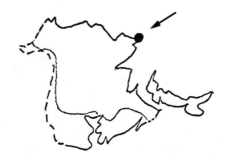

CARAQUET—MISCOU

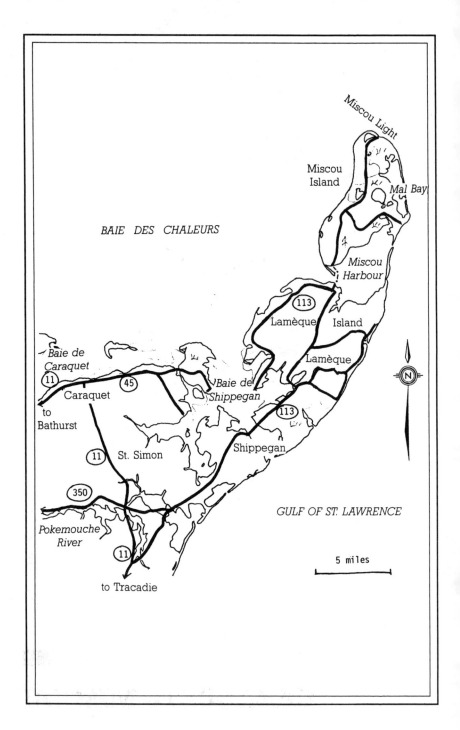

Miscou Light

Miscou Island

Mal Bay

BAIE DES CHALEURS

Miscou Harbour

113

Lamèque Island

Lamèque

Baie de Caraquet

11

45

Caraquet

Baie de Shippegan

113

to Bathurst

11

St. Simon

Shippegan

350

Pokemouche River

GULF OF ST. LAWRENCE

11

to Tracadie

5 miles

The peninsula and islands extending northeast into the Gulf of St. Lawrence were almost entirely dependent on fishing until the recent opening of the Village Acadien at Caraquet. People are now beginning to discover the beauty of the area which is unlike anywhere else in New Brunswick. The island of Lamèque is connected to the mainland at Shippegan by a bridge, but Miscou Island can only be reached by ferry. Although there are few birdwatchers in the area they have been quite active in fall and early winter.

Caraquet has not received much attention of late, but the sheltered harbour looks like a good place for waterfowl and gulls. The Christmas Bird Count usually has large numbers of **Oldsquaw** and a few **Common Eider and Red-breasted Merganser**, but the main feature is the high count of both **Iceland and Glaucous Gulls** which occur in larger numbers than anywhere else in the province. A **Bald Eagle** in mid January was a little further north than usual in winter. **Snow Bunting and Common Redpoll** are quite common in winter, and there have been occasional **Mourning Dove, Three-toed Woodpecker, Horned Lark, Brown Creeper, American Robin, Cedar Waxwing, Song Sparrow, Rusty Blackbird, Common Grackle and Brown-headed Cowbird** to supplement the usual boreal residents. A **Pine Warbler** on the 1988 Caraquet Christmas Bird Count was well off range.

Brant are common on spring migration and appear around the same time as **Surf Scoter** start to build to an early May peak of **5000**. **Northern Gannet** are commonest in the middle of May, when an occasional **Northern Shoveler** might appear, along with an off-course **Gyrfalcon** and a wandering **Wilson's Phalarope**. Local fishermen might be willing to charter their boats for trips to the islands or into the Baie des Chaleurs to look for pelagics which occasionally wander into the bay from the Gulf of St. Lawrence. While shorebirds are not all that common in fall, Caraquet has reported **75 Short-billed Dowitcher** in late July.

The sheltered bay south of Bas Caraquet may have waterfowl until it freezes over, although the only winter reports from St-Simon have been of flocks of **Snow Bunting and Common Redpoll** in early-mid April. Spring migration at Shippegan appears to be both small and late — **Willet** appear in late May. By late June, the nesting **Killdeer and Piping Plover** both have young. There are usually a few **Greater and Sooty Shearwater** to be seen offshore in summer and early fall, and **Pomarine Jaeger** are already heading south in late July.

The spits to the southeast are hard to get to, but they do appear to offer good locations for shorebirds. **Short-billed Dowitcher** are the first of the southbound shorebirds in early July, and **Sanderling** may remain on the beaches until mid November. **Bald Eagle and Peregrine** have been seen in the early stages of migration in late July. Both **Glaucous and Iceland Gulls** are common in winter, as a count of **476 Iceland Gull** in late December shows.

Lamèque is connected to Shippegan by the Highway 113 bridge. I have not visited the area and have not seen any reports other than the Christmas Bird Counts, Maritime Shorebird Surveys and a few records from the 1970s, but I suspect that gulls and shorebirds are numerous on migration. **Brant** are common in spring, a **Northern Hawk Owl** appeared one November, and a **Boreal Owl** in late December was a surprise count visitor. In fact, owls are a feature of the area with **Snowy Owl** in winter, and **Great Horned, Northern Saw-whet, Boreal and Long-eared Owls** all calling in mid-March one year. **Black-crowned Night Heron and Eurasian Wigeon** have waited until late June to visit Shippegan.

Birding does not end with fall migration as winter reports of **Northern Hawk Owl and Three-toed Woodpecker** indicate. A **Cattle Egret** in mid October was about as far north as any in Atlantic Canada, and **Blue-gray Gnatcatcher, Dickcissel and Indigo Bunting** the same month were well north, too. Shorebirds are best seen just west of Lamèque at Pointe Alexandre, where **385 White-rumped Sandpiper, 85 Dunlin and Short-billed Dowitcher, 35 Whimbrel, 30 Red Knot and 20 Hudsonian Godwit** have been counted in fall. The marshes and dunes are restricted to the southeast corner of Lamèque Island.

Winter conditions are a little better for waterfowl than on the mainland and the result is a better selection of wintering species. **Oldsquaw** are again the major species, but **Common Eider, Common Goldeneye, Common and Red-breasted Mergansers** occur in small numbers, and **Great Blue Heron, Canada Goose, Black Duck, Mallard, Barrow's Goldeneye, Harlequin and Hooded Merganser** have appeared. The Lamèque count also has as many as **270 Black Guillemot** overwintering, and this concentration sometimes persuades a few **Common Murre** to remain. **Glaucous and Iceland Gulls** are quite common, but the typical winter gull is the **Great Black-backed Gull**. **Snow Bunting and Common Redpoll** are the only widespread songbirds in winter, but there have been **Black-backed Woodpecker, Horned Lark, Red-breasted Nuthatch, American Robin, Northern Shrike, Bohemian and Cedar Waxwings, Song and White-throated Sparrows, and Common Grackle** to vary the fare.

The best birding may well be on Miscou Island, the furthermost point of the archipelago. It does not get heavy summer visitation from tourists and a toll-free ferry connects it to Lamèque. Most visits have been made in fall, when shorebirds are common on the tidal flats around the harbour and the shallow lagoons of Mal Bay North, more than a mile south of the Birch Point light—a good place to see **Northern Gannet** and other waterbirds. Large numbers of **Whimbrel** feed on the berries in fall, but the treed bogs have only nesting **Palm Warbler and Lincoln's Sparrow** to commend them in summer. Good numbers of **American Bittern** nest on the island, and the breeding **Northern Harrier** have been joined by **Peregrine and Long-eared Owl** in mid September. Only the northwest and southern sections of Miscou Island are wooded. The odd **Gyrfal-con** may zip by in spring, usually mid-late May. **Northern Mockingbird and Logger-head Shrike** are possible, though still rare, in summer.

Dunlin

As many as **500 Dunlin** and three-figure counts of **Black-bellied Plover, Greater and Lesser Yellowlegs, Red Knot, White-rumped and Semipalmated Sandpipers, Sanderling and Hudsonian Godwit** have been reported from Mal Bay South, which is reached by walking a short distance north from Wilson Point. Smaller numbers of **Semipalmated and Piping Plovers, Ruddy Turnstone, Whimbrel, Short-billed Dowitcher and Least Sandpiper** have been supplemented by an occasional **Purple or Buff-breasted Sandpiper**—the latter appearing in early September on a regular basis. **Piping Plover** nest in the dunes and should not be disturbed. Mal Bay is divid-ed into two bays—known as MacGregors and Windsors Mal Bays. The sandbar shelters a lagoon and marshy area with brackish ponds.

Shorebirds are not the only attraction on Miscou. Pelagics can be seen flying by from May to October. The few **Long-tailed Jaeger** reported in these waters may well be attracted by the large flocks of gulls and terns found around the lagoons on the east coast of the island. These flocks may contain **2500 Great Black-backed Gull** in early September. The September gull flocks at Miscou have attracted **Common Black-headed and Little Gulls, and White-winged Tern**. **Red-throated Loon** also arrive inshore in early September, when ducks and **Canada Geese** are quite common. A **Greater White-fronted Goose** with a late October flock was a Mal Bay bonus one year.

The Christmas Bird Count turns up good numbers of **Common Eider, Oldsquaw, Red-breasted Merganser and Black Guillemot**, as well as a few **Canada Goose, Black Scoter and Dovekie**. The 1988 count also turned up a **Northern Gannet**. Owls are a winter and spring feature of Miscou Island and, in good flight years there are **Snowy Owl**— 14 in 1988-89, and even a **Northern Hawk Owl** to supplement the **Boreal and Northern Saw-whet Owls** on territory in March.

This is, however, a pretty bleak area in winter for landbirds and a total of fewer than 30 species is considered normal for the count. There were, however, a small number of **Red-breasted Nuthatch, American Robin and Yellow-rumped Warbler** on the 1988 count, and a **Northern Shrike** to make their lives even more miserable.

Other places to visit from this area
Although Newcastle and other communities of the Miramichi do not have a premier birding site, Harry Walker's bird column was always filled with information on the wealth of nesting birds, unusual migrants and birds wintering at local feeders. Spring is usually fairly quiet, but a pair of **Northern Hawk Owl** made an interesting spring visit to nearby Chatham, and the first New Brunswick **Clay-colored Sparrow** was discovered in late May. Up to **300 Common Nighthawk** stream by along the river in late August. **House Wren, Eastern Meadowlark, and Vesper Sparrow** have appeared within urban limits, plus several **Eastern Bluebird** on spring and fall migration.

In summer Newcastle attracts the usual urban species plus several pairs of **Yellow Warbler and American Redstart** to its shade trees and shrubbery. **Red-eyed and Warbling Vireos** are also widespread, and there is a good chance of finding **Eastern Wood-pewee and Northern Oriole**. Other regular summer visitors include **Chimney Swift, Olive-sided and Least Flycatchers, Tree, Barn and Bank Swallows, Veery, Common Yellowthroat, Bobolink, Evening Grosbeak, Purple Finch, Chipping Sparrow and Pine Siskin**. Non-passerines reported regularly in summer include **Common Merganser, Killdeer, Spotted Sandpiper, Mourning Dove and Belted Kingfisher**. Nearby Mercury Island has had both **Black-backed and Three-toed Woodpecker** in summer, plus many **Brown-headed Cowbirds**.

Many birds are persuaded to remain into the winter months by a growing number of feeders, the most obvious beneficiaries being the **35 Red-breasted Nuthatches** and the **600 Evening Grosbeaks** recorded on the 1988 Christmas Bird Count. **Northern Mockingbird, Eastern Meadowlark and Northern Cardinal** have all stayed, and a small number of **American Robin** were joined by a **Hermit Thrush** late one January. Any wintering **Northern Shrike** may have **Common Grackle and Brown-headed Cowbird** in their sights, but usually have smaller prey to hand. The town is also host to small numbers of **Bohemian Waxwing**. Rarer winter visitors to Newcastle include single **Three-toed Woodpecker, Yellow-rumped Warbler** and stray **Dickcissel** and **House Finch**. Other unusual wintering birds have included **Double-crested Cormorant, Cooper's Hawk, Three-toed Woodpecker, White-breasted Nuthatch, Cedar Waxwing and Northern Cardinal**.

The best birding site close to town is the small saltmarsh known as Strawberry Marsh along the Miramichi River. The first **Horned Lark** pass through in mid April, but many birds are still on the move when the first broods of ducks are being raised. Breeding birds include **American Bittern, Black Duck, Green- and Blue-winged Teal, Northern Harrier, American Kestrel, Killdeer, Common Snipe, Sora, Short-eared Owl,**

Eastern Kingbird, Bobolink and Sharp-tailed Sparrow. A few Wilson's Phalarope are now making summer visits. Strawberry Marsh has also attracted Black-crowned Night Heron, Glossy Ibis and American Coot.

Fall migration starts with Semipalmated Plover, Least and Semipalmated Sandpipers and a few Lesser Yellowlegs and Short-billed Dowitcher in late July, and continues as long as there is open water. Killdeer are regular in fall, and so are Pectoral and White-rumped Sandpipers. Rarer migrants like Lesser Golden-plover, Solitary Sandpiper, Red-necked and Wilson's Phalaropes are most likely to be seen in September.

Fall also brings an assortment of waterfowl. This is a good place to look for Mallard, Northern Shoveler, American Wigeon, Wood and Ruddy Ducks. While songbirds are in general not all that common, flocks of Horned Lark and Lapland Longspur do occur in fall and early winter. When the marsh freezes over, Snow Bunting are common, and Glaucous and Iceland Gulls join the wintering gull flock. There is a chance of adding Redhead, Canvasback and Lesser Scaup, and a Green-backed Heron stayed at Miramichi Lake until mid October.

The river valley west of Newcastle has a wide range of woods and pasturelands for breeding songbirds. The area between Sunny Corner and Beckett Brook provides a good indication of what can be found. The commoner nesting species include Alder Flycatcher, Veery, Tennessee Warbler and Rose-breasted Grosbeak, and there are also some Yellow-bellied Flycatcher, Cliff Swallow, Gray Catbird, Bay-breasted, Blackburnian and Canada Warblers, and Cedar Waxwing and boreal species. The commonest non-passerines are American Bittern, Sharp-shinned Hawk, American Woodcock and Common Nighthawk. Other birds of prey are probably present but less regularly seen. There have been summer visits to the Miramichi woods by Ruby-throated Hummingbird, Great Crested Flycatcher and northward-expanding Purple Martin, Wood Thrush, Solitary Vireo, Black-throated Blue Warbler and Indigo Bunting. The local Christmas Bird Count has large numbers of Blue Jay, Common Redpoll and Evening Grosbeak, and fewer waterfowl, gulls, woodpeckers and songbirds.

I spent just over an hour one late June in the woods west of the river near Doaktown and found a good variety of boreal and hardwood species. Merlin, Pileated Woodpecker and Yellow-bellied Sapsucker were all present, as were the three more common woodpeckers, Yellow-bellied and Olive-sided Flycatchers, Common Raven, Boreal Chickadee, Red-breasted Nuthatch, Winter Wren, Cedar Waxwing, Solitary Vireo, Evening Grosbeak and Red Crossbill. Both Hermit and Swainson's Thrush are common, and there are a few Gray-cheeked Thrush and the odd Wood Thrush. Warblers seen on my visit included Nashville, Cape May, Blackpoll and Mourning Warblers. Black-and-white and Blackburnian Warblers, and Northern Parula were common in the mature hardwoods, where I saw Rose-breasted Grosbeak and Purple Finch.

Bank, Tree and Barn Swallows are common in the small communities along the Miramichi. A few Cliff Swallow may also be found, along with Killdeer, Belted Kingfisher and good numbers of Common Grackle. The picnic site at Upper Blackville may be worth a brief stop. A **Chipping Sparrow** was in full song on my visit, along with **Northern Parula and Swainson's Thrush**. A trail into the woods yielded several breeding thrushes and warblers, **Ruby-crowned Kinglet and Solitary Vireo**.

Portage Island, situated in the middle of Miramichi Bay, is accessible by boat from Neguac. Administered as a wildlife area by the Canadian Wildlife Service, it is ideally located with sandbars to the north. Waterfowl and seabirds breed on the island, which has herons, birds of prey and shorebirds during migration periods. Songbirds are also numerous and conspicuous on migration. The best time to visit is late June-late August when both breeding birds and migrants are present. Al Smith has recorded 65 species in about a week of birding, so a concentrated birding visit would add some new species. The best of the more regular species so far recorded on the island have been **Northern Gannet, Osprey, Ring-billed Gull, and Sharp-tailed Sparrow**.

A good movement of shorebirds takes place from late July to early September and most species could be expected. Up to **20 Whimbrel and Hudsonian Godwit** are regular, and there are somewhat smaller parties of **Piping Plover, Ruddy Turnstone and Red Knot** passing through at the same time. Some more unusual visitors include **Black-crowned Night Heron, Black-billed Cuckoo, Veery, Bay-breasted Warbler and Rose-breasted Grosbeak**.

Neguac to the north has a **Ring-billed Gull** colony. Up to **400 Great Cormorant** have been counted in mid June, and there are still a few **Piping Plover** and the odd **Wilson's Phalarope** to be seen in summer. Burnt Church to the south has **Northern Mockingbird** year round — the species reaches its northern wintering limits here and has nested. The Neguac to Tabusintac coast offers similar habitats with tidal rivers and sandbars providing resting places for migrant gulls, terns and shorebirds late summer and early fall.

Tabusintac has a **Ring-billed Gull** colony and is also a popular stopover point for **Canada Geese. Piping Plover** are regular on migration, although **Short-billed Dowitcher and Least Sandpiper** are the most common shorebirds — **Piping Plover** were common in the early 1900s but are very rare now. Ducks are also common as **107 American Wigeon** in late July clearly show, and there have also been some **American Coot** in late May and a drake **Eurasian Wigeon** in summer. **Brant** pass through in good numbers on spring migration, and **Short-eared Owl, Black-backed Woodpecker, Nashville Warbler and Vesper Sparrow** all nest.

Tracadie, a short distance to the north on Highway 11, is better known, partly because it has one of the best sand beaches in Atlantic Canada at Val Comeau some 5 miles further south. This is a good place to look for shorebirds and gulls. A **Laughing Gull** has been seen in the Tracadie **Ring-billed Gull** colony in summer, and small numbers of **Piping Plover and Short-billed Dowitcher** have been reported from the area. A further 11 miles on, just south of Highway 350, there is a **Double-crested Cormorant** colony on a small island off Pokemouche. This is one of the most photographed colonies in the province, but little else is known of this area. The Christmas Bird Counts have been notable for high numbers of **Common Eider, Oldsquaw and Snow Bunting**, two **Barrow's Goldeneye**, count period **Belted Kingfisher and American Robin**, a **Red-winged Blackbird**, and a small flock of **Lapland Longspur**.

Bathurst to the west on Highway 11 is a reliable birding site, although the dominant pulp and paper mill and the area's mining make it a less than pleasant place to be at times. **Hooded Merganser and Bufflehead** obviously disagree as they are often found for a brief period in fall and early winter, and **Canada Goose and Black Duck** can be common in spring and fall.

The best viewpoints are at the mouth of the Tetagouche River on the west of the harbour and at Carron Point near the harbour mouth — best viewed from Riverbank Drive on the south side of the rivermouth. Gulls and shorebirds feed on the tidal flats and retreat to the small islands at high tide. Youghall Park offers excellent views of shorebirds and gulls, and waterbirds such as **Great Blue Heron, Double-crested Cormorant and Red-breasted Merganser**. Bathurst Harbour forms a natural shallow estuary of four rivers and is almost enclosed by two sandbars extending across Nepisiguit Bay. These sandbars provide feeding and roosting sites for good numbers of fall shorebirds, especially **Lesser Golden-plover, Killdeer, Ruddy Turnstone, Hudsonian Godwit, Greater and Lesser Yellowlegs, Short-billed Dowitcher, Least and Semipalmated Sandpipers**. **Whimbrel, Willet, Red Knot and Dunlin** are also regularly seen in the Bathurst area.

Material brought to the surface in dredging operations has been dumped to form four small islands. The largest off Carron Point to the east of town had nesting **Herring Gull and Common Tern** as early as the 1940s, but three others close by and west of wooded Indian Island now also have gull and tern colonies. Until the late 1970s the first island had mainly **Great Black-backed and Herring Gull** nests, but there were also a few **Ring-billed Gull, Common Tern, Red-breasted Merganser and Spotted Sandpiper** pairs, too.

By the late 1970s **Ring-billed Gull and Common Tern** colonies were established on all four islets. The maximum count in 1985 was **700 Ring-billed Gull and 895 Common Tern** nests, but numbers have fluctuated and so has the choice of islet. There are now close to **100 pairs of Great Black-backed and 300 pairs of Herring Gull** on the islands, and an **Arctic Tern** has been noted on several occasions. **Bonaparte's Gull** stage here in early June, when **350** have been counted. **American Bittern** are common around Bathurst, which also has nesting **Killdeer**.

Pileated Woodpecker is to be found among the resident **Hairy and Downy Woodpeckers**. Apart from a few **Oldsquaw, Common Goldeneye and Red-breasted Merganser** and the north's only wintering **Ring-billed Gulls**, Bathurst's winter counts usually turn up only landbirds, and even they are in small numbers. **Snow Bunting, Pine Grosbeak, Common Redpoll, Pine Siskin and Evening Grosbeak** totals are usually higher than those of other boreal species. There are, however, nearly always a few **Northern Flicker, Gray Jay, White- and Red-breasted Nuthatches, Purple Finch and American Goldfinch** to keep them company. A few **American Tree Sparrows** wintering in 1988-89 were more unusual. Interesting summer records at Bathurst have been **Indigo Bunting and Grasshopper Sparrow**, and the best winter finds have been **Three-toed Woodpecker and Tufted Titmouse**.

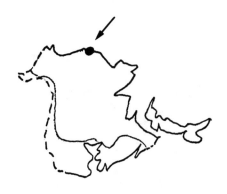

EEL RIVER CROSSING

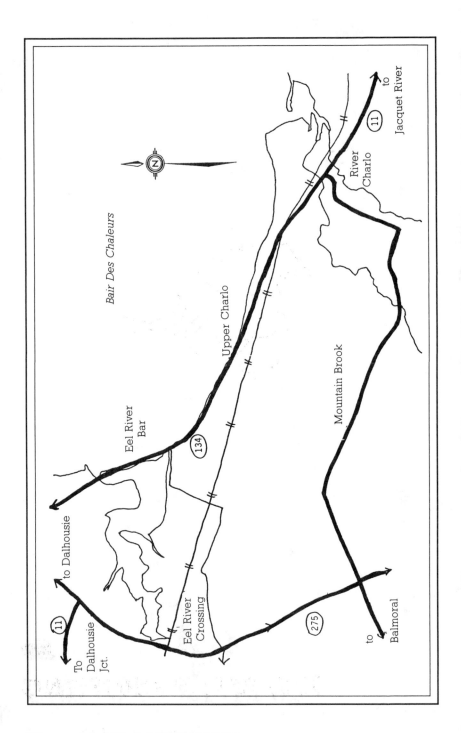

The inner reaches of the Baie des Chaleurs have steep sandstone cliffs, but these give way to sand beaches and dunes between Dalhousie and Bathurst. Very few people visit this region which is used as an approach to the Gaspé, so the number of reports is very low and far from complete. The bay gets its name from the mists that sweep up the long arm of the sea at different times of the year. Its warm waters in winter provide a feeding place for waterfowl — especially **Barrow's Goldeneye** which are commoner than anywhere else in Atlantic Canada.

The best birding spot is a barrier beach, sandbar and saltwater lagoon along Highway 11 just east of Dalhousie. Eel River Crossing is now known as Chaleur Park, but it remains an excellent place to watch ducks, herons, shorebirds and gulls at all times of year except midsummer when sailboards are more in evidence than birds. The coastline from here to New Mills should be carefully checked in spring and fall migration periods when rarer ducks, gulls and shorebirds are most often found. Eel River Bar has a nesting colony of **Double-crested Cormorant, Great Blue Heron, Black-crowned Night Heron, and Black Guillemot** at the aptly-named Heron Island. The best sighting at Heron Island was of a **Black-necked Stilt** in late May.

The spring migration of herons and ducks nearly always produces a few surprises. **Green-backed Heron, Glossy Ibis, Gadwall, Northern Shoveler and Canvasback** wait until mid-late May to put in a rare appearance at Eel River, and this is one of the few places where **Little and Laughing Gulls** may both be seen in late May and June. Rarer shorebirds found in early May include **Upland Sandpiper and Wilson's Phalarope**. The first **Black-crowned Night Heron and Northern Pintail** arrive in April, and the last **Oldsquaw** may linger into late June. **Pied-billed Grebe** nest in the area, and both **Common Moorhen and Wilson's Phalarope** have checked the area out. Shorebirds and gulls also appear in reasonable numbers, and the tern flocks should also be checked out as **Black Tern** are regular early summer visitors. **Ruddy Turnstone** have found enough to detain them until mid June.

My only recent visit was in late June and it was a very rewarding one. Just after dawn I walked past a roosting flock of **Ring-billed Gull** and disturbed some feeding **Great Blue Heron and Black-crowned Night Heron**. I then walked across the sluice gates and put up nesting **Spotted Sandpiper** pairs and a number of waterfowl, including good numbers of **Double-crested Cormorant, Black Duck and American Wigeon** and a few **Blue-winged Teal**. The lagoon also had at least one pair of **Common Loon** and a drake **Northern Shoveler**.

Great Blue Heron

It is worth continuing beyond on the wooded bar to check out a wealth of songbirds. Some of my better finds in a two-hour walk were **Yellow-bellied Flycatcher, Gray Catbird, Warbling Vireo, Canada Warbler, Rose-breasted and Evening Grosbeaks**. I tallied 11 species of warblers but there were doubtless more. A **Connecticut Warbler** in June suggests that they should be carefully watched. On the landward side of the lagoon there was less variety but **Merlin and Evening Grosbeak** both appeared to be nesting and there were two **Gray Catbird** waging a war over territory. **Great Cormorant, Mallard, Northern Pintail and American Wigeon** were all seen alongside Highway 134 to Campbellton. Summer ends with parties of **Common Nighthawk** flying by in early August.

Fall migration is also eventful with ducks, shorebirds and gulls again fairly plentiful. Most ducks can be looked for, and there have been several parties of **Redhead** to satisfy the visiting birder. Shorebirds are conspicuous along the beaches and around the marsh in early August. Numbers are generally small, although **60 Red Knot** in late August is a reasonable count, but the later flocks tend to be bigger. The marshes and sandbar are appealing enough to persuade **Black-bellied Plover, Ruddy Turnstone, Dunlin**

and White-rumped Sandpiper to stay as late as mid November. **Common Moorhen** have also appeared in early August, and later shorebirds have included **Curlew Sandpiper**.

The first flocks of southbound **Bonaparte's Gull** arrive in August and can be studied for accompanying **Common Black-headed Gull and Black-legged Kittiwake**. The possibility of a **Sabine's Gull** is always there, especially in late August and September. Parties of **Common and Arctic Terns** from Baie des Chalèurs colonies may attract a few **Caspian and Black Terns**. There have also been a few "wrecks" of pelagics after mid-late fall storms, including **several hundred Leach's Storm-petrel** one November.

Other places to visit from this site
Jacquet River and Belledune to the east also have small numbers of gulls and shorebirds, and **Black Tern** are regular here and at Nigadoo. The usual wintering birds are a few **Canada Geese and Oldsquaw**, but numbers are much higher in April, when **Oldsquaw and Black Scoter** are quite common. **Winter Wren** arrive in the area as early as late April, and they are soon followed by the odd **Snow Goose** and nesting **Rusty Blackbird**. Some of the more interesting breeding species include **Whip-poorwill, Black-backed Woodpecker, Eastern Phoebe, Veery and Bobolink**. Fall migration is fitful with **White-crowned Sparrow** among the commoner migrants, but there have been a few **Cliff Swallow, Yellow-breasted Chat, Scarlet Tanager, Northern Oriole and Rose-breasted Grosbeak** sightings to liven things up. **Pine Grosbeak** are common year round, as a count of **75** in early January shows.

Charlo just to the east of Eel River Bar has small counts of shorebirds in fall, but New Mills is a little more productive. **Great Blue Heron** are common in August, when parties of **Common Nighthawk** fly by on their way south. New Mills is most active in mid fall when **500 Surf Scoter** have been counted off Heron Island.

Dalhousie a few miles to the west of Eel River Bar has one of New Brunswick's largest newsprint mills. The area is best known for its wintering flock of **150+ Barrow's Goldeneye**, and the rafts of **200 Red-throated Loon and 5000 Black Scoter** that may appear on the bay in mid-late April. Point La Nim to the west is the centre for **Surf Scoter**, with numbers building up from **8400** in late April to as many as **20,000** in early May. Dalhousie also has a gull colony on the pulp mill slash pile. This mixed colony has **300+ pairs of Ring-billed, 50 pairs of Herring and 20 pairs of Great Black-backed Gulls**. Regular **Gyrfalcon** along the area's steep cliffs from December to mid March are gone two full months before large numbers of **White-crowned Sparrow** pass through in May, and a few parties of **Semipalmated Sandpiper** follow in early June. Several **Little Gull** have been noted in town and in the small bay north of Eel River Crossing.

The Kedgwick River road between St. Leonard and Campbellton provides good summer birding with a wide variety of flycatchers, thrushes, vireos, warblers and finches. A trip off the main road along Highway 265 is strongly recommended for its scenery — farmland, secondgrowth, alder swamps, conifers and deciduous guarantee a good selection of nesting species.

The commonest species are **American Robin, Barn and Tree Swallows, Northern Flicker, Cedar Waxwing, Common Raven, Song Sparrow, Common Grackle, Red-winged Blackbird, American Kestrel, Chipping Sparrow, Blue Jay, American Redstart, Rose-breasted Grosbeak, White-throated Sparrow, Eastern Kingbird, American Crow and Purple Finch. Black Duck, Ruffed Grouse, Killdeer, Bank Swallow, Black-capped Chickadee, Common Yellowthroat, Bobolink and House Sparrow** are also widespread in the area, which has nesting **Wood Thrush** as well as boreal species. The Maritime Breeding Bird Atlas turned up **Green-backed Heron, Hooded Merganser, Brown Thrasher, Eastern Bluebird and Northern Oriole** in the Campbellton area.

Beyond lies the mythical "Republique de Madawaska" with its own flag and coat of arms. Both **Brown Thrasher and Gray Catbird** are common nesting species throughout this region. Edmundston is the capital of Madawaska County and has a pulp and paper mill and St. Louis College. There's a good chance of hearing **Gray-cheeked Thrush** songs before dawn in the mixed and young coniferous forests close to town — hardwoods are likely to turn up a few **Philadelphia Vireo**. The 107-acre Jardins de la Republique is close to Edmundston and is probably the best place to camp.

The best birding is certainly in the forests, so it's a good idea to call in and get a forest road map from Fraser Companies before doing any exploring. Remember that logging truck drivers don't expect to meet anyone coming the other way and travel at a fair clip on the narrow gravel roads! Some of the best birding may be along the Upper Green River (Riviere-Verte) north of Edmundston.

Spruce-fir forest with white birch supports northern breeders like **Spruce Grouse, Three-toed and Black-backed Woodpeckers, Blackpoll Warbler, Pine Grosbeak and Fox Sparrow**. Most of the boreal warblers are common, and there are a few **Solitary Vireo** in summer — younger forests have colonies of **Gray-cheeked Thrush**. Where there are hardwoods, **Philadelphia Vireo and White-winged Crossbill** are found, and the maple-beech-birch forests have commoner hardwood species like **Least Flycatcher, Red-eyed Vireo, Ovenbird and American Redstart** in good numbers, and **Wood Thrush** can now be numbered among guaranteed species. There's also a chance of adding **Blackburnian Warbler and Scarlet Tanager**.

The final attraction of the Saint-Jacques area is a **Black-crowned Night Heron** rookery. Winter counts are sparse in terms of numbers with high numbers of **Black-capped Chickadee** and a few **Red-breasted Nuthatch**, and **Mallard and Northern Shrike** the only surprises reported so far.

Just west of Edmundston, Lac Baker offers a similar variety of birds. **Barred Owl** are often heard from deciduous woodlots, and other more boreal raptors can be looked for. **Ruby-throated Hummingbird and Philadedlphia Vireo** are common, and other nesting species include **Whip-poor-will, Eastern Phoebe, Wood Thrush and Veery**. One of the commonest of the spruce forest warblers is the **Cape May Warbler**, but secondgrowth attracts **Chestnut-sided Warbler**, and more mature forest and glades have numbers of **Pine Grosbeak**.

Grand Falls on the St. John River contains a mixture of coniferous forests with extensive bogs and riverine hardwoods. **Common Goldeneye** stay on the river until early January, but winters can be pretty bleak here. Many warblers stay to nest, **Eastern Phoebe** nest by the streams, **Mourning Dove and Bobolink** now nest on the local farmlands, and other species could be expected to follow. A little further downriver is another major border crossing between Fort Fairfield, Maine and Aroostook. This region is characterized by a wide variety of habitats. The river and marshlands provide feeding and nesting places for several ducks and occasional **Common Loon, American Bittern, Great Blue and Green-backed Herons**. They have also been odd pairs of **Northern Shoveler** in spring.

Extensive wooded areas are composed of mixed forests with pure stands of deciduous or coniferous trees. Typical nesting species include **Belted Kingfisher and Pileated Woodpecker**, a good variety of thrushes and warblers, and both **Evening and Rose-breasted Grosbeaks**. Farmland areas attract **Bank Swallow** and a few **Northern Oriole**, and there have been a few **Black-billed Cuckoo** in early summer.

The best time to visit is mid April-early May when waterfowl and the first **Osprey** arrive, and in June when most of the warblers and other songbirds return. A **Northern Shoveler** in May represented a more inland location than usual for this species which is increasing in Atlantic Canada. Few birds stay for the winter months when only **Common Merganser and American Tree Sparrow** have reached double figures on the Christmas Bird Count. Boreal species are, however, usually common outside Perth-Andover, with winter finches very well represented, and there may also be a few **Common Goldeneye, Canada Geese, Black Duck, and Bald Eagle** by the river.

The most productive route out of Perth-Andover takes in the valley of the Tobique River, which joins the St. John River at the Tobique Narrows hydro-electric dam. You can drive either side of the river on Highway 109 through Odell or Highway 390 to Plaster Rock. **Black-backed Woodpecker, Gray-cheeked Thrush, Golden-crowned Kinglet and Blackpoll Warbler** are common in the conifers, and there are **Eastern Wood-pewee, Eastern Bluebird and Fox Sparrow** nesting in the mixed woods and clearings. **Northern Shoveler** have been found nesting at Perth-Andover, and **Solitary Sandpiper** provided a rare breeding record at Beadle Mountain. Brian Dalziel's efforts in the Maritime Breeding Bird Atlas were rewarded by breeding **Great Crested Flycatcher, Eastern Phoebe, Brown Thrasher, Warbling Vireo and Northern Oriole** as far upstream as Nictau. Yvon Beaulieu found a pair of **Indigo Bunting** with young near Plaster Rock, where Mark Phiney reported the most northerly colony of **Purple Martin** in the province.

Plaster Rock has a very productive Christmas Bird Count. As many as 32 species have been found which is surprising for a site so far north and inland. **Snow Bunting and Evening Grosbeak** are by far the commonest winter birds. **Great Gray Owl and Northern Hawk Owl** have both been seen at Plaster Rock in midwinter, and the local count recently included **Common Grackle and Eastern Meadowlark. American Kestrel, Merlin, Great Horned, Snowy and Northern Saw-whet Owls** have also been seen in winter, when the resident woodpeckers are very conspicuous. **Hairy and Downy Woodpeckers** are quite common, with **Pileated, Black-backed and Three-toed Woodpeckers** also present in small numbers at Plaster Rock and Wapske. **Gray Jay,**

White- and Red-breasted Nuthatches, Brown Creeper, Winter Wren, Bohemian Waxwing, Northern Cardinal, Chipping and White-throated Sparrows, White-winged Crossbill, Red-winged Blackbird, Common Grackle and Brown-headed Cowbird round out the winter counts.

Equally productive is the river gorge between Riley Brook and Nictau which lie halfway to Mount Carleton. The mainly coniferous woods have all the boreal species, including **Three-toed Woodpecker**, broods of **Common Loon, Common Goldeneye and Common Merganser**, and several southern species, including **Great Crested Flycatcher, Brown Thrasher and Northern Oriole**.

A pair of **Golden Eagle** have been seen year round in the Nictau area. A **Dickcissel** in late April, **Yellow-throated Vireo** in early July, and **Northern Cardinal** in late October suggest that Riley Brook and Nictau are worth visiting at any time, and this area should be checked out more often than at Christmas. A surprising number of **Common Goldeneye and Common Merganser** remain into the winter, when **Canada Goose, Hooded Merganser, Bald Eagle, Northern Shrike and Rusty Blackbird** have also been reported.

There are also several **Pileated, Black-backed and Three-toed Woodpeckers** in the woods with **White-breasted Nuthatch, Brown Creeper, Golden-crowned Kinglet, Pine and Evening Grosbeaks, Purple Finch, Pine Siskin** and the odd **Barred Owl, American Robin, Brown-headed Cowbird and White-throated Sparrow**. The local count has yielded as many as **33 Gray and 140 Blue Jays** and somewhat fewer **Boreal Chickadee, White- and Red-breasted Nuthatches**.

The high plateau region of Northumberland County includes Mount Carleton — the highest peak in Atlantic Canada at over 2500 feet. This is now part of a new provincial park with a wilderness aspect demonstrated by the lack of a road — visitors are urged to backpack in. The park has a number of hiking trails of varying distance and difficulty. The Mount Bailey trail winds 4 miles through hardwood stands to a summit offering spectacular views of Nictau Lake, Mount Carleton, Sagamook Mountain and Bald Mountain Brook valley. The trails up Mount Carleton are moderately demanding, and the Sagamook trail offers great views of the Nepisiguit and Nictau Lakes and links up to the Mount Head trail.

Boreal species are common in the park, especially **Boreal Chickadee, Red-breasted Nuthatch, Pine Grosbeak, Purple Finch, Red and White-winged Crossbills, Common Redpoll and Pine Siskin**, which are reported as common in winter. A good number of **American Pipit** also nest on the mountains. **Ruffed Grouse, Hairy, Downy, Black-backed and Pileated Woodpeckers, Gray Jay, Golden-crowned Kinglet, and American Goldfinch** have been counted in small numbers, but **Common Redpoll** is the typical winter finch. **Northern Goshawk, Barred Owl, Brown Creeper, White-breasted Nuthatch, Northern Shrike and Purple Finch** stayed long enough to be added to the Mount Carleton Christmas Bird Count. **Three-toed Woodpecker** is another resident here and at nearby Upsalquitch Lake, where **Whip-poor-will** have been reported in summer.

Other trails lead through spruce-fir forests to waterfalls, alongside Big Brook, and through a red pine stand by Nepisiguit Lake. **Harlequin** summer on the Nepisiguit River and **Golden Eagle** may also breed in the area where **Gray-cheeked Thrush** are very common. **Gray Jay, Boreal Chickadee, Fox Sparrow**, and a variety of boreal warblers and finches can be found in summer — there has also been a **Northern Saw-whet Owl** nest along the Little Tobique.

CACOUNA

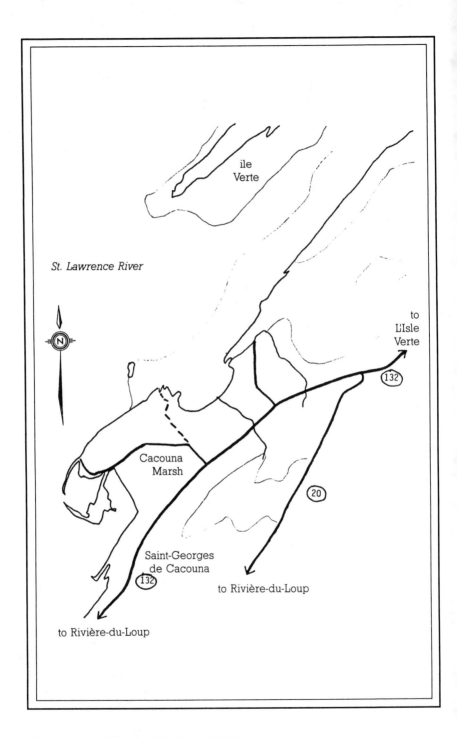

île
Verte

St. Lawrence River

to
L'Isle
Verte

132

Cacouna
Marsh

20

Saint-Georges
de Cacouna

132

to Rivière-du-Loup

to Rivière-du-Loup

The St. Lawrence South Shore is quite different from the rugged North Shore, in terms of its varied habitats, easier accessibility and large population. The forest cover mainly consists of mixed woods with patches of conifers along river valleys. Large areas of fresh and saltwater marshes north of Rivière-du-Loup are among the best waterfowl and marshbird habitats in the region, and almost all eastern bird species have been found. Ferry crossings to the North Shore from Rivière-du/Loup to Saint-Siméon and from Trois-Pistoles to Escoumins provide possibilities of seeing pelagic species year round, but especially in the fall.

Waterfowl often stage on the St. Lawrence in spring and fall, and the coastal marshes attract large numbers of marshbirds in summer. The same marshes are also very popular with shorebirds in fall — several species can be found as early as the end of June and numbers can be quite high in early August when waterfowl become increasingly common.

The Bas-Saint-Laurent marshes are not visited as often as they deserve, but birders from Rimouski keep an eye on them and reports have increased in recent years. This came about partly as a result of the visit of a Eurasian vagrant in 1980, although local birders were already aware Cacouna held good numbers of birds on migration. Few people visited the oil tanker port until that year, but it has become more popular since then.

In spring, up to **500 Mallard, 500 Black Duck, 1500 Northern Pintail, 500 Green-winged Teal and 70 American Wigeon** have been tallied in the dabbling duck flocks on the marshes. A few **Wood Duck** have also appeared at the tail end of spring migration. Diving ducks prefer to swim offshore and can be quite numerous in late April and May, when **125 Greater and 30 Lesser Scaup, 80 Ring-necked Duck, and 500 Surf Scoter** may be counted. **Redhead, Bufflehead, King Eider, Common, Red-breasted and Hooded Mergansers** are all seen in May. **Black Guillemot** also gather offshore in spring, and a **Razorbill** may provide a bonus.

Family parties of **Gadwall and Blue-winged Teal** may be a welcome addition to the usual feeding groups of **Black Duck and Green-winged Teal**. At the time of my visit in late June, a few **Northern Pintail and American Wigeon** were also present on the marshes and may breed. Groups of young **Common Eider** are conspicuous along the shoreline, and there are usually **Greater Scaup and Common Goldeneye** during the summer, and even a few **Snow Geese** and a **Ross's Geese** in April and May.

Equally impressive are the summer concentrations of marshbirds—with **Great Blue Heron and Black-crowned Night Heron** the most numerous species. **Virginia Rail and Sora** both nest, and **Great and Snowy Egrets** are quite regular in late spring and summer. **Glossy Ibis, Tri-colored, Little Blue and Green-backed Herons, Sandhill Crane and American Coot** have all appeared in spring, and there is the chance of adding a **Common Moorhen or Yellow Rail**. With so many marshbirds around, the arrival of the **Little Egret** in the summer of 1980 was not too surprising, and its lengthy stay from June to September suggested that its arrival was not entirely accidental.

Shorebirds are not a feature of spring migration, so a mid May count of **800 Black-bellied Plover and 550 Red Knot** in full breeding plumage is quite astonishing, as is the arrival of a **Greater Golden-plover** in the summer of 1989. Birds of prey are quite common as they await suitable conditions for crossing the river. **Northern Harrier and Short-eared Owl** were interesting bonuses on my visit, and **Cooper's and Rough-legged Hawks, Peregrine and Gyrfalcon** are all possible with the commoner migrants in April and May. Six **Rough-legged Hawk** in early July were more unusual.

The marshside woods are quite likely to be filled with songbird migrants in spring, and the shoreline is worth checking to find **Lapland Longspur** among the flocks of **Snow Bunting** in late April and early May. Numbers of songbirds are low in late June, but breeding **Bobolink and Sharp-tailed Sparrow** on the marshes and a singing **Warbling Vireo** in the woods were interesting enough on my visit. The few summering **Eastern Meadowlark** should be carefully scrutinized as **Western Meadowlark** have been reported here in the summer months.

Bobolink

In about six hours of birding from dawn to noon at the end of June I was able to see good numbers of ducks, marshbirds and shorebirds, and even a few birds of prey. This was a good haul, but I am assured that my totals were quite normal for summer and that the marshes are even more interesting in July and August when numbers of most species peak. The tides play an important role in the feeding habits of most birds, and a low-tide visit is recommended if shorebirds are the object of interest—ducks are sometimes more visible when the marshes are inundated.

Fall starts early as far as the shorebirds are concerned. Perhaps the most interesting aspect of my late June visit was the abundance of shorebirds at a time migration should have been over for the spring and not yet underway for the fall. Apart from the regular breeding species, I tallied **Killdeer, Black-bellied Plover, 60 Short-billed Dowitcher, Lesser Yellowlegs** and some "nesty" **Wilson's Phalarope** pairs. My totals were far below the maximum counts of late July and early August. These include **260 Short-billed Dowitcher, 110 Lesser Yellowlegs and 85 Least Sandpiper**. Later in August, there are regular visits from **Stilt and Solitary Sandpipers**, up to **30 Pectoral Sandpiper**, and rarer migrants such as **Baird's, Buff-breasted and Western Sandpipers, and Red-necked Phalarope**. Vagrant shorebirds like **Long-billed Dowitcher and Western Sandpiper** have been noted later in fall.

Red-necked Grebe are common on fall migration, and a few **Pied-billed Grebe** can be looked for on the ponds, but ducks dominate in terms of numbers. Large flocks of **Northern Pintail, American Wigeon, Green- and Blue-winged Teal** flash colourfully among the drabber **Black Duck and Mallard**, and there are smaller groups of **Northern Shoveler and Gadwall**, and the occasional **Eurasian Wigeon**, to add spice. **Lesser Scaup** are quite common in the bay among rafts of diving ducks worth scanning for **Canvasback, Redhead, Ruddy Duck and Hooded Merganser**, and I have noted a party of five **Barrow's Goldeneye** in early July. A few pelagics occasionally stray inshore in September after the large flock of **Ring-billed Gull** has dispersed. These have included **Parasitic Jaeger**, which find occasional **Common Black-headed, Laughing and Franklin's Gulls** to pursue.

Other places to visit from this site

The best birdwatching is east of Rivière-du-Loup, but the immediate area has yielded some interesting species. Some of the rarer nesting species include **Black-billed Cuckoo, Eastern Kingbird, Eastern Phoebe, Eastern Wood-pewee, House Wren, Gray Catbird, Eastern Bluebird and Scarlet Tanager**. In fall **Double-crested Cormorant and Common Eider** are regularly seen with **Common and Red-throated Loons** and good numbers of **Ring-billed Gull and Black Guillemot**. **Thayer's Gull** has wintered in Rivière-du-Loup, and so have **Short-eared Owl and House Finch**—the first to visit the region. The Saguenay rivermouth is reached by driving east along Highway 138 from Quebec City, taking the Saint-Siméon ferry from Rivière-du-Loup or the Escoumins ferry from Trois-Pistoles. The latter is the more productive with many pelagic species reported between April and mid September. The Les Escoumins ferry is quite productive in spring, with May and early June crossings turning up **Red-throated Loon, Northern Fulmar, Oldsquaw, Razorbill, Common Murre, Black Tern, Parasitic and Long-tailed Jaegers**. There have also been as many as **200 Black Guillemot** in early

April and **150 Arctic Tern** in mid June. As the summer progresses, the chances of **Razorbill and Parasitic Jaeger** increase. In late summer, the ferry has the added possibility of **Pomarine and Long-tailed Jaegers, Little, Franklin's, Laughing and Sabine's Gulls.**

Leach's and Wilson's Storm-petrels, Northern Fulmar, Greater Shearwater, Great Skua and Atlantic Puffin are also being reported more often on fall crossings. The most recent list I have seen from early September had **Northern Fulmar, Razorbill, Parasitic and Pomarine Jaegers** as its best birds. In September a few **Red-necked Phalarope** may pass through—with as many as **8 Pomarine Jaeger, Sooty and Manx Shearwaters, Little and Sabine's Gulls** and a few **Horned Grebe** for company.

To the east of Cacouna on the south shore, the similar but larger coastal marshes of the Isle Verte National Wildlife Area attract the same species but access is more restricted. Dabbling ducks are known to stage in good numbers, with **Northern Pintail and Green-winged Teal** abundant in spring, when **Eurasian Wigeon** is possible. **Brant** are also common, but the most abundant species is the **Snow Goose**, represented by upwards of **40,000 birds** in late April. The flock should be carefully scutinized for **Ross's Goose** which has been seen several times in May. **Common Eider** are also very conspicuous, especially in late summer and early fall when the young are in the water. The **Little Egret** of 1980 could be seen here when disturbed from its regular place at Cacouna.

Isle Verte is also an excellent place to see shorebirds, including as many as **50 Semipalmated Plover and 500 Lesser Golden-plover** in late May. A **Lesser Golden-plover** appeared at Isle Verte in early April when shorebirds are decidedly rare and a **Greater Golden-plover** a distinct possibility. **Whimbrel, Hudsonian Godwit and Willet** are also conspicuous among the commoner shorebirds in July and August, and there is always the chance of a rarity like a **Baird's Sandpiper** anytime in the fall. The marshes attract up to **60 Black-crowned Night Heron** from the breeding colony on Isle-Verte in early summer, and fairly regular **King and Virginia Rails**—**Snowy Egret** are sometimes reported here in summer.

Birds of prey often stop by on migration. Late spring and summer have turned up **Turkey Vulture, Rough-legged Hawk and Peregrine**, and **Short-eared Owl** is a widespread nesting species on the sanctuary. **Rough-legged Hawk and Northern Harrier** are known to winter, and the odd **Mourning Dove** may, too. The only interesting nesting songbirds are **Sharp-tailed Sparrow** which are abundant.

Further east, the Trois-Pistoles area is best known for its seabird islands just offshore. Ile-aux-Basques, the most westerly of all the St. Lawrence colonies, and Iles Razades are maintained as seabird sanctuaries by the Provancher Society who alone can give permission to visit. The commonest breeding bird is the **Common Eider**—with about **700 nests** in 1984 on Iles Razades—but there may be a few **Ring-billed Gull**, and even a **Laughing Gull**, in the flourishing **Herring Gull** colony. The coastline is attractive to **Brant and Black Scoter** in spring, and **Gadwall** sometimes appear. Waterfowl are also common in fall, with good numbers of ducks present offshore in October. **Black Duck and Common Eider** are abundant, and as many as **150 White-winged Scoter and 300 Surf Scoter** have been reported from mid September. Wintering **Bufflehead** arrive late in October.

The coastline also attracts good numbers of fall shorebirds, with late August counts of **150 Semipalmated Plover, 25 Whimbrel and 500 Semipalmated Sandpiper. Purple Martin** have nested, and **Northern Mockingbird, Brown Thrasher, Eastern Bluebird and Rufous-sided Towhee** are all irregular visitors. It is also worth checking in the fall for migrant **Boreal Owl** and occasional **Yellow-billed Cuckoo, Northern Mockingbird, House Wren and Yellow-breasted Chat**.

The inland lakeland area from Degelis to Cabano and north to Squatec is perhaps best known for its wintering waterfowl, especially along the Madawaska River at Degelis. Small numbers of **Black Duck** regularly winter, attracting a few **Mallard**. A **Wood Duck** was an unexpected companion of **Black Duck and Mallard** at Squatec in February. Diving ducks are more numerous, with **Common Goldeneye** flocks augmented by as many as **15 Barrow's Goldeneye** and occasional **Greater Scaup**. Merganser numbers tend to be lower, with an odd **Red-breasted or Hooded Merganser** a rarity among the **Common Merganser** parties. **Northern Goshawk** is another regular winter resident. Fewer visits outside the winter months partly account for the lack of records, but a **Little Blue Heron** has occurred in late May in the Squatec area, where **Green-backed Heron** are more regular. There have also been several reports of summering **Indigo Bunting** in this area, and even a nesting record. The Lac Pohenegamook area has attracted **Brown Thrasher and Warbling Vireo** in June, and **Wood Thrush** has been found on territory in July.

RIMOUSKI

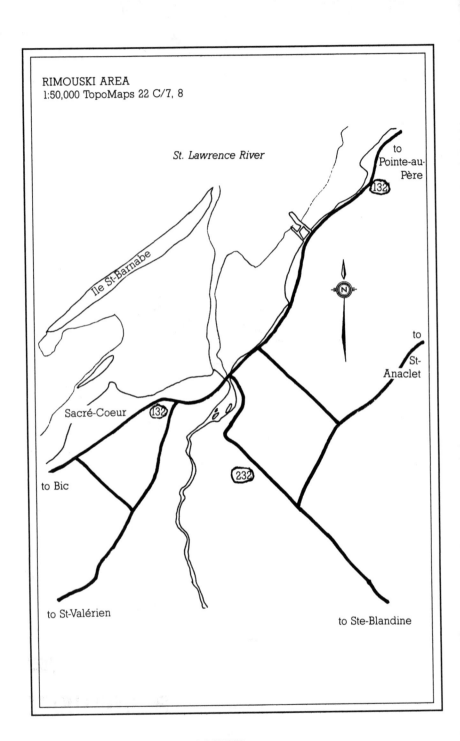

RIMOUSKI AREA
1:50,000 TopoMaps 22 C/7, 8

St. Lawrence River

to
Pointe-au-
Père

132

Île St-Barnabe

N

to
St-
Anaclet

Sacré-Coeur   132

232

to Bic

to St-Valérien

to Ste-Blandine

The shoreline from Rimouski to Point-au-père is one of the best studied areas in the region, so the abundance of records is not surprising. Rimouski is the largest town along the St. Lawrence South Shore and has a number of avid birders and the "Le Naturaliste" birding supplies company among its 28,000+ residents. This coastline has attracted **Great Cormorant, Wilson's Storm-petrel, Long-tailed Jaeger and Sabine's Gull** in September, so a coastal scan may be a good idea. Most of the smaller communities have birding sites within walking distance, and this is an excellent place to set up temporary headquarters for birding the Gaspé.

One of the best areas to see birds in spring and summer is the saltwater marsh just west of town known as marais de Sacré-Coeur. I had the pleasure of spending several hours there in the evening and early morning in late June and I know it to be an excellent place to visit year round. A series of trails provides access to regenerating fields, deciduous woods, a flooded area of fresh and brackish water, saltmarshes and the river itself. The marsh sanctuary is maintained by the City of Rimouski, and I commend the residents for setting aside so large an area of the coastline for wildlife.

From the records I have seen, spring starts as early as April when a **Gyrfalcon** ruffled a few feathers before the marshbirds were settled in. Marais de Sacré-Coeur has a roost of **Great Blue Heron and Black-crowned Night Heron**, and has attracted **Great, Snowy and Cattle Egrets** on a fairly regular basis. My count of **38 Black-crowned Night Heron and 14 Great Blue Heron** was probably low, and I didn't have any other marshbirds except a calling **Sora**. **Common Moorhen** are also on the increase in the area, and **Sora, Virginia Rail and American Coot** are all summer visitors to the marsh. **Little Blue, Tri-coloured and Green-backed Herons, and Glossy Ibis** are rare vagrants in spring and late summer.

Shorebirds are largely absent in spring, although **American Avocet, Willet, Ruff, Marbled Godwit, White-rumped, Solitary and Stilt Sandpipers, and Wilson's Phalarope** have all appeared in spring. Occasional summering **Lesser Golden-plover, Red Knot and Wilson's Phalarope** make colourful additions to the breeding birds, and **Marbled Godwit** has appeared in late June and early July. I found a large number of **Black Duck and Common Eider** feeding along the marsh edges in the early morning. It was difficult to judge which were which until the sun came up, and I also identified **Mallard, American Wigeon, Blue-winged Teal**, plus a few **Common Loon and Double-crested Cormorant** offshore.

Common Black-headed, Franklin's and Laughing Gulls make spring and summer visits even more interesting at times. A **Common Nighthawk** might also be expected after dark in summer. Songbirds might be considered a minor attraction, although both **Northern Mockingbird and Brown Thrasher** may join the several pairs of **Gray Catbird**. I also found **Veery, Common Yellowthroat, Song and Swamp Sparrows, American Goldfinch, Common Grackle and Red-winged Blackbird** extremely common in their preferred habitats. **Philadelphia Vireo** appeared to be commoner than either **Redeyed or Solitary Vireos**, and I tallied few warblers. The small area of grassy salt-marsh has a few **Sharp-tailed Sparrow** pairs. Fewer visits have been made in fall, but an early October **Boreal Owl** was a good sighting. Winter visits are even rarer, but an early December **Palm Warbler** and a mid December **Gyrfalcon** indicate they may yield some surprises.

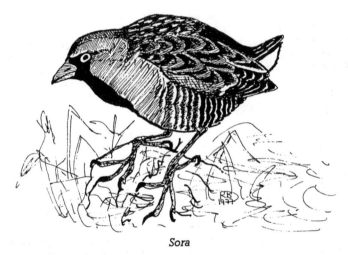

Sora

This and other local marshes attract marshbirds and shorebirds as early as late April, when up to **50 Great Blue Heron and 20 Black-crowned Night Heron** may be present. There have been several outstanding finds in the local marshes in spring, including **Great and Snowy Egrets, Little Blue and Green-backed Herons, Sandhill Crane, Sora and Virginia Rail. Red Knot, Short-billed Dowitcher and Pectoral Sandpiper** are also possible in mid May, when numbers of **Greater Yellowlegs, Semipalmated and Least Sandpipers** may build up to over **150** apiece. In addition, upwards of **100 Semipalmated Plover, 45 Killdeer and 325 Lesser Yellowlegs** have been counted in late May and early June.

Rimouski is also known for its waterfowl, especially in spring. The first migrants arrive in early April when up to **300 Oldsquaw** have been seen along with a few **White-winged and Black Scoters**. By late in the month, the number of **Canada Geese** may reach **500**, and up to **300 Green-winged Teal and 55 Greater Scaup** can be expected until early in May when the **500+ Oldsquaw** are joined by a few **Red-throated Loon**. As far as sheer numbers go, the staging of northbound **Snow Geese** in May is very impressive. The flocks have contained **Ross's Goose** on three different occasions and a **Greater**

White-fronted Goose on another. Occasional **Canvasback, Gadwall and Northern Shoveler** turn up at Rimouski in April—strays such as **Ruddy Duck** tend to wait until May. **Common Teal, Eurasian Wigeon, Wood Duck, Redhead, Bufflehead, Barrow's Goldeneye, King Eider and Hooded Merganser** may also put in a late spring appearance, but the best duck was a late May **Cinnamon Teal**. The June migrants have included regular groups of **Mallard and Blue-winged Teal** and smaller numbers of **Gadwall and American Wigeon**.

Gulls are also common along the shore with as many as **110 Glaucous Gull** counted in late March, and April brings a sprinkling of **Black-legged Kittiwake, Common Black-headed and Bonaparte's Gulls**—most of which have left by May when **Caspian Tern** occasionally appear. **Common Black-headed, Franklin's and Laughing Gulls** can make spring and summer visits even more interesting. By late summer it's hard to find any other gulls among the **1100+ Ring-billed Gull** gathering.

Raptors are well represented in spring—with sightings of up to **40 Sharp-shinned Hawk**, small numbers of **Northern Harrier, Osprey and American Kestrel**, and occasional **Golden and Bald Eagles, Cooper's Hawk, Peregrine and Gyrfalcon** indicative of spring movements. **Short-eared Owl** has been known to nest, and a **Red-shouldered Hawk** has been found in mid August. **Snowy Owl** are more likely in fall and early winter in open areas. April always brings a few **Northern Saw-whet** to the area, and **Short-eared and Great Horned Owls** are conspicuous from May. **Boreal and Long-eared Owls** have also appeared around Rimouski in recent springs, and what may well have been the first **Burrowing Owl** was seen by a local farmer in May. A **Black-billed Cuckoo** may appear in midsummer, but **Mourning Dove** is more likely.

Woodpeckers are quite common—**Pileated Woodpecker** are rare residents, and **Three-toed and Black-backed Woodpeckers** can be looked for in late March. Songbirds are widespread in spring, and some species arrive early. Up to **2000 Bohemian Waxwing** have been seen in the first half of April, and there are large flocks of **White-throated and White-crowned Sparrows** in early May. By the end of the month, up to **500 Horned Lark** can be seen on the fields. **Northern Mockingbird** are regular in spring. Small parties of **Nashville Warbler, Bobolink and American Goldfinch** also appear on spring migration. **Purple Martin, Gray-cheeked Thrush, Warbling Vireo, Eastern Meadowlark, Northern Oriole and Scarlet Tanager** have all been seen, too.

Occasional **House Wren and Clay-colored Sparrow** may appear, and other spring sightings include **Western Kingbird, Great Crested Flycatcher, Eastern Phoebe, Wood Thrush, Orange-crowned and Pine Warblers, Northern Parula and Blue-gray Gnatcatcher**. The sparrow flocks attracted a **Harris' Sparrow** one spring. Of great interest to birders were the first sightings of **Western Meadowlark** in late June and **Prairie Warbler** in early July—the former may be a regular spring and early summer visitor.

This is one of the few areas where **Loggerhead Shrike** can be looked for with much hope of success and there have been nesting records. Also nesting in the local thickets and denser woods are **Northern Mockingbird, Brown Thrasher and Blackburnian Warbler**—**Common Yellowthroat** is a particularly abundant species here and at nearby Sainte-Odile.

In late July, good numbers of **Semipalmated Plover, Lesser Yellowlegs and Short-billed Dowitcher** are joined by occasional **Hudsonian Godwit, Long-billed Dowitcher, Stilt and Buff-breasted Sandpipers** and wandering southern and arctic gulls. In September over **100 Ring-billed Gull** are in the area with good numbers of **Greater and Lesser Yellowlegs, Short-billed Dowitcher and Semipalmated Sandpiper**, and the last of the **Hudsonian Godwit. Pectoral, Western and Baird's Sandpipers** may also appear in early fall, and late shorebird flocks are swelled by up to **1000 White-rumped Sandpiper and 250 Dunlin** in late October.

The gull flocks fall in October but may contain as many as **15 Glaucous and 200 Iceland Gulls** in November. **Snowy Owl** have appeared as early as mid September but usually wait until late October when **Gyrfalcon** pass through. **Peregrine** are more regular migrants and pass through until mid November with large numbers of **Rough-legged Hawk**.

Waterfowl numbers are highest in fall — with **Black Duck and Blue-winged Teal** well represented, and as many as **450 Oldsquaw** offshore. **American Wigeon and Hooded Merganser** can be looked for among the earlier flocks with **Lesser Scaup and Barrow's Goldeneye** later on. **Wood Duck and Redhead** have both appeared early and most other diving ducks gather in the area late. **Ruddy Duck and Canvasback** are fall possibilities at Rimouski, and loons swimming offshore should be checked as possible **Pacific Loon** have appeared in July and October. Among marshbirds, **Green-backed Heron and Cattle Egret** have both turned up in early fall, but most of the area's marshes are taken over by ducks, shorebirds and gulls after late July. A **Great Egret** in late October was both very late and off course.

The wooded areas and secondgrowth harbour good numbers of migrant songbirds in August-mid September, as counts of **500 Tennessee Warbler, 44 Rose-breasted Grosbeak and 50 Chipping Sparrow** clearly show. There have been as many as **5 Orange-crowned Warbler** present at the same time, too. Sparrows are also common in the more open areas. **Purple Martin, Great Crested Flycatcher, Northern Wheatear, Gray-cheeked Thrush and Blue-gray Gnatcatcher** have been notable fall migrants, along with **Warbling and Philadelphia Vireos, Blue-winged, Prairie and Connecticut Warblers, and Yellow-breasted Chat. Indigo Bunting, Hoary Redpoll, Rufous-sided Towhee, Clay-colored and Field Sparrows, and Northern Oriole** have all been reported in fall.

Small parties of **Bohemian Waxwing** appear in the early winter, when **Three-toed Woodpecker** can be looked for. **Gray Catbird and Northern Mockingbird** are also normal in November, when as many as **150 White-winged Crossbill** have been joined by a few **Red Crossbill**. The weather normally turns cold early in December, but **Pileated, Black-backed and Three-toed Woodpeckers** are guaranteed to brighten a winter day if they stray into town. **Yellow-rumped and Pine Warblers, Northern Cardinal and White-crowned Sparrow** have overwintered, as have **Brown Creeper, Winter Wren, Northern Mockingbird, Song Sparrow** and small parties of **Common Grackle, Brown-headed Cowbird and American Goldfinch. Common Redpoll and Evening Grosbeak** are occasionally quite numerous in winter. **Bohemian and Cedar Waxwings, and Northern Shrike** are also seen most winters, but an overwintering **White-breasted Nuthatch** must be considered unusual.

Good numbers of **Glaucous Gull** join the harbour flocks in winter, and there may be an odd **Northern Gannet or Dovekie**. There may also be a few lingering **Common Black-headed Gull** among the wintering **Iceland Gull** flock, which has also contained a **Thayer's Gull**, but waterfowl and raptors tend to attract more attention. **Barrow's Goldeneye, Harlequin, King Eider, White-winged and Surf Scoters** are quite regular into the Christmas Count period. The only unusual winter waterbird reported is a mid December **Snow Goose**. Most birds of prey leave, but **Great Horned Owl** are resident and an occasional **Gyrfalcon or Peregrine** scatter the wintering flocks. **Cooper's and Rough-legged Hawks, Long-eared and Boreal Owls** have also been seen in winter.

Rimouski's Christmas Bird Count usually has small numbers of diving ducks, especially **Oldsquaw, Common Eider, Common and Barrow's Goldeneyes**, but rarely any **Black Duck** or other dabbling species. Other species recorded on a fairly regular basis are **Surf Scoter and Greater Scaup**, with **Common Loon, Canada Goose, King Eider, Harlequin, White-winged and Black Scoters** less likely. The wintering flock of **Iceland Gull** also include equal numbers of **Herring and Glaucous Gulls**, but **Ring-billed Gull and Black-legged Kittiwake** are irregular in winter. **Snowy Owl** is the only regular raptor, although **Northern Goshawk, Sharp-shinned and Rough-legged Hawks, Gyrfalcon, Great Horned and Short-eared Owls** have appeared.

Landbirds are common throughout the winter, with high counts of **Mourning Dove, Hairy and Downy Woodpeckers, Common Raven, Black-capped Chickadee, Bohemian Waxwing, Snow Bunting, Common Redpoll and Evening Grosbeak**. A few **Ruffed Grouse** sometimes visit feeders, and there are usually a few **Pileated and Black-backed Woodpeckers, Northern Flicker, Red-breasted Nuthatch, Brown Creeper, American Robin, Northern Shrike**, sparrows and blackbirds to liven things up on a cold winter's day. **White-throated and Song Sparrows, Common Grackle. Red-winged Blackbird and Brown-headed Cowbird** are all regular winter residents.

Some of the better birds on the Rimouski Christmas Bird Count include **Mew Gull, Thick-billed Murre, Three-toed Woodpecker, White-breasted Nuthatch, Northern Mockingbird, Yellow-rumped and Pine Warblers, Northern Cardinal, White-crowned Sparrow, Lapland Longspur and Hoary Redpoll**. A little more unusual are **Peregrine, Dark-eyed Junco, Field and Sharp-tailed Sparrows**. A **Townsend's Solitaire** was not alone for long one January, and another western vagrant was an adult male **Rufous-sided Towhee** of the western race.

Other places to visit from this site
Southeast of Rimouski, the upland woods of Neigette, Sainte-Blandine and Mont-Lebel have attracted wintering species and several unusual migrants. Lac à l'Anguille has as many as **60 Green-winged Teal** and a few **Pied-billed Grebe, Solitary Sandpiper and Wilson's Phalarope** in May, but it lacks the breeding habitats of Lac des Joncs, although a few **Ring-necked Duck** probably raise young. **Sora, Virginia Rail and American Coot** are also possible at Lac à l'Anguille in late spring and summer. Fall sightings of **Wood Duck and Solitary Sandpiper** and a surprising **5 Cattle Egret** in November suggest that freshwater levels vary.

Lac Macpès to the west also has **American Bittern and Wood Duck** in spring. Lac Poire has had **15 Pied-billed Grebe** and smaller numbers of **Sora, Common Moorhen and American Coot** in summer. Mont-Lebel is an excellent place to look for spring migrants. Good counts of **Common Snipe, Northern Flicker, Yellow-bellied Sapsucker, Dark-eyed Junco, Chipping and White-throated Sparrows** have been made in the first half of May.

Possibly the more productive area except in winter is Sainte-Blandine. **Bank Swallow** are common in late May and early June, when as many as **15 Veery, 50 Tennessee Warbler, 30 Ovenbird, 10 Northern Oriole and 45 White-crowned Sparrow** have been seen in the riverside woods. The main migration period is mid May-early June, although a **Pileated Woodpecker** has been noted with the usual wintering **Black-backed Woodpeckers** in early March.

Among May migrants at Sainte-Blandine, **Peregrine, Upland Sandpiper, Ruby-throated Hummingbird, Great Crested Flycatcher, Wood Thrush, Warbling Vireo and Scarlet Tanager** are all worth a mention. **Wood Thrush** are regular in summer and **Warbling Vireo** are certainly worth searching out. **Barred Owl** are summer residents, while **Great Horned Owl and Bald Eagle** are more likely to be seen with commoner raptors in late October and November. Both **Pileated Woodpecker and Brown Creeper** have been found in winter, and **Red-winged Blackbird and Brown-headed Cowbird** may winter in small numbers. Neigette is a good place to visit in spring when **Northern Flicker and Winter Wren** are quite common and **Solitary Vireo and Northern Oriole** regular. **Eastern Wood-pewee, Cliff Swallow, Wood Thrush, Warbling Vireo, Northern Oriole and Rose-breasted Grosbeak** are all present in summer.

The woods are very popular with migrants in August, and an indication of abundance are counts of **20 Eastern Kingbird, 100 Bobolink and 1000 Red-winged Blackbird** early in the month. **Short-eared Owl** sometimes appear at Neigette in spring, and there have also been several **Cooper's Hawk** in the area. Perhaps the most notable raptor records at Neigette have been **Northern Saw-whet and Boreal Owl** in winter and spring and **Red-shouldered Hawk** in fall. The area is quite good in winter, especially for **Pileated, Three-toed and Black-backed Woodpeckers**. Small numbers of **Red-breasted Nuthatch and Brown Creeper** may winter and **Lapland Longspur** are possible.

Saint-Anaclet, which can be reached by driving out of Rimouski on rue Cathédrale and turning left at the T-junction, attracts good numbers of spring songbirds. There are feeding areas for **Snow Geese**, which have totalled **2500** in early October, and **Wood Duck**, which is regular in spring. Raptors have also been reported on the few visits made, including spring sightings of **Northern Harrier, Snowy and Short-eared Owls**.

I had not seen any summer reports, but a morning's inspection of woods close to the intersection of rue Cathédrale and rue des Près revealed a wide diversity of birds in late June. A woodlot with a central core of oldgrowth cedars opposite Ranche La Seigneure turned up a good variety of warblers, including several territorial **Northern Parula, Magnolia, Blackburnian, Bay-breasted and Canada Warblers, Ovenbird, Northern Waterthrush and American Redstart**.

A trail around the edge of the woodlot and linking up with open trails by the powerline added **Nashville and Mourning Warblers** and two pairs of **American Kestrel**. A number of **Winter Wren and Swainson's Thrush** were also in full song. Hardwoods added **Eastern Wood-pewee, Least Flycatcher, Veery, Red-eyed and Philadelphia Vireos, Scarlet Tanager and Rose-breasted Grosbeak**, and mixed woods **Black-capped Chickadee, Red-breasted Nuthatch, Hermit Thrush, Golden-crowned Kinglet and Evening Grosbeak**. A small marshy area had **Common Moorhen and Rusty Blackbird**. For such a small area, a total of 42 species in less than two hours was very impressive.

L'Anse au Lard is about two miles to the east of Rimouski along a side road bordering the river between Pointe-au-père and Sainte-Luce. It is best known as a haven for shorebirds—hence its alternate name of L'Anse aux Bécasseaux. The best place to see pelagics is just left of Stella Maria at the bay's western edge, as the raised point offers a clear view of pelagics from August to mid December. Storm conditions or strong easterlies offer the best hope of seeing birds.

Most species have occurred, including **Leach's Storm-petrel, Parasitic Jaeger, Dovekie, Common and Thick-billed Murres**. In October and November, **Red-throated Loon and Red-necked Grebe** are quite common, and **Purple Sandpiper** seen from late October. Even in mid February there is a good chance of finding **Oldsquaw, Common and Barrow's Goldeneyes, and Black Guillemot** offshore, and an outside chance of adding **Dovekie and Thick-billed Murre**.

Shorebirds can be seen in good numbers without leaving your car and often venture close to the road. The peep flocks are worth checking for **Baird's and Western Sandpipers** in August and September, although the majority of birds are likely to be **Semipalmated, Least and White-rumped Sandpipers, and Sanderling** interspersed with **Ruddy Turnstone, Black-bellied Plover and Pectoral Sandpiper**.

To the west, Saint-Fabien and the adjoining Saint-Fabien-sur-mer are good places to find birds. The coastal settlement is particularly productive during spring migration with counts of **50 Red-necked Grebe, 70 American Wigeon, 100 Barrow's Goldeneye, 435 Common Eider and 170 Surf Scoter**.

Raptors are also well represented with counts of **28 Bald Eagle, 155 Sharp-shinned Hawk, 300 Red-tailed Hawk, 115 Rough-legged Hawk and 10 Merlin**. Songbird totals camn be impressive with **300 Rusty Blackbird, 1000 Common Redpoll and 6000 Snow Bunting** reported in late April-early May. **Golden Eagle, Northern Harrier, Cooper's Hawk, Northern Goshawk, Peregrine, Gyrfalcon, Barred and Great Horned Owls** are also regular migrants at this time or slightly earlier. By the middle of May up to **100 Broad-winged Hawk** and even greater numbers of **Sharp-shinned and Red-tailed Hawks** are possible. A **Turkey Vulture** appeared as early as mid April.

Smaller parties of ducks, including **White-winged Scoter**, can be seen in mid May, and a **Pomarine Jaeger** has been seen in late June. Family parties of **Common Eider** and loafing **Black-crowned Night Heron and Double-crested Cormorant** are common in summer, and there are several pairs of **Killdeer and Spotted Sandpiper** dotted along the coast. **Great Horned Owl and Black-backed Woodpecker** have been reported in the winter months.

Lac des Joncs is located southeast of Saint-Fabien off the Ladrière Road. This is a good place to look for ducks and marshbirds. **Pied-billed Grebe** are common early in summer and certainly breed, along with **Ring-necked Duck, Sora, American Coot and American Bittern.** **Green-backed Heron and Virginia Rail** have also been noted in May at Lac des Joncs, which is also one of the best places to look for owls. **Great Horned and Barred Owls** are both resident, and **Northern Saw-whet** have been seen in May. **Broad-winged Hawk** may also nest in the area, having been noted in June. **Black-backed Woodpecker** nests have been located, and songbirds find the bushes very attractive on migration. Counts of **300 Horned Lark, 20 Northern Waterthrush, 30 Least Flycatcher, 15 Canada Warbler and 50 American Redstart** in May and early June are fairly typical. **Chimney Swift, Black-throated Blue Warbler and Scarlet Tanager** can also be looked for in summer.

POINT-AU-PÈRE

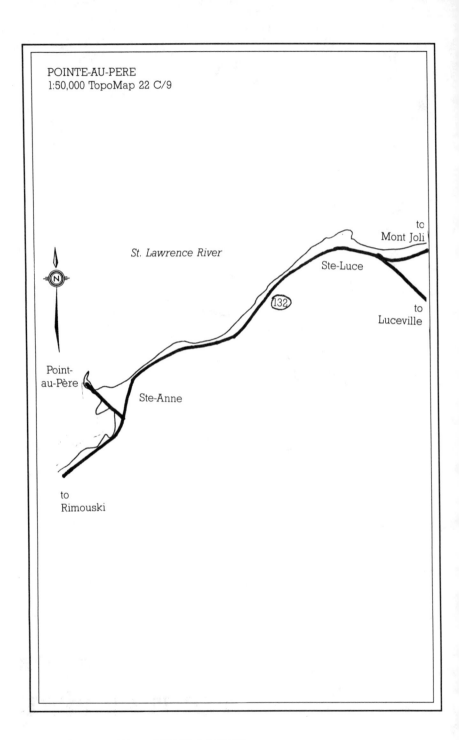

POINTE-AU-PERE
1:50,000 TopoMap 22 C/9

St. Lawrence River

to
Mont Joli

Ste-Luce

132

to
Luceville

Point-
au-Père

Ste-Anne

to
Rimouski

The coastal area just east of Rimouski is yet another excellent birding site along the St. Lawrence South Shore. Pointe-au-père is at its most productive in migration periods and should not be missed if you are in the area during May-June or August-November. Spring migration really starts in March and April with **Northern Gannet, Double-crested Cormorant and Oldsquaw** numerous and **Brant, Northern Shoveler and Hooded Merganser** all regular. A recent spring raptor survey also revealed over **300 Red-tailed and 70 Rough-legged Hawks** in one late April day, and sightings of **Northern Goshawk, Cooper's and Broad-winged Hawks, Golden Eagle and Peregrine** in April and early May show the variety. The only unusual raptor reported in spring was a mid May **Turkey Vulture**.

Gatherings of **75 Red-throated Loon and 60 Great Blue Heron** in the first part of May are unique to this area, and almost any waterfowl species can be expected offshore. A **Pacific Loon** in late June and two non-breeding birds in late July indicate that not all are **Common and Red-throated Loons**. **Horned and Eared Grebes, Great Cormorant, Greater White-fronted Goose, Redhead, Canvasback, King Eider and Hooded Merganser** have all been recorded in May or early June at Pointe-au-père. The number of marshbirds is also very high with **Snowy and Great Egrets, and American Coot** appearing with the more numerous **Great Blue Heron and Black-crowned Night Heron**. A **Tri-colored Heron** and the Cacouna **Little Egret** in spring are the best marshbirds.

Shorebirds are common in late May — with counts of **500 Semipalmated Plover, 250 Greater Yellowlegs, 125 Red Knot, 500 Short-billed Dowitcher and 515 Least Sandpiper** very impressive. Other birds noted in May include **Lesser Golden-plover, Piping Plover, Willet, Upland and Pectoral Sandpipers, Ruff, Dunlin, White-rumped Sandpiper and Wilson's Phalarope**. A May **Western Sandpiper** rates a mention, but the most interesting shorebird was an early June **Black-tailed Godwit** looking for its nesting grounds far to the east. A **Marbled Godwit** at the same time and a **Hudsonian Godwit** a month later are less surprising. **Great Black-backed Gull** is another abundant species in May. **Laughing, Common Black-headed and Bonaparte's Gulls** are sometimes noted with a few **Arctic Tern**. Alcids are another spring possibility, especially after northerly or easterly winds.

Although songbirds have not elicited the same interest as other groups, the point does provide a resting place for large numbers of north- and eastbound migrants. **Great**

Crested Flycatcher, Orange-crowned Warbler, Clay-colored and Harris' Sparrows rate among the more unusual species in May and June, but an early April **Fieldfare** was obviously a holdover from an earlier invasion. A late July **Black-billed Cuckoo** was a little beyond its normal range. **Eastern Meadowlark** has appeared in midsummer, but the most intriguing report was that of a singing **Willow Flycatcher**.

The marshes and bordering waters again come into prominence in early August when upwards of **750 Double-crested Cormorant, 1000 Common Eider, 150 Surf Scoter and 45 Great Blue Heron** may be joined by a few **Northern Shoveler and Hooded Merganser**. Shorebirds are also greatly in evidence in late July with maxima of **900 Ruddy Turnstone, 400+ Black-bellied Plover and Semipalmated Sandpiper, 150 Least Sandpiper** and parties of **Greater Yellowlegs, Killdeer, Whimbrel and Spotted Sandpiper** joined by a smattering of **Lesser Golden-plover, Red Knot and Sanderling**. **Stilt Sandpiper** may also turn up as early as the first week of July and again later in the month.

By August there may be as many as **500 Black-bellied Plover, 300 Ruddy Turnstone, 200 Red Knot, 50 Lesser Golden-plover, and 30 Pectoral Sandpiper** on the point, plus an odd **Solitary, Purple, Stilt or Baird's Sandpiper. Ruff, Willet, Western Sandpiper and Wilson's Phalarope** have all appeared in August. Later flocks are dominated by **Black-bellied Plover, White-rumped Sandpiper and Dunlin** which appear in large numbers. **Whimbrel, Buff-breasted, Pectoral and Purple Sandpipers, Long-billed Dowitcher and Hudsonian Godwit** are rarer mid September-October migrants. As many as **85 Purple Sandpiper** are also present in the winter months.

Waterfowl take over again in late September-mid October, when up to **15 Red-throated Loon, 1000 Canada Geese, 800 Black Duck and 350 Common Goldeneye** are joined by smaller numbers of **Red-necked Grebe, Northern Gannet, Snow Goose, Gadwall, Northern Shoveler, Harlequin, King Eider, White-winged, Surf and Black Scoters**. A **Great Cormorant** was another rare visitor in mid September, and a **Ross's Goose** recently made the scene in late September. There has been a report of a **Western Grebe** in mid October when **Horned Grebe** parties are conspicuous and the first of the wintering **Oldsquaw** arrive — by late October as many as **550 Oldsquaw** can be counted.

Gull flocks are also worth scanning as **Black Tern, Laughing and Franklin's Gulls** have been seen in late spring, and could be expected again in fall. **Parasitic Jaeger, Common Black-headed and Bonaparte's Gulls** have been sighted as the **Iceland Gull** flock reaches its peak in mid fall. **Leach's Storm-petrel** have been blown here in early October and late November, and the **200+ Iceland Gull** wintering in the harbour should be scanned for an infrequent early winter **Ivory Gull**. Alcids are also common offshore, with **Razorbill** in summer and both **Dovekie and Thick-billed Murre** in winter.

Birds of prey are also readily seen in fall with **Red-tailed Hawk, Northern Harrier and Merlin** regular and **Peregrine** a distinct possibility. The situation with owls is even more intriguing as **Short-eared Owl** first arrive in early August and have to share the point with other migrant owls for two months — by then the first wintering **Snowy Owl** is likely to have taken up residence. **Long-eared and Boreal Owls** have been noted in October and November. Landbirds use the point as a migration marker, and there are often **Yellow-bellied Sapsucker** in with the **Northern Flicker** parties. Songbirds, especially finches and sparrows, are very much in evidence. Maximum counts have included **250 Evening Grosbeak, 20 Red and 10 White-winged Crossbill** in early August when **Rose-breasted Grosbeak** are quite common. By late September as many as **1000 Horned Lark** may mass here, and October has seen a flock of **450 American Robin** winging south.

Songbirds pass through the area well into October with **Snow Bunting and Lapland Longspur** arriving among the **Horned Lark** flocks. As many as **1400 Snow Bunting** have been counted in November when **50+ Common Redpoll** are normal. The flocks may be scattered by a **Northern Shrike** in winter, and a **Common Grackle** made it through the winter one year.

Winter flocks of nearly **4000 Oldsquaw** have included **Red-throated Loon, Red-necked Grebe, Harlequin and Black Scoter**. Other high counts in early December are **45 Red-breasted Merganser, 275 Black-legged Kittiwake, 150 Black Guillemot** and a few **Purple Sandpiper**. Later in the month, as many as **350 Iceland Gull** have joined the wintering flock. **Horned Grebe, Surf Scoter, Mew and Ring-billed Gulls, and Dovekie** have all been noted in December, and wintering raptors have included **Gyrfalcon and Snowy Owl**.

Other places to visit from this site

The resort town of Bic a few miles to the east can be quite productive in spring. **Bufflehead, Lesser Scaup and Gadwall** are regular, and **Blue-winged Teal** evident among the large flocks of **Green-winged Teal**. **100 Great Blue Heron** have been counted in early May, and **Green-backed Heron** are irregular in spring. Shorebirds are also prominent in late May, when **Lesser Yellowlegs and Least Sandpiper** are common, and **Wilson's Phalarope, Solitary and Upland Sandpipers** can be looked for. **Eurasian Wigeon, Wood Duck, Ruddy Duck, King Eider, Hooded Merganser and American Avocet** have all appeared at Bic in spring, and a **Glossy Ibis** has been noted in early May.

A recent survey of migrant raptors revealed **125 Red-tailed Hawk** in late April, and **400 Broad-winged Hawk and 18 Osprey** in early May. There were also sightings of **Cooper's Hawk, Bald and Golden Eagles, Peregrine, Northern Hawk, Boreal and Northern Saw-whet Owls** on migration — suggesting that this is a favoured crossing point.

Songbird reports are more scattered, although both **Chipping and Vesper Sparrows** are common in April and May — when **Cliff Swallow and Brown Thrasher** might be expected. **Philadelphia Vireo** is a regular attraction in June, and there have been visits from **Eastern Bluebird**.

The offshore island of Bicquette (Petit Bic) has more than **10,000 pairs** of **Common Eider** under the zealous protection of the Thibault family. Poachers had reduced numbers on St. Lawrence island colonies to as low as **8000** in 1965, and Bicquette had only **500 pairs** in the 1930s when the present guardians supervised the eiderdown industry. Nesting birds come ashore in May when the females build their nests among the windblown spruces away from **Herring Gulls and American Crows** and less numerous **Great**

Black-backed Gulls and Great Horned Owls. An interesting raptor is the **Great Gray Owl** on Ile Bicquette in October — one bird was found dead but another was very much alive. By mid July most breeding birds have left for marine waters, so it's best to visit in June when family parties can be seen from the Bic shore.

The real action starts when shorebird numbers start to pick up in August and September, and rarer species like **Marbled Godwit** have been known to pay a visit, but the greatest movement is in October when **Red-necked Grebe** and diving ducks are in good supply. Upwards of **10,000 Surf Scoter and 150 White-winged Scoter** have been reported in mid September. A few songbirds nest in the area and may include **Northern Mockingbird and Brown Thrasher**. Songbirds are less conspicuous in fall, although August sees small flocks of **Cedar Waxwing and Red-breasted Nuthatch** in temporary residence. A few **Great Blue Heron, Killdeer and Greater Yellowlegs** linger with the later migrants and have to contend with occasional **Peregrine**. Rarities may turn up unannounced late in the migration period, as did a **Pine Warbler** at Bic in November.

Winter visits have turned up fair numbers of **Common Eider and Oldsquaw**, and an occasional **Common Loon and Black Guillemot**. The woods are fairly quiet, but there may be a **Northern Goshawk, Black-backed Woodpecker or Brown Creeper** among the commoner winter residents and visitors. **White-winged Crossbill** sometimes appear in good numbers. **Mourning Dove and Brown-headed Cowbird** have overwintered and other interesting birds include **Horned Grebe, Three-toed Woodpecker, White-crowned Sparrow** and **40 Cedar Waxwing** in late February.

MATANE

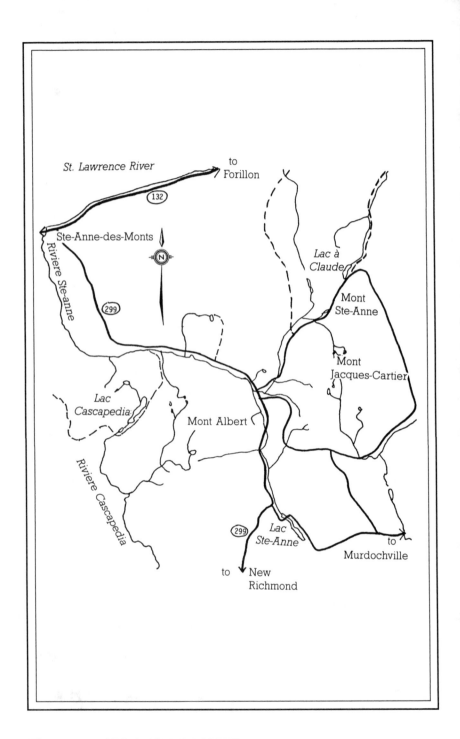

Matane is the ferry terminal for Godbout and Baie-Comeau on the St. Lawrence North Shore. It does not receive the same attention as Rimouski from birders—salmon fishing is a more popular pastime here, and Matane's shrimp are celebrated in an annual festival. Matane is also the access point to the Chic-Chocs—the Canadian continuation of the Appalachian mountain chain. Parc Matane has been very lightly reported, but Parc de la Gaspésie is a very popular destination for birders who wish to list boreal species.

The community of Matane has not reported all that much in the way of birds, but there have been some interesting sightings. The Matane River is worth checking for songbirds—especially **Gray-cheeked Thrush** which passes through each year from late May. Waterfowl flocks in fall can be quite large, and there have been counts of **1000 Common Eider and 100 Barrow's Goldeneye** in December. As many as **300 Iceland Gull** gather in December and a few make it through the winter with up to **20 Glaucous Gull**. Small numbers of **Brown-headed Cowbird** are also present in the first half of the winter, and **Brown Creeper and Red-winged Blackbird** have made it through the remainder.

Fairly regular reports of **Golden Eagle** in spring, **Red-shouldered Hawk and Common Moorhen** in early May, and **Upland Sandpiper** in late June are the best Matane spring sightings. Saint-Ulric and Saint-Leandre to the west have added **American Avocet** in late May, and a pair of **Eastern Bluebird** and a **Loggerhead Shrike** on spring migration. **Turkey Vulture** in early August and **Cattle Egret** in mid September added to fall visits. The list of Matane's fall vagrants also includes **Gadwall and Greater White-fronted Goose**.

Parc Matane to the southeast has not been visited by birders all that much, although **Golden Eagle** may well be regular in summer and there are a few **Pied-billed Grebe** close to the edge of their breeding range. A **Red-shouldered Hawk** has also been found in early May, but most visitors are looking for moose, caribou, black bear or trout. Breeding songbirds are most likely to emphasise the boreal nature of the woods, with boreal finches common some summers and **Great Horned and Boreal Owls** occasionally flushed from cover.

The farming area close to Matane is good for **American Kestrel, Mourning Dove, Cliff Swallow and Bobolink**—all of which I noted on my only visit in late June. Over the adjoining farmlands and open areas, swallows, including **Cliff Swallow**, are quite common, along with **Bobolink, Brown-headed Cowbird, Savannah and Song Sparrows, and American Goldfinch. Northern Harrier and American Kestrel** are the main predators.

Perhaps the most interesting side trip is some 55 miles east along the coast to Sainte-Anne-des-Monts. The deep harbour allows fishing to continue most of the year which means gulls year round, including an occasional **Ivory Gull** in winter. The inshore waters also have good numbers of **Common Goldeneye, Oldsquaw and Black Guillemot** in winter. Parties of **Harlequin** along the river in early fall and **Eastern Bluebird** in mid August could represent nesting birds. Spring brings a few **Cooper's Hawk** and occasional **Eastern Bluebird, Loggerhead Shrike, Warbling Vireo and Orange-crowned Warbler** to Sainte-Anne-des-Monts, and summer sightings have included **Green-backed Heron, Eastern Meadowlark and Scarlet Tanager**. An early June **Snowy Owl** and a mid September **Northern Wheatear** were obviously vagrants.

Highway 299 leads from here into the Chic-Chocs and the majestic Parc de la Gaspésie. The high mountains dominate the scenery and provide a habitat for arctic-alpine plants and boreal birds. It is possible to see black bear, moose, whitetailed deer and woodland caribou in the same place, as well as a number of rarer local breeding birds such as **American Pipit and Common Redpoll**. Fastflowing streams cascade down gorges and steepsided valleys—excellent places for salmon and trout fishermen to try their luck. The roads to the interior are closed in winter, but they provide a relaxing drive at other times of the year.

Common Redpoll

Mont Albert is approached by a series of roads and nature trails, which start at the Gite du Mont Albert campground reception centre—several other trails climb other peaks and border mountain lakes and streams. Mont Jacques-Cartier probably has the best nesting birds. A trail leads from Camp Galène on the loop road east of Mont Albert—the summit provides a magnificent view of the mountains and clear lakes. Stunted conifers crowd the lower slopes, while higher areas are typically arctic-alpine barrens.

Most boreal birds, including **Pileated, Black-backed and Three-toed Woodpeckers**, are found in good numbers. Both **American Pipit and Common Redpoll** nest near the summits, and recent sightings of **Boreal Owl** in April suggest they may, too. There have been reports of **Broad-winged Hawk, Golden Eagle and Northern Hawk Owl** from the Mont Albert area. Parc de la Gaspésie also has **Snow Goose, Mallard, Peregrine, Baird's Sandpiper, Northern Saw-whet, Wood Thrush, Eastern Bluebird, Loggerhead Shrike and Scarlet Tanager** on its checklist.

Other places to visit from this site

The two-hour ferry trips across the St. Lawrence can be very rewarding from late May to early December with most pelagic species reported. Late May crossings have offered **Northern Fulmar, Red Phalarope and Pomarine Jaeger**, and early June trips add a few more **Northern Fulmar, Wilson's Storm-petrel, Glaucous and Iceland Gulls** and an early northbound **Long-tailed Jaeger** to the peak numbers of **Red-throated Loon**. **Northern Gannet** are the commonest species in July when **Northern Fulmar, Wilson's and Leach's Storm-petrels, and Parasitic Jaeger** occur in small numbers, together with rather more **Greater and Sooty Shearwaters**. There are usually a few **Manx Shearwater, Red Phalarope and Caspian Tern**, but sightings of **Pomarine Jaeger** are less frequent.

Early August trips may yield an occasional **Greater or Manx Shearwater** or a **Wilson's Storm-petrel**. Trips in mid August may turn up a few **Greater and Sooty Shearwaters, and Leach's Storm-petrel**, along with a smattering of **Manx Shearwaters** and the odd **Wilson's Storm-petrel, Pomarine and Parasitic Jaegers**. As many as **50 Red-necked Phalarope** have been reported in late August, and **Black-legged Kittiwake** flocks build up in September. **Red Phalarope, Great Cormorant, Lesser Black-backed Gull, Pomarine, Parasitic and Long-tailed Jaegers** have been seen in August. **Greater Shearwater, Pomarine Jaeger, Atlantic Puffin, Red Phalarope, Little and Laughing Gulls** pass through in September. A few **Northern Fulmar** regularly stray upriver in October. The Baie-Comeau ferry has also turned up **Sabine's Gull** in fall. A **Pacific Loon** in mid October represents a rather late southward movement. Birds can still be seen heading south into November when the **Black-legged Kittiwake** numbers have dropped. By early December a few wintering **Dovekie and Thick-billed Murre** appear and are joined by **King Eider and Black Guillemot**.

The mixed forest, ponds, lakes, bogs, streams and farmlands around Saint-Tharcisius on Route 195 from Matane to Amqui have a good selection of common species. **Black Duck, Green- and Blue-winged Teal, and Ring-necked Duck** are the commonest breeding waterfowl and share the wetter areas with **American Bittern, Common Goldeneye, Killdeer, Common Snipe, Spotted Sandpiper, Belted Kingfisher, Red-winged and Rusty Blackbirds**. In the woodlands and secondgrowth, flycatchers are represented by **Eastern Kingbird, Eastern Phoebe, Alder and Least Flycatchers**, and there are nesting **Ruffed Grouse, Ruby-throated Hummingbird and Cedar Waxwing**.

The selection of nesting thrushes, warblers and sparrows indicates the mixed nature of the woodlands. **Veery, American Robin, Ovenbird, Chestnut-sided, Black-throated Blue and Wilson's Warblers, American Redstart, Rose-breasted Grosbeak and Chipping Sparrow** prefer broadleaf trees and open areas, but most nesting species are more boreal in preference. These include **Hermit Thrush, Ruby-crowned Kinglet, Yellow-rumped, Cape May, Magnolia and Bay-breasted Warblers, Northern Waterthrush, Fox and Swamp Sparrows.** Flocks of **Evening Grosbeak** are joined by good numbers of **Snow Bunting, American Tree Sparrow and Dark-eyed Junco.** The **Common Redpoll** flocks should be checked as **Hoary Redpoll** are quite regular until mid April.

The Sayabec area to the southwest of Matane was a major forestry area, but only a forestry museum now remains to indicate just how active logging was a hundred years ago. Lac Matapedia has a small but active **Great Blue Heron** colony and a number of interesting breeding species, including **Veery.** The river valley alongside Highway 132 is one of the most scenic in Canada and has been called "the river of 222 rapids". Boreal species are common all along the valley, and it is not difficult to find **Northern Goshawk, Gray Jay, Boreal Chickadee and Evening Grosbeak.**

Métis Park is owned by the province of Quebec and provides a glorious setting for flowering plants among a variety of lakes and streams, conifers, hardwoods and lawns. The former owners transformed the Reford estate at Grand-Métis into one of the most famous botanical gardens in North America with over 2500 varieties of plants—this alone ensured admission into the Royal Horticultural Society. Songbird migrants abound in early morning, but few visits have been made by birders. **Great Horned Owl and Three-toed Woodpecker** have both been reported in the surrounding woodlands. An early September **Western Tanager** provided a bonus for birders at Métis Park.

Nearby Métis-sur-mer is very popular with waterfowl of all kinds. Up to **12,000 Snow Geese and 1200 Canada Geese, 1000 Double-crested Cormorant, 450 Black Scoter, 150 Surf Scoter and 100 Barrow's Goldeneye** have been tallied in May. Spring vagrants include obviously storm-blown **Pied-billed Grebe and Least Bittern** at the end of March, **Harlequin and King Eider** from March to May, **Common Moorhen, Willet and Upland Sandpiper** in the first half of May, and **Green-backed Heron** and a pair of **Ruddy Duck** in the second half of the month. A **Northern Hawk Owl** has also been found in early May. Nearby Les Boules' bird reserve has also produced a **Short-eared Owl** in mid April and **3500 Snow Bunting** at the end of the month. The appearance of a **Long-billed Curlew** in mid July suggests that summer visits may also be rewarded.

This area is most productive in the fall migration period. Up to **500 Double-crested Cormorant** and several **Lesser Golden-plover, White-rumped and Pectoral Sandpipers** have appeared in late July, but the best time to visit is from early September to mid October when waterfowl again arrive in large numbers. Counts of **1000 Black Duck, 500 Common Goldeneye, 2000 Common Eider, 300 Double-crested Cormorant and 75 Surf Scoter** are not unusual. There have also been fall counts of **300 Mallard and 75 Northern Pintail.** September sightings of **Greater White-fronted Goose, Broad-winged Hawk** and some lingering shorebirds round out the fall migration period. Winter is distinguished by flocks of up to **55 Barrow's** and somewhat fewer **Common Goldeneye** and the odd **Bufflehead.** Small parties of **Purple Sandpiper** search the rocks in winter and are scattered by the odd **Gyrfalcon. Three-toed Woodpecker** has been reported on several occasions.

The town of Mont-Joli is best known for the successful nesting of a few pairs of **Upland Sandpiper** at the airport — as many as two dozen birds have been counted in June and July. The nearby woodlands have attracted nesting **Eastern Bluebird** and visits from **Cooper's and Red-shouldered Hawks, and Eastern Screech Owl**. The open areas outside town have attracted up to **300 Horned Lark, 50 Lapland Longspur** and a few **Eastern Meadowlark** in late April and May. There may be some rarer species at Mont-Joli such as **Purple Martin and Western Meadowlark**, and vagrant **Northern Wheatear and Rufous-sided Towhee**. A **Redhead** has been noted in May on a small pond just outside town at Saint-Joseph-de-Lepage.

Christmas Bird Counts can be quite interesting with good numbers of **Barrow's Goldeneye, Oldsquaw, Glaucous and Iceland Gulls, White-winged Crossbill** and as many as **1650 Snow Bunting**. A few **Mallard, Black-legged Kittiwake, Red-breasted Nuthatch, Northern Shrike and Brown-headed Cowbird** winter, and there have been **Surf Scoter, Northern Goshawk, Gyrfalcon, Snowy Owl, Pileated and Three-toed Woodpeckers**.

The most westerly birding site in this area is where Highway 132 divides to loop around the Gaspé at Sainte-Flavie. Sainte-Flavie is worth visiting year round, although a **Snowy Owl or Gyrfalcon** might be the only tangible reward in the dead of winter. Other December sightings have included **Three-toed Woodpecker and Red-winged Blackbird**, but small parties of **Common Redpoll and Brown-headed Cowbird** are more likely. The most surprising wintering bird at Sainte-Flavie was a **Rufous-sided Towhee**. Migrant sparrows move through the coastal woods and have been joined by **Western Meadowlark and Field Sparrow** — both possible breeding species some time in the future.

Pied-billed Grebe, Northern Gannet, Glaucous Gull and up to **100 Black Guillemot** may be present in late March, and by May **Horned Grebe, King Eider, Piping Plover, Short-billed Dowitcher and Black Tern** could be added to the list. There have also been **300 Semipalmated Sandpiper** passing through in late May. Outside these peak periods there are concentrations of **Common Loon and Black Scoter** in late June. Late June was the time chosen to visit by a **Pacific Loon** three decades ago. **Franklin's and Laughing Gulls** have also enlivened June visits. The greatest concentration of birds is in late July-early August, when up to **400 Ruddy Turnstone** have been noted, and in October, when as many as **600 Common Eider and 250 Surf Scoter** are joined by a few **Red-throated Loon and Hooded Merganser**. As many as **80 Black Scoter** are usually present later in the month, when there are a few **Black Guillemot**.

Shorebirds are found well into October, when counts of **200 Lesser Golden-plover** and small numbers of **Black-bellied Plover, White-rumped Sandpiper, Dunlin and Sanderling** are normal. A few **Upland Sandpiper** can be expected in August and a **Baird's Sandpiper** has been found in mid September. Good numbers of gulls appear on the beach, with flocks of **Ring-billed Gull** early on and an occasional **Glaucous Gull** from late October.

CAP-DES-ROSIERS TO PENOUILLE

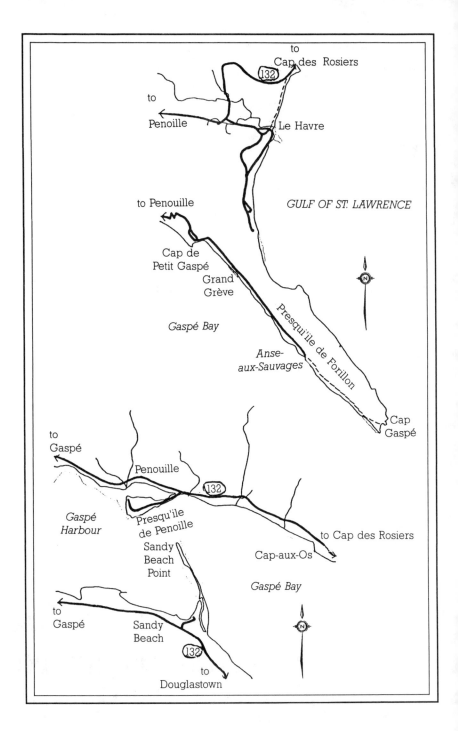

Quebec's most easterly national park, Forillon, occupies a rugged peninsula jutting into the Gulf of St. Lawrence north of Gaspé. The combination of mountains, mixed and boreal forests, and alpine tundra is found elsewhere on the Gaspé Peninsula, but the nature of the marine waters and the spectacular coastal scenery make Forillon much different. Hiking is the best way to enjoy the park with trails to most of the different habitats. Maxime St.-Amour, the park naturalist, has written an excellent guide to the park, and the Gaspésie bird club maintains sales outlets at the interpretation centres.

The park is divided into northern and southern sections with their own campgrounds and interpretation centres. I stayed in the southern section and camped at Petit Gaspé which is close to the Mont Saint-Alban trail which proved to be an excellent trail. I understand Le Castor trail alongside Cap-des-Rosiers Brook, Les Graves trail along the shore to Cap Gaspé, and Les Lacs trail into the interior provide a representative selection of habitats in the northern section. Moose, whitetailed deer, black bear, porcupine, woodchuck, muskrat, red squirrel and eastern chipmunk are all common, and there are usually good numbers of seals, whales and harbour porpoises in summer. The most recent bird checklist I have seen lists nearly 230 species, including several at the extreme edge of their ranges.

The whole peninsula resembling a dolphin's beak and ending at Cap Gaspé is called Presqu'ile — an appropriate name as it is almost an island. Most of the park's breeding songbirds are found along it, including good numbers of more local species such as **Yellow-bellied Flycatcher, Red-breasted Nuthatch, Golden-crowned Kinglet, Solitary Vireo, Yellow and Bay-breasted Warblers**. This is also a good place to look for **White-crowned and Vesper Sparrows** on migration. The western section of the peninsula is the best place for birds of prey, especially **Cooper's Hawk, Gyrfalcon and Peregrine** on migration.

The point is also a good place to look for raptors which use it as a migration landmark — **Cooper's Hawk** are possible during spring or fall, but **Peregrine** are more regular in August than any other time. Among the more unusual species at Cap Gaspé, **Cooper's Hawk and Boreal Owl** have been found in summer, and **Gyrfalcon** at the turn of the year. Many of the commoner species are regularly seen along the nature trails, and **Northern Harrier and Short-eared Owl** use the coastal marshes in fall. **Snowy Owl** are fairly regular winter visitors, and **Northern Goshawk** are also seen in winter, when the same waterfowl as at Cap-des-Rosiers can be expected.

The northern shore of Cap Gaspé also has breeding **Black-legged Kittiwake, Herring Gull, Black Guillemot and Double-crested Cormorant** colonies, as well as a few **Northern Gannet and Great Cormorant** flying by from April to September. This is also one of the few places you can expect to find **Common Murre and Atlantic Puffin** in summer. There are a few **Bufflehead** among the wintering **Oldsquaw, Surf Scoter and King Eider**, and there are often **Red Knot** in September, although most shorebirds avoid the rocky cape. **Mourning Dove and Common Raven** are quite common, and songbirds can also be found in good numbers, especially migrant **Red-breasted Nuthatch, Bohemian Waxwing, Red-winged Blackbird, Evening Grosbeak and Snow Bunting**. Rarer migrants on the north shore of Cap Gaspé have included **Scarlet Tanager, Dickcissel and Indigo Bunting**. A **Yellow-billed Cuckoo** was found in mid November, and there have been reports of **Blue-gray Gnatcatcher, Yellow-breasted Chat and Rufous-sided Towhee**.

The rocky coastline from Le Havre to Cap Bon-Ami, with its unique arctic-alpine flora, contains two campgrounds and most of the breeding seabirds. Over **1000 pairs of Black-legged Kittiwake** nest with smaller numbers of **Double-crested Cormorant and Herring Gull**, and there are a few pairs of **Razorbill** among the **60+ pairs of Black Guillemot**. The only **Ruddy Duck** seen was off Le Havre, but **Horned Grebe and Great Cormorant** are more regular in spring. **American Coot** are also regular migrants, and **Pectoral Sandpiper** are common in September.

The area is attractive to landbirds—with **Yellow-billed Cuckoo** quite often reported in November. There have been summer sightings of **Great Crested Flycatcher and Field Sparrow** around Cap Bon-Ami. During the summer months the campground areas shelter **Alder Flycatcher, Eastern Wood-pewee, Solitary Vireo, Bobolink, Eastern Meadowlark and Savannah Sparrow**. In the fall, the shoreline and open areas have parties of **American Tree Sparrow, Lapland Longspur and Snow Bunting**.

The coastline south of Cap-des-Rosiers offers a good chance of seeing migrants and nesting seabirds. **Pied-billed Grebe** appear in spring and fall, and the offshore waters offer **Red-throated Loon and Red-necked Grebe** in early May and October. Waterfowl are also plentiful on migration with most eastern species represented. Regular spring and fall migrants include **Green- and Blue-winged Teal, Bufflehead, Oldsquaw, White-winged, Surf and Black Scoters** as well as additions to the nesting **Black Duck and Northern Pintail** population. Rarer dabbling ducks, such as **American Wigeon, Northern Shoveler and Wood Duck**, are now present into the summer months, and they are joined by a few **Ring-necked Duck and Lesser Scaup. Mallard** have also nested in Forillon National Park.

This is also one of the best beaches in the park area for fall shorebirds, and there are a few **Killdeer, Semipalmated Plover, Dunlin and Semipalmated Sandpiper** in spring, too. During the main late July-mid October migration period, **Semipalmated Plover, Ruddy Turnstone, Whimbrel, Greater Yellowlegs, Semipalmated Sandpiper and Sanderling** are common. Shorebirds seen less often around Cap-des-Rosiers have included **Lesser Golden-plover, Willet, Lesser Yellowlegs, Dunlin, Baird's Sandpiper and Red-necked Phalarope**.

Marsh habitats have attracted **Green-backed Heron, Least Bittern, Glossy Ibis and Virginia Rail**, and the beaches have yielded **Upland and Baird's Sandpipers** in the fall. Other marshbirds have included **Glossy Ibis** and **Least Bittern**. This is also a good area for gulls, with **Black-legged Kittiwake** abundant in summer and both **Glaucous and Iceland Gulls** very common in winter. The cliffs and offshore waters also attract large numbers of **Razorbill and Black Guillemot** in summer.

The variety of habitats in the Cap-des-Rosiers area goes a long way towards explaining the appearance of southern songbirds like **Blue-gray Gnatcatcher, Scarlet Tanager, Indigo Bunting and Field Sparrow**. Recent reports have added **Great Crested Flycatcher, Purple Martin, Brown Thrasher, Eastern Bluebird, House Wren, Loggerhead Shrike, Eastern Meadowlark, Dickcissel, Rufous-sided Towhee and Clay-colored Sparrow** in summer.

Winter, especially February, is the time to look for **Great Cormorant, Common and Barrow's Goldeneyes, Bufflehead, Oldsquaw, Common Eider, Red-breasted Merganser, Black Guillemot and Dovekie**, and **Purple Sandpiper** winter in small numbers. **Double-crested Cormorant, Lesser Scaup, King Eider, Common Merganser** and all three scoters are a possibility here, too, and several **Red-necked Grebe** have been found in early January. **Great Black-backed and Iceland Gulls** can be quite common, but gulls and raptors are less a feature of the Forillon Christmas Bird Count than elsewhere. **Greater White-fronted Goose, Mallard and Greater Scaup** have been noted in fall, and **Red-throated Loon** has been seen in winter.

Songbirds are not a major feature, although **Hoary Redpoll** may be seen in winter among flocks of **Common Redpoll, Purple Finch, Snow Bunting, Pine Siskin and White-winged Crossbill**, and both **Pine and Evening Grosbeaks** are sometimes common, too. Signs of **Pileated Woodpecker** have been noted south of Cap-des-Rosiers, and **Red-breasted Nuthatch and Brown Creeper** may appear in winter. Other songbirds tend to be scarcer here than in more urban regions, with just 11 species noted on the 1989 Christmas count.

The southern shore of Presqu'ile has about **100 pairs of Black Guillemot and Herring Gull** and the only nesting **Great Black-backed Gulls**. The Les Graves trail is recommended for songbirds, which have included **Gray Catbird and Great Crested Flycatcher** in summer and **Northern Shrike** in winter. Access is possible from the northern section of the park by using trails linked to the Mont Saint-Alban trail.

The Petit-Gaspé area also has marshes for **Sora and Virginia Rail** in summer, when **Green-backed Heron, Black-crowned Night Heron and Common Moorhen** might be present. A few pairs of **Herring Gull and Black Guillemot** nest in the area, but gulls and terns are largely absent, except in winter when **Glaucous Gull** are regular. Landbirds are quite plentiful and have included one or two vagrants. The campground and picnic areas are packed in the short summer tourist season, and there are few birds to see apart from a few thrushes and warblers. Late summer and fall **Black-billed Cuckoo**, a few May **Purple Martin**, spring **Eastern Meadowlark**, and fall **Northern Oriole** have, however, been noted in this area.

A short walk past the church provides access to the beach below where **Double-crested Cormorant and Black Guillemot** are regular in summer and waterfowl, gulls and shorebirds in season. There are also several pairs of **Alder Flycatcher, Solitary Vireo, Chipping Sparrow, American Goldfinch and Common Grackle** by the trail, as well as a reasonable selection of thrushes and warblers.

At the steep trail to the beach turn left and return to the highway—the start of the trail system linking up with the northern section of the park is a short distance beyond the bridge. I walked only the four-mile-long Mont Saint-Alban trail, but my three hours were extremely well spent. The trail wends its way up the ridge through a variety of woodlands and offers some excellent views of the park and its coastline along the way. I highly recommend it, especially if you only have a day to visit as I did in late June. More time would allow other trails to be added. I was, in fact, a short distance behind a black bear, but, fortunately, our paths never crossed or my narrative may have been much different.

I counted a total of 50 bird species on my walk. The commonest were **Yellow-bellied Flycatcher, Swainson's and Hermit Thrushes, American Robin, Winter Wren, Golden-crowned Kinglet, Solitary Vireo, Magnolia, Black-throated Green, Blackburnian and Black-and-white Warblers, American Redstart, White-throated Sparrow, Evening Grosbeak and American Goldfinch**. A count of 14 warblers and 12 finches and sparrows indicates the diversity. My better sightings included broods of **Ruffed Grouse**, and single **Brown Creeper, Philadelphia Vireo, Tennessee and Black-throated Blue Warblers, Northern Waterthrush, Rose-breasted Grosbeak, Fox Sparrow and White-winged Crossbill**. **Least Flycatcher, Eastern Wood-pewee, Northern Parula and Red-eyed Vireo** were restricted to the mature hardwoods, while **Boreal Chickadee and Pine Siskin** were seen only in the conifers.

The tiny peninsula of Penouille is an excellent place for birds throughout the year—its sand dunes and saltmarshes are unique on the Gaspé Peninsula. The cliffs to the east have **Black Guillemot and Herring Gull**, but the sheltered waters provide the main attraction to birds. Good numbers of **Northern Gannet, Great and Double-crested Cormorants** fish Gaspé Bay in summer, and the parties of **Great Blue Heron** along the shoreline are sometimes joined by **Black-crowned Night Heron**. Waterfowl also pass through in good numbers with good-sized parties of **Canada Goose and Brant** in spring. **Mallard, Northern Pintail and American Wigeon** all drop in to feed, and **Greater Scaup, Black Scoter and Common Merganser** are more common than anywhere else in the park—a **Lesser Scaup** also paid a visit in May.

Birds of prey regularly seen on the peninsula include **Northern Goshawk, Osprey and Peregrine**, and the shorebird flocks are often scattered by **Sharp-shinned Hawk, American Kestrel and Merlin**. Good numbers of **Killdeer, Semipalmated and Black-bellied Plovers, Whimbrel, Greater and Lesser Yellowlegs, Red Knot, Dunlin, Least and Semipalmated Sandpipers** arrive between late July and the end of October. This is also one of the few places where **Common Nighthawk** are at all regular and **Whip-poor-will** likely, but landbirds are not a major attraction. The coastal woods and interconnecting trails provide a good selection of songbirds.

Glaucous, Iceland, Great Black-backed and Herring Gulls all winter in the area, but the number of songbirds overwintering is quite low, with **Red-breasted Nuthatch, Northern Shrike, Hoary Redpoll and White-winged Crossbill** the most interesting. Both **Black-capped and Boreal Chickadees** are, however, quite common, and flocks of **Common Redpoll** can be quite large some winters.

Winter, especially February, is the time to look for **Great Cormorant, Common and Barrow's Goldeneyes, Bufflehead, Oldsquaw, Common Eider, Red-breasted Merganser, Black Guillemot and Dovekie**, and **Purple Sandpiper** winter in small numbers. **Double-crested Cormorant, Lesser Scaup, King Eider, Common Merganser, Thick-billed Murre** and all three scoters are a possibility here, too, and several **Red-necked Grebe** have been found in early January. **Great Black-backed and Iceland Gulls** can be quite common, but gulls and raptors are less a feature of the Forillon Christmas Bird Count, although **Snowy Owl** is seen most years and **Northern Goshawk, Rough-legged Hawk and Barred Owl** have also appeared. Signs of **Pileated Woodpecker, Black-backed and Three-toed Woodpeckers** have been seen on the Forillon count.

Other places to visit from this area

The Rivière-au-Renard rivermouth attracts parties of waterfowl and shorebirds in spring and fall, as well as occasional marshbirds and birds of prey. The coastline west of Forillon is characterized by high cliffs. **Boreal Owl** sometimes appear in summer, and so do **White-breasted Nuthatch** where there are hardwoods, but a **Northern Shrike** was an unusual mid July visitor—the species is regular in winter. Winter is also a good time to look for **Thick-billed Murre** and the odd **Ivory Gull** among wintering **Glaucous and Iceland Gulls**. The Gaspésie naturalists maintain a sales desk at the park's interpretive centre by the highway.

To the west of Presqu'ile, the L'Anse-au-Griffon estuary is a good place to look for **Gyrfalcon and Peregrine** on migration, and **Barred Owl** is another raptor found on the floodplain year round. **Osprey, Northern Goshawk, Rough-legged and Red-tailed Hawks** also use the estuary and valley, and **Common Snipe and Belted Kingfisher** are common.

The number of songbirds in the area grows with the addition of **Eastern Bluebird, Veery, Chestnut-sided Warbler, Bobolink, White-winged Crossbill and White-crowned Sparrow** on migration. A **Snowy Egret** in late May and an **Ivory Gull** in mid December are among the rarer species listed for the community of L'Anse-au-Griffon. It has also received visits from **Ruby-throated Hummingbird, Red-headed Woodpecker and Yellow-bellied Sapsucker**.

A bicycle/riding trail crosses the park and can be reached by driving west of L'Anse-au-Griffon. The first mile is characterized by steep wooded slopes on the right and a broad open floodplain over-run by heaths and secondgrowth on the left. One attractive feature in June and early July is the flowering of several lilac trees alongside the trail. **Alder Flycatcher, Magnolia Warbler, Chipping, White-throated and Song Sparrows, American Goldfinch and Red-winged Blackbird** were the commonest species, but I also recorded **Northern Harrier, Ruby-throated Hummingbird, Hermit and Gray-cheeked Thrushes, Cedar Waxwing, Solitary and Philadelphia Vireos, Northern**

Parula, Yellow Warbler, American Redstart, Common Yellowthroat, Swamp Sparrow, Evening Grosbeak and Purple Finch.

The Lacs trail loops off the central road to take in a primitive campsite at Lac-au-Renard, where **Common Goldeneye** nest. **Gray Jay** are also regular visitors to the campsite, but most of the better birds are found along the trail itself. **Spruce Grouse** are resident and usually seen, but **Nashville Warbler** requires a more careful search in the bordering secondgrowth. Woodlands are quite varied with elm, ash, maple, yellow birch and balsam fir well in evidence. The most common species are those of the boreal forest — **Dark-eyed Junco, Tennessee and Blackpoll Warblers**, and **Canada Warbler and Northern Waterthrush** are also quite widespread. The trail system also takes in habitat suitable for **Philadelphia Vireo, Northern Parula, Magnolia, Cape May, Black-throated Blue, Blackburnian, Bay-breasted, Palm and Wilson's Warblers**. Boreal finches, including **Pine Grosbeak, Pine Siskin, Red and White-winged Crossbills**, can be looked for with some degree of certainty in summer. Trails east of the valley probably have a similar selection of species.

The southern shoreline of Gaspé Bay offers a similar selection of birds to that in the national park. The saltmarshes at the mouths of the Dartmouth, York and Saint John Rivers are all worth visiting — they have produced broods of **Ring-necked Duck**. The Gaspé Bay saltmarshes have also produced a **Wood Duck** nest and spring sightings of **Gadwall and Canvasback**. Scoters and **Common Eider** form rafts of nonbreeding birds in summer, and there is an excellent fall migration.

The largest numbers are, however, reserved for the winter months when concentrations of diving ducks can be staggering in comparison with other coastal bays. Counts of **45,000 Oldsquaw** in February are not unusual, and there are large numbers of **Common Eider, Barrow's and Common Goldeneyes** throughout the winter.

A good birding site for other bird groups is the community of Gaspé situated at the mouth of the York River just beyond the intersection of Highways 132 and 198. Waterfowl, shorebirds and gulls gather here. The best shorebird location is the long sandspit just east of the community at Sandy Beach. This attracts large numbers of all eastern species and is perfectly placed to hold flocks of later-migrating **Black-bellied Plover and White-rumped Sandpiper. Semipalmated Plover, Ruddy Turnstone and Sanderling** are all common, and this would seem to be the best beach on the Gaspé to look for **Piping Plover, Buff-breasted Sandpiper**, gulls and terns. There have been sightings of **Canvasback, Common Moorhen and Marbled Godwit** at Gaspé.

Birds of prey also drift over from Penouille on the far shore of Gaspé Bay. **Northern Harrier and Short-eared Owl** are regular in fall, and both **Gyrfalcon and Snowy Owl** have put in winter appearances. The surrounding farmland and forest is attractive to landbirds and there have been a number of interesting reports in recent years. Summer visits by nonbreeding **Peregrine** may eventually lead to a nesting record, but the return of the **Yellow Rail** colony of the 1950s is unlikely. Large flocks of **Bank and Cliff Swallows** should be checked for **Rough-winged Swallow and Purple Martin** in May and June. Both **Northern Mockingbird and Brown Thrasher** reports are increasing along this coastline, and Sandy Beach also attracted a **Black-billed Cuckoo** in mid July. A **Northern Cardinal** was an interesting addition at Wakeham, as was an **Orange-crowned Warbler** at Douglastown.

BONAVENTURE ISLAND—
BARACHOIS

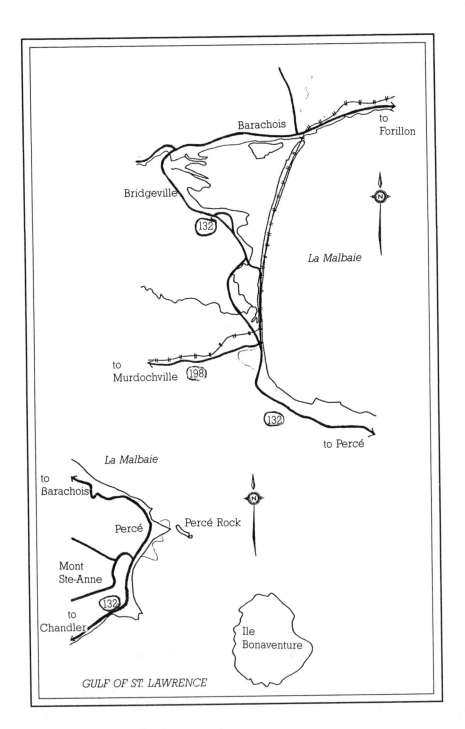

This section of coastline receives more visits than any other part of the Gaspé. It's not hard to see why when you're on the boat out to Bonaventure Island and its colony of **Northern Gannet**. This island colony drew visitors to the Gaspé long before the idea of creating a national park at Forillon materialized, and most people also took in a visit to Percé Rock with its natural arch. Centuries of settlement have led to large areas of cleared land along the coast, which has helped the local populations of whitetailed deer and red fox and provided nesting habitats for open-country birds. Percé Rock and Bonaventure Island were sanctuaries as early as 1919. The Percé Wildlife Interpretation Centre staff helped write this site guide before budget cuts forced the centre's closure a few years ago. However, it has reopened and is better than ever, and an interpretation program is offered during the summer months on Bonaventure Island.

The tourist and resort centre of Percé has developed along the shore between Belvedere and Cap Blanc. When Jacques Cartier arrived in 1534, Percé Rock was still part of the mainland, but wind and wave action has toppled a previous stack and sculptured the present one into a stack and an arch. You can still walk to the rock at low tide by walking along the sandbar from the foot of the hill but watch out for the incoming tide! The best scenic views are from above the town and there are excursions to the nearby fishing communities in summer. The interpretive centre itself lies on the hillside south of the community and is well worth a visit to find out what is around and to take in the interpretive displays. A small trail leads through the fields and woodlots, and there are guided walks and other events in summer.

The area's breeding bird list includes **Yellow-bellied Flycatcher, Cliff Swallow, Winter Wren, Ruby-crowned Kinglet, Cedar Waxwing and Philadelphia Vireo**. Nesting warblers include **Nashville, Cape May, Black-throated Blue, Bay-breasted, Mourning, Wilson's and Canada Warblers**, and **Pine and Rose-breasted Grosbeaks, and Sharp-tailed Sparrow** also nest. The number of nocturnal migrants can be gauged by undertaking a night-time tryst on Mont Sainte-Anne—preferably with a flask of hot coffee or whisky and a close friend! The greatest movements are from late August to mid September. Trails to the top start behind the church and by the Gargantua Restaurant at the top of a steep climb up the mountain. **Great Horned Owl, Olive-sided Flycatcher, Common Raven, Boreal Chickadee, Gray-cheeked Thrush, White-winged Crossbill, Pine Grosbeak and Fox Sparrow** can all be found in summer.

Strays are very likely and the list is very impressive, with **Rock Ptarmigan, Black-billed Cuckoo, Red-headed Woodpecker, Say's Phoebe, Great Crested and Willow Flycatchers, Purple Martin, White-breasted Nuthatch, Yellow-breasted Chat, Orchard Oriole, Scarlet Tanager, Dickcissel, Lark and Field Sparrows** being just a few of the birds reported around Percé.

The cliffs and Percé Rock itself have nesting **Great and Double-crested Cormorants, Razorbill, Black Guillemot, Great Black-backed and Herring Gulls, and Black-legged Kittiwake** and a few pairs of **Common Murre**, as well as a cliff-nesting colony of **Common Starling** — the only mention of the species I will allow in this book! The summer months usually offer large numbers of **Greater Shearwater**, and **Green-backed Heron and Glossy Ibis** are the most likely summer additions to **Great Blue Heron and Black-crowned Night Heron**. **Mallard and Northern Shoveler** are regular visitors, and **Harlequin** also breed in the area and so do **Sora**. Other likely breeding additions are **Willet and Upland Sandpiper**, both frequently seen in the summer months.

An early September **Turkey Vulture** caused a stir and an early January **Peregrine** set hearts aflutter. **Golden Eagle and Gyrfalcon** are regular enough to elicit little local excitement — **Snowy and Short-eared Owls** are both found in winter. Pelagics are frequently seen close to shore by Percé Rock, and have included **Sooty Shearwater, Wilson's Storm-petrel, Long-tailed Jaeger, Thick-billed Murre and Caspian Tern**. **Chimney Swift, Eastern Kingbird, Eastern Wood-pewee and Bobolink** are recent additions to the area's breeding bird list.

Fall migration can be spectacular with rafts of scoters, **Common Eider and Red-breasted Merganser** supplemented by **Harlequin and King Eider**, regular in winter, when storms bring in **Northern Gannet, Razorbill, Dovekie and Ivory Gull**, and **Horned and Pied-billed Grebes** are occasional fall visitors. **Greater White-fronted and Snow Geese** have both been noted at Percé. **Oldsquaw, Common and Barrow's Goldeneyes, Common Eider and Red-breasted Merganser** are the commonest of the wintering waterfowl, but **Common Loon, Red-necked Grebe, Great Cormorant, Black Duck, Surf, Black and White-winged Scoters and Black Guillemot** are all regularly seen. Numbers of **Thick-billed and Common Murres, and Dovekie** are usually small, and **Harlequin and Hooded Merganser** are rarities in winter. Gulls are also rare in winter, despite the appearance of **150 Black-legged Kittiwake** one count, and **Snowy Owl** is the most likely raptor, although **Northern Goshawk, Rough-legged Hawk, Gyrfalcon, Merlin and Great Horned Owl** have also been reported.

Common Raven, Common Redpoll and Snow Bunting are the most conspicuous wintering landbirds, and there are small numbers of **Blue Jay, Boreal Chickadee, American Robin, Evening Grosbeak and White-winged Crossbill**. A few **Black-backed Woodpecker, Gray Jay and Red-breasted Nuthatch** are also present year round, but **Brown Creeper and Golden-crowned Kinglet** are less regular. **Three-toed Woodpecker, Northern Shrike, Yellow-rumped Warbler, Bohemian and Cedar Waxwings, American Tree Sparrow, Lapland Longspur, Song Sparrow, Red Crossbill and Red-winged Blackbird** have also appeared on the Percé count.

Bonaventure Island is located two miles off Percé and can be reached by taking the boat cruise. A ferry operates during the daytime from June to October, but no overnight camping is allowed. In the summer months when the seabird colonies are in full swing, landings can be made in the morning with a return in the afternoon. The best time to visit is from June to mid August. More than 175 bird species have been noted on the island.

The regular cruises in summer circle the island and offer views of nesting birds, but the best views are from the top of the island itself, which is composed of rather crumbly rocks with 75 meter-high cliffs. The trail from the dock to the island plateau is steep but not too strenuous and begins in grassy fields. The lower spruce-fir forest is an excellent place to look for boreal warblers and finches — **Tennessee Warbler and Fox Sparrow** are common. **Winter Wren** is apparently making a comeback and over 150 landbird species have been recorded on Bonaventure Island. A few **Bald and Golden Eagles** may be found in summer but do not nest.

Northern Gannet

The best seabird colonies are on the eastern cliffs — those to the northeast are favoured by **Black-legged Kittiwake and Black Guillemot** with smaller numbers of **Razorbill, Common Murre and Atlantic Puffin**. **Northern Gannet** also nest on these high cliffs — most of the **18,000+ pairs** prefer the flat top or larger ledges. A rail restricts too close an approach both for the safety of the birds and visitors — younger birds on the cliffs suffer greater losses. Bonaventure Island also has good numbers of **Razorbill and Common Murre** from June to early August, as well as a few **Atlantic Puffin — Thick-billed Murre and Dovekie** have also been noted in summer and on the water in winter when the deserted ledges have a few **Great Cormorant**.

The island is also home to around **100 pairs** of **Leach's Storm-petrel**, and a few **Northern Fulmar** may nest in the future. **Greater and Sooty Shearwaters** are seen offshore in summer, and fall is the best time to look for **Bonaparte's Gull** and an occasional **Brant**. **Harlequin** are a common sight in winter and may linger into the summer months—a July 9 count of 24 drakes indicates an improved eastern population.

Birders visiting Bonaventure Island in summer guarantee a few unusual reports. **King Eider, Ruddy Duck, Cooper's Hawk, Willet, Baird's Sandpiper, Red Phalarope, Laughing, Common Black-headed and Little Gulls, Parasitic Jaeger and Snowy Owl** have decorated various lists. Among songbirds, the best sightings are a mid June **Summer Tanager** and late June **Fork-tailed Flycatcher**, but **Brown Thrasher, Northern Mockingbird, White-breasted Nuthatch, Orange-crowned Warbler, Yellow-breasted Chat, Orchard Oriole and Field Sparrow** in early summer, and **Yellow-breasted Chat, Eastern Meadowlark, Northern Oriole, Indigo Bunting, Lark and Field Sparrows** in fall all rate a mention. **Red-headed Woodpecker, Great Crested Flycatcher and Purple Martin** round out the migrants, and a **Red-bellied Woodpecker** overwintered recently.

Barachois and Bridgeville on either side of the Riviere Malbaie estuary provide excellent opportunities to look for rarities. The barachois pond and sandbar at Barachois are used by large numbers of waterbirds and shorebirds from early spring to late fall, and there is always the chance of a vagrant. **Double-crested and Great Cormorants** are fairly common in late summer, and there are often groups of **Black-legged Kittiwake** inshore. The largest flocks of gulls in September and October are composed mainly of **Bonaparte's Gull**, although there are always a few **Common Black-headed Gull** mixed in with them. Marshbirds are another feature in summer and early fall with sightings of **Great Egret, Little Blue Heron, Glossy Ibis and American Coot**. A few **Willet** have taken up summer residence, and there are also reports of **Virginia Rail and Wilson's Phalarope** at the northeastern edge of their ranges.

Good numbers of **Brant** drop by in spring, when dabbling ducks are also common. Waterfowl are common in summer—the usual **Wood Duck** being supplemented by prospecting **Gadwall, American Wigeon, Northern Shoveler and Redhead** of late. **Pied-billed Grebe** are now considered regular summer residents until mid September, when the waterfowl migration is again in full swing. Groups of **Common and Red-throated Loons, Oldsquaw, Black, White-winged and Surf Scoters, Common and Red-breasted Mergansers** are common on the salt water. **Snowy Owl** have summered— which makes life a little more dangerous than usual for the nesting **Sharp-tailed Sparrow**. The gravel roads behind the community can be very productive, but take care to park off the roadway and watch out for logging trucks which zip along the dry roads at tremendous speeds and kick up clouds of dust.

A short walk inland will often produce a good yield of songbirds in the early morning, including good numbers of warblers, **Olivesided and Yellow-bellied Flycatchers, Ruby-crowned Kinglet, Solitary Vireo, Pine Grosbeak, White-winged Crossbill** and other boreal species. I found **Magnolia Warbler and American Redstart** particularly common, and sightings of red fox and eastern chipmunk were interesting.

Pied-billed Grebe is now considered a regular summer resident. A report of **Sandhill Crane** and several July reports of **Yellow Rail**—formerly a regular nesting species along this coast and still a possibility in summer at Barachois, are indicative of the habitats available. Late spring and early fall provide rarities like **Little Gull and Caspian Tern**, and any gulls are worth checking out throughout the year. There is even a record of a **Eurasian Wigeon** and summer stopovers by **Brant, Ruddy Duck, Lesser Scaup** and even a **Greater White-fronted Goose**. Other unusual summer visitors to Barachois include **Red-throated Loon, Horned Grebe**, a blue phase **Snow Goose**, and a **Greater Shearwater**. Another interesting mid June addition in the Barachois area was a singing **Willow Flycatcher**—one of very few Canadian records until quite recently. Among the better fall migrants have been an early August **Northern Wheatear**, October **Blue-gray Gnatcatcher** and late October **Rufous-sided Towhee**.

Other places to visit from this area

The deep waters off Pointe-Saint-Pierre (Ile Plate) and Belle-Anse have large concentrations of alcids and seaducks in winter. **Bufflehead and Harlequin** have both wintered, and **Thick-billed Murre** may join the parties of **Black Guillemot**. This headland also has a wintering flock of **Purple Sandpiper**. A **Common Eider** colony on a small rocky island in front of the cape may also have resting **Great Cormorant**—a telescope is needed to see the birds.

The exposed cape is also a good place to look for seabirds such as **Common Eider, Oldsquaw, White-winged Scoter and Red-breasted Merganser**. The coastline to the south has also provided a few surprises. Cap-d'Espoir is an excellent place to look for pelagics, as well as a "'ghost ship" wrecked here in 1711. More regular in their appearances are **Wilson's Phalarope, Black Tern, Northern Saw-whet, Yellow- and Black-billed Cuckoos, and Purple Martin**. Nearly **2000 pairs** of **Black-legged Kittiwake** nest on the cliffs and there is a report of an **American Coot** nest in the area. The more notable vagrants at Cap-d'Espoir include **Greater White-fronted and Snow Geese, Ruddy Duck, Hooded Merganser, Cattle Egret, Ivory Gull, Western Kingbird, Say's Phoebe and Dickcissel**—several have appeared outside their normal migration periods.

Cape Cove, 10 miles west of Percé, is another good spot for pelagics—a secondary road leads to the light from Route 132. The communities between Cap-d'Espoir and Chandler have turned up **Turkey Vulture, Common Black-headed and Ivory Gulls, Boreal Owl and Field Sparrow**. **Wilson's Phalarope** appear in spring at Chandler, and **Great Egret, Virginia Rail and Little Gull** have enlivened summer visits. A calling **Whip-poor-will**, the first recorded on the Gaspé peninsula since 1923, was a recent late spring surprise at Chandler. **Ruff, Baird's and Buff-breasted Sandpipers** are all possible in fall. A mid May **Say's Phoebe** and mid November **Townsend's Solitaire** were well off course but not entirely unexpected given sightings in Newfoundland. The small bay south of Chandler is the best birding site along this coast—as a total of **105 Hudsonian Godwit** in early August shows. Similar habitats exist at Port-Daniel which has a fine sand beach. Both Port-Daniel and Anse-aux-Gascons are worth visiting for gulls and shorebirds.

Port-Daniel's sandy beach and fringing saltmarsh has gulls, shorebirds and marshbirds on migration—**Black-crowned Night Heron** are quite often seen. In winter the deep bay attracts a few **Great Cormorant and Bufflehead**, and the first returning **Northern Gannet** migrants. There have also been sightings of **Little Gull** in spring and **Black Tern** in early fall at Port-Daniel.

The wildlife reserve situated eight miles along a secondary road from Port-Daniel is one of the most beautiful spots in the province with the Port-Daniel River surrounded by spruce forests dotted liberally with white birch. **Harlequin** have nested along the river and there are numerous lakes accessible by the park's road system. I visited a few lakes and trails and especially recommend the short trail by the river. A **Pileated Woodpecker** flew over my head, and I also saw **Osprey, Hairy Woodpecker, Yellow-bellied Sapsucker, Olive-sided Flycatcher, Philadelphia Vireo, Rose-breasted Grosbeak and Rusty Blackbird**.

This is a favourite location for **Golden-crowned Kinglet** and boreal finches. The park's featured species is the **Evening Grosbeak** and both **Red and White-winged Crossbills** are common in irruption years. I had tallied nine warbler species in less than two hours without departing far from the roads.

Saint-Godefroi has good numbers of **Double-crested Cormorant, Great Black-backed and Herring Gulls** in late June, but an immature **Glaucous Gull** and a pair of **Canada Geese** added to the visit. Saint-Siméon has had a **Loggerhead Shrike** in mid April, although my visit in late June revealed very little of interest.

The birdlife of the Chaleur Bay area has received very little attention, but the shoreline from Miguasha to Carleton is certainly worth visiting. The more unusual landbirds along the inner bay shore have included **Merlin and Rufous-sided Towhee** in winter, a **Loggerhead Shrike** in early May, **Indigo Bunting** in mid May, and a mid July **Blue-gray Gnatcatcher**. The park at Carleton is an excellent place to spend a few days. Two colonies of **Great Blue Heron** fish the sandy beach at Carleton, where they are joined inshore by **Northern Gannet and Arctic Tern**. A **Pomarine Jaeger** has also arrived as early as late March, and the two sandbars have hosted nesting **Northern Shoveler** and the Gaspé's largest colony of **Common Tern**, which sometimes attracts **Black Tern** in summer. **Herring Gull** nest alongside a gravel road to the beach. I also noted **Killdeer** and what looked like a non-breeding **Semipalmated Sandpiper** in late June. The best shorebird at Carleton so far has been an adult summer-plumaged **Curlew Sandpiper** in late May.

The bars are also good for shorebirds in July and August—**Baird's Sandpiper** has appeared at least twice and there have also been visiting **Piping Plover and Green-backed Heron** in early August, although the latter prefers the small marsh to the west at Saint-Omer where I found a good variety of birds in late June but nothing spectacular. Paspébiac attracted the only **Tri-colored Heron** found on this coast in mid May.

Chaleur Bay is home to **thousands** of all three scoters in spring and good numbers of **Red-necked Grebe** in fall. The ferry offers views of large numbers of diving ducks at the right time of year, usually May and October. Wintering flocks of **Common and Barrow's Goldeneye** are joined by smaller numbers of **Great Cormorant and Black Guillemot**. Waterfowl are abundant in spring, too, when **thousands** of **Brant, Black Duck, Northern Pintail and Green-winged Teal** are joined by other dabbling ducks. It is also quite normal to find **20 Osprey** in the air together at one time during migration— a testimonial to the excellent fishing in the bay.

New Carlisle is best known for its counts of **5000 Surf and 3000 Black Scoters** in early May. **Piping Plover** sometimes nest in the area, and **Little and Laughing Gulls** are quite regular. Another small marsh at Saint-Siméon is used by herons, sandpipers, **Red and Red-necked Phalaropes**. **Great Cormorant** winter between New Carlisle and New Richmond. The mouth of the Cascapedia River is good for aquatic birds in spring and fall—herons and egrets are possible and **Wood Duck** have appeared in summer. The mixed woods may turn up **Great Crested Flycatcher, White-breasted Nuthatch, Philadelphia Vireo and Scarlet Tanager** near the northern limits of their nesting ranges, and a **Warbling Vireo** in late June was a particularly good find.

The New Richmond Christmas Bird Count has small numbers of **Great Cormorant, Canada Goose, Black Duck, Common and Barrow's Goldeneye, Common and Red-breasted Mergansers**, the occasional party of **Oldsquaw** and the odd **Double-crested Cormorant or Red-necked Grebe**. Gulls are scarce once the ice moves in, although **Ring-billed Gull** have wintered, and **Bald Eagle** is the most likely raptor. Several **Mourning Dove** in winter at Bonaventure, and there is usually a **Pileated Woodpecker** in the vicinity. Flocks of **Pine and Evening Grosbeaks, Common Redpoll, Pine Siskin and Snow Bunting** parcel out the available food supply, and are joined by a few **Blue Jay, American Robin, Red-breasted Nuthatch and Bohemian Waxwing**. **American Tree Sparrow and Hoary Redpoll** are less regular. New Richmond has added **Three-toed Woodpecker and Ruby-crowned Kinglet** on its count.

Pied-billed Grebe, Greater White-fronted Goose, Hooded Merganser, Glossy Ibis, Laughing Gull and Arctic Tern have all been noted just outside Bonaventure. There have also been **Turkey Vulture, Whip-poor-will, Western Kingbird and Northern Oriole** in summer at Bonaventure. The Maria area has had **Hooded Merganser and Scarlet Tanager** in spring and early summer.

The woods and rivers to the west of Miguasha do not receive much attention from birders who prefer to take the ferry to Dalhousie, but Escuminacs sometimes provides a few interesting birds. Ducks and marshbirds are abundant close to the bridge joining the community with Campbellton. **Sharp-tailed Sparrow** also nest at Point-à-la-Garde, and both **Scarlet Tanager and Field Sparrow** have been reported from nearby communities in summer. If a return is being made along the Matapedia River valley, a stop at Routhierville is recommended for songbirds.

BIBLIOGRAPHY

Books (Field and Identification Guides/Local Interest)

Bruun & Singer, **Larousse Guide to Birds of Britain and Europe**, Larousse & Co. Inc. 1978

Bull & Farrand, **Audubon Society Field Guide to North American Birds: Eastern Region**, Alfred A. Knopf/Random House of Canada Ltd.

Farrand, John Jr., **The Audubon Society Master Guide to Birding** (three volumes), Alfred A. Knopf/Random House of Canada Ltd.

Finlay, J.C., **A Bird-Finding Guide to Canada**, Hurtig Publishers Ltd. 1984

Gendron, Guy and Yves Gauthier, **Les Oiseaux du Bas St.-Laurent**, Gouvernement du Quebec 1984

Godfrey, Earl, **The Birds of Canada**, National Museums of Canada 1986

Grant, P.J., **Gulls**, Buteo Books 1982

Harrison, Peter, **Seabirds**, Croom Helm Ltd./A.H. & A.W. Reed Ltd. 1983

Heinzel, Fitter, Parslow, **Birds of Britain and Europe with North Africa and the Middle East**, Collins 1977

Hogan, Geoff, **Birds of PEI**, Ragweed Press 1991.

National Geographic Society, **Field Guide to the Birds of North America**, National Geographic Society 1987

Peterson, Roger T., **A Field Guide to the Birds East of the Rockies**, Houghton Mifflin Company 1980

Robbins, Bruun, Zim, Singer, **Birds of North America**, Golden Press 1983

Sharrock, J.T.R., **Frontiers of Bird Identification**, MacMillan Journals 1980

Squires, W.A.,**The Birds of New Brunswick**, New Brunswick Museum 1976

Stephenson, Marylee, **Canada's National Parks**, Prentice-Hall Canada, Inc. 1983

Booklets (Local Sites Only)

Christie, David, **Finding Birds around Saint John**, New Brunswick Museum 1978

Guide to Fredericton and Vicinity, Fredericton Nature Club 1989

Magazines and Journals (National and Local)

American Birding Association, **Birding**, bimonthly USA

Club des Ornithologues du bas Saint-Laurent, **Kakawi**, quarterly QUE

Club des Ornithologues du Quebec, **Bulletin Ornithologique**, quarterly QUE

Maybank, Blake et al., **Canadian Birding**, quarterly CAN

National Audubon Society, **American Birds**, bimonthly USA

Natural History Society of Prince Edward Island, **NHSPEI Newsletter**, monthly PEI

New Brunswick Federation of Naturalists, **NB Naturalist**, bimonthly NB

Province of Quebec Society for the Protection of Birds, Inc., **PQSPB Newsletter**, monthly QUE

Checklists (International, National, Provincial and Local)

Border Region, Nova Scotia-New Brunswick, **Checklist of Birds**, Canadian Wildlife Service 1974

British Trust for Ornithology, **List of the Birds of the Western Palearctic**, British Trust for Ornithology

Cape Jourimain National Wildlife Area, **Check-list of Birds**, Canadian Wildlife Service 1980

Club des Ornithologues du Quebec, **Oiseaux du Quebec** 1979

Forillon National Park, **Check List of Birds**, Parks Canada 1979

Fundy National Park, **Check List**, Parks Canada

Kouchibouguac National Park, **Check List**, Parks Canada 1977

New Brunswick Federation of Naturalists, **Check-list of New Brunswick Birds**, New Brunswick Museum 1985

Parc de la Gaspésie, **Liste des Oiseaux**, Gouvernement du Quebec

Prince Edward Island, **Field Check List of Birds**, Dept. of Tourism, Parks and Conservation 1978

Tintamarre National Wildlife Area, **Check-list of Birds**, Canadian Wildlife Service 1980

Provincial and Local Natural History Societies

Chignecto Naturalist Club, Mount Allison University, Sackville, New Brunswick, Canada, E0A 3C0

Club des Ornithologues de la Gaspésie, CP 245, Percé, Quebec, Canada, G0C 2L0

Club des Ornithologues du bas Saint-Laurent, Inc., CP 118, Pointe-au-Père, Quebec, Canada, G0K 1G0

Club des Ornithologues du Quebec, Inc., 8191 Zoo, Orsainville, Quebec, Canada, G1G 4G4

Fredericton Field Naturalists' Club, CP 542, Fredericton, NB, Canada, E3B 5A6

Kennebecasis Naturalists' Society, c/o Mrs. Gladys Bickford, 24 Stewart Ave, Sussex, NB, Canada, E0E 1P0

Lady Slipper Naturalists, Prince County, PEI, Canada

Miramichi Naturalists' Club, c/o Harry Walker, 276 Heath Court, Newcastle, NB, Canada, E1V 2Y5

Moncton Naturalists' Club, c/o Dr. Mike Majka, Regional Laboratory, Argen St, Moncton, NB, Canada, E1C 4B7

New Brunswick Federation of Naturalists, New Brunswick Museum, 277 Douglas Ave, Saint John, NB, Canada, E2K 1E5

PEI Natural History Society, PO Box 2346, Charlottetown, PEI, Canada, C1A 8C1

Province of Quebec Society for the Protection of Birds, Inc., PO Box 43, Station B, Montreal, Quebec, Canada, H4Z 1A6

Saint John Naturalists' Club,New Brunswick Museum, 277 Douglas Ave, Saint John, NB, Canada, E2K 1E5

Index to Sites